How to Find Work that Works for People with Asperger Syndrome

of related interest

**Employment for Individuals with Asperger Syndrome
or Non-Verbal Learning Disability**
Stories and Strategies
Yvona Fast and others
ISBN 1 84310 766 X

Asperger Syndrome Employment Workbook
An Employment Workbook for Adults with Asperger Syndrome
Roger N. Meyer
ISBN 1 85302 796 0

Asperger's Syndrome
A Guide for Parents and Professionals
Tony Attwood
Foreword by Lorna Wing
ISBN 1 85302 577 1

Succeeding in College with Asperger Syndrome
A Student Guide
John Harpur, Maria Lawlor and Michael Fitzgerald
ISBN 1 84310 201 3

Build Your Own Life
A Self-Help Guide for Individuals with Asperger Syndrome
Wendy Lawson
Foreword by Dr Dinah Murray
ISBN 1 84310 114 9

Understanding Autism Spectrum Disorders
Frequently Asked Questions
Diane Yapko
ISBN 1 84310 756 2

Pretending to be Normal
Living with Asperger's Syndrome
Liane Holliday-Willey
Foreword by Tony Attwood
ISBN 1 84310 749 9

How to Find Work that Works for People with Asperger Syndrome

The Ultimate Guide for Getting People with Asperger Syndrome into the Workplace (and Keeping Them There!)

Gail Hawkins

Jessica Kingsley Publishers
London and Philadelphia

First published in the United Kingdom in 2004
by Jessica Kingsley Publishers
116 Pentonville Road
London N1 9JB, UK
and
400 Market Street, Suite 400
Philadelphia, PA 19106, USA

www.jkp.com

Library of Congress Cataloging in Publication Data
Hawkins, Gail, 1964-
How to find work that works for people with Asperger syndrome : the
ultimate guide for getting people with Asperger syndrome into the workplace (and keeping them there!) / Gail Hawkins.
p. cm.
Includes bibliographical references and index.
ISBN 1-84310-151-3 (pbk.)
1. People with disabilities--Vocational guidance. 2. Asperger's syndrome--Patients--Vocational guidance. 3. Asperger's syndrome--Patients--Employment. I. Title.
HV1568.5.H38 2004
362.196'8588--dc22

2003026952

British Library Cataloguing in Publication Data
A CIP catalogue record for this book is available from the British Library

ISBN-13: 978 1 84310 151 2
ISBN-10: 1 84310 151 3

Printed and Bound in Great Britain by
Athenaeum Press, Gateshead, Tyne and Wear

Contents

Part 1: The players

Part 2: The foundation

List of figures

Acknowledgments

Thanks to:

Margaret and Terry Hawkins, who brought me up to believe that anything is possible and gave me the encouragement and support to *know* I can do it

My sister Janet, who is my best friend, biggest fan and voice of reason, and to her husband Mike who fed me, encouraged me, listened to me, and occasionally helped me think of the right word

Baby Adelaide, who is my heart, hope, wonder, and teacher

Norm, Peter, Sheila, Tyson, and Amber who believe in me

My staff at Mission Possible who supported me by doing their jobs above and beyond and who shared their wisdom and insights

Lucille Blainey for her "wise words" in supporting my efforts to get this book off the ground

Grandma Hawkins for the light inside me

My dear friends Jon, Leslie, Colleen, Kat, Debbie, Denise, Ingrid, Tanya, and Yvonne

My clients, who have transformed my life and allowed me to grow and learn about Asperger Syndrome and myself: I am forever grateful to the riches you have brought to my life

Margaret Whelan, Neil Walker, and the Geneva Centre for Autism who believed in my vision and in me

PBN, for the power of networking

Cubby and Marshall

My publisher Jessica Kingsley for believing in this cause

Every person with Asperger Syndrome on and off the planet, I believe in you

Introduction

This book is about a journey. Although it focuses on helping find work that works for people with Asperger Syndrome, it is also about helping them find happiness and success in life. These are things that take time to foster and no one should have to do it alone.

This book is also about hope. I want people to know that anything is possible when they believe in it and work hard enough for it. It has been this conviction that has allowed me to move employers to take a chance on hiring someone who is different, and they have not regretted their decisions.

Asperger Syndrome is a pervasive developmental disorder that has been attracting increasing attention in the media in recent years. It is considered to be a high-functioning form of autism. People with this disorder are often of average or superior intelligence but have difficulty interacting socially with others. They are known for their reliability, special talents and dedication and, when given the right opportunity and clear direction, make outstanding employees.

You may never have heard of Asperger Syndrome before, or even been aware of autism, but you have seen its face on film, on television, and in your community.

Numerous characters have portrayed traits of Asperger Syndrome in the media. Leonard Nimoy as Dr. Spock in "Star Trek" displayed the low emotional affect typical of many people with Asperger Syndrome. Jack Nicholson as writer Melvin Udall in the film "As Good As It Gets" exhibited the symptoms of obsessive-compulsive disorder. His inappropriate comments and intense need for routine and regimen were also typical of Asperger Syndrome. Likewise, Tony Shalhoub as former police detective Adrian

Monk in the television series "Monk" models how obsessive-compulsive characteristics can be an asset in the right job. Vincent D'Onofrio as Detective Robert Goren on "Law and Order, Criminal Intent," depicts physical twitches and a fascination for detail associated with Asperger Syndrome.

An astonishing number of people are showing up with what the *New York Times* in June of 2000 called the "Little Professor Syndrome." It is estimated by some that there are millions of people in the world who have this disorder. Many of these people want desperately to get a job and keep it. But most of them won't succeed in the workplace because of their unique differences. Estimates of underemployed or unemployed people with Asperger Syndrome soar well into the 80 percentile range. Even those individuals who are formally educated with post-secondary degrees have low employment rates. The employment issues of people with Asperger Syndrome are complex. The solutions therefore are not simple, but they are also not impossible.

There are few supports in place that help people with cognitive differences adequately transition from school into the workplace. These vary from country to country, but are typically offered through social service or disability agencies for which funding and trained resources are always in short supply. Counselors struggling to help people with physical, emotional, and cognitive differences often have little or no understanding of this particular disorder and its unique challenges. Regular employment agencies are not equipped to help the candidate with Asperger Syndrome. Where then can families, teachers and professionals find the guidance and support they need to help?

How to Find Work that Works for People with Asperger Syndrome: The Ultimate Guide for Getting People with Asperger Syndrome into the Workplace (and keeping them there!) aims to help everyone who wants to see people with this disorder succeed in competitive employment.

> Readers will find wisdom, user-friendly assessments, teaching techniques and practical tools to help their Asperger relative, friend, client or student succeed.

This book is the product of more than fifteen years of experience and success in finding meaningful work for people with Asperger Syndrome. Over this period I have enjoyed a 92 per cent success rate in finding employment for people with Asperger Syndrome by blending business with social work. This approach achieves success by looking at all aspects of a person's life and customizing the most effective solution for each individual.

The process of finding work that works described in this book has helped hundreds of people with Asperger Syndrome to achieve their employment potential in companies of all sizes and from a wide range of industries.

How to Find Work that Works for People with Asperger Syndrome guides readers through this proven system of finding competitive employment.

This system works because it demonstrates how to identify the relevant strengths and challenges that impact employment and shows the reader how to make the uniqueness of the Asperger Syndrome into a benefit. Readers will learn how to use Asperger Syndrome to open doors and show employers the long-term benefits of hiring someone with this disorder. Readers will gain insight into the specific challenges faced by people with Asperger Syndrome in the workplace and how to address them. They will also learn what jobs are best suited to people with Asperger Syndrome and what jobs to avoid.

Anyone who has not worked with someone with Asperger Syndrome will find it challenging to understand the complexities and nature of the disorder. Those who are familiar with the disorder may find it difficult to anticipate how it can impact performance on the job. This book can help both groups.

The system explained in this book lets the reader know ahead of time what to look for, what to expect and how to deal with the obstacles and challenges that arise when finding employment for this population. If readers follow this prescription, there is no reason why they cannot successfully find meaningful employment for their Asperger friends, family members, students, or clients.

I have seen this system work for hundreds of people. I have witnessed people with no self-esteem become confident, contributing employees and have seen their lives jump from hopeless to successful. And I have cheered as reluctant employers were converted into enthusiastic supporters.

I am excited to share stories of successful employees with Asperger Syndrome and pass on the lessons shared by those who are still in the process of finding work. Much of my insight comes from the employers and family members with whom I have worked alongside and, of course, the employees themselves.

Over the past few years, I have watched the number of clients coming through my door double, double again, and then double again. I have been asked to provide services all over the world. There is clearly a dire need for specialized services for adults with Asperger Syndrome. How could I get this system out there for others to use? This book is my response.

How to Find Work that Works for People with Asperger Syndrome shares real-life stories of clients with Asperger Syndrome, their struggles and successes, along with assessment tools and strategies such as the "Employment Toolbox" and the "Four Pillar Teaching Technique," a solid teaching strategy for people with Asperger Syndrome. These strategies are transferable to all other aspects of their lives and will not only help them to realize their employment goals and potential, but also to lead happier and more productive lives in general.

Part 1
The players

1 There is hope

What you should know about finding work that works for people with Asperger Syndrome

Imagine playing a computer game where around every corner is something you have to decipher before you can move to the next level. Now imagine living that computer game day in and day out. Take a moment to feel how exhausting that would be. Picture how stressful it would be to never know what was next, what was going to jump out at you or what test might stump you and keep you stuck in that spot for a long time.

If you can envision this, then perhaps you can relate to what it must be like to have Asperger Syndrome. To have a life that is a constant game of strategy and endurance. People with Asperger Syndrome are real-life heroes who are seen as underdogs in our society. Yet they really are not underdogs. They are amazing, beautiful people who can succeed and prosper if they are given the right support and have people around them who believe in them and give them a chance. Finding work that works is achieved by building on strengths and finding effective strategies. It is about helping people with Asperger Syndrome (candidates) win the game of competitive employment.

1.1 The gift of Asperger Syndrome

Asperger Syndrome is a gift, not a curse, an affliction, or a sentence. People with Asperger Syndrome are just regular folks who happen to see the world in a unique and interesting way. I owe a great deal to my clients with

Asperger Syndrome. They have taught me about patience, endurance, fear, love and success. I admire my clients because they get up every morning to face a world that does not make a lot of sense to them. They face each day with few friends and few people who take the time to understand them. They are often isolated and scapegoated in their communities and schools and yet they keep going. They get out of bed and try again and again to face a world that is often intolerant and cruel. This takes a resilience, courage and stamina that few other people will ever have to match in a lifetime.

Think of a person with such stamina, resilience, and determination. Think of a person who is driven to succeed. Now think of the qualities an employer values. It is hard to imagine an employer who does not want an employee who is reliable, resilient, motivated, and driven to be successful. The trick is to put these two people together and teach them how to get what they need from one another.

People with Asperger Syndrome are an untapped gold mine to employers. Only most of them do not know this. Part of your job in finding work that works for people with Asperger Syndrome is to show employers the wealth that is available to them in these employees and how they can tap into it.

1.2 The magic

People with Asperger Syndrome make great employees. This has been demonstrated repeatedly. Sometimes it's not how long they stay in a job that is important, but rather the impact they have while they are there. It is amazing to watch the attitude in workplaces transform because of one such employee.

Alex was a young man with Asperger Syndrome who got a job in a small warehouse. The company had about fifteen employees and Alex came on staff as a picker/packer in their warehouse. It didn't take long for him to learn the job, which impressed the employer because there was so much to remember in the warehouse. Alex was slight and had a very quiet, shy personality. He struggled to lift boxes that the other guys in the warehouse tossed around like sponges. His social skills were adequate at best, until he became comfortable. He would only ask questions when it was absolutely necessary and would only answer questions when approached directly. Otherwise, he kept to himself.

After about three months, Alex slowly started to come out of his shell; sitting with his coworkers during breaks he would listen and smile as the others chatted and joked. Then one day he told a joke. No one remembers whether or not the joke was funny but everyone was so shocked and thrilled to hear him that they laughed anyway. From that day forward, Alex began to take part in the daily rituals of break time. He got a reputation for being a very reliable, hard worker who could come up with clever "one-liners" that would catch everyone off guard. It was amazing to go into that warehouse and see these big bulky guys include him in their banter. At the same time it was apparent that they respected him. The energy in that warehouse shifted when they hired Alex.

Then the company was sold. The new owner had to make some deep cuts and let go several employees, including Alex. Pete, the warehouse manager sat in a chair as he waited for Alex to come into the meeting room. He really respected Alex and had tried desperately to save his job. When he met Alex, Pete recalled that he was afraid of him; he didn't know what to say or how to talk to him. Over time, however, it was as if Alex's disability disappeared. All Pete could see in Alex now was this great guy who worked harder than anyone else he'd ever hired. It was a rough meeting but Alex took the news like a trouper. At the end, Alex said, "Well, I guess it's time for me to move on anyway. I need to learn more things."

The whole company showed up for Alex's last day. He left his first job with his head held high, feeling like he belonged and was valued, and is now happy and successful working in another warehouse.

Since then, as some of his coworkers at the first warehouse moved on to other companies, they have inquired about how to bring someone like Alex into their new workplace. Alex not only contributed to that company but also paved the way for others like him.

There is hope for every person with Asperger Syndrome to do the same. I personally have seen employees have a similar impact in banks, government offices and high-tech companies. The environment doesn't matter. It's the people that create the magic.

1.3 Why it's important to find work that works

Work and family are the basic building blocks of society. Both constitute a network of relationships and responsibilities that to a large extent define who we are as individuals, as a group, and as a community.

Relationships in the workplace exist between employers and employees, coworkers and customers, suppliers, shareholders, stakeholders, regulators, and competitors. They can be complex and challenging even for people with well-honed interpersonal skills.

Work that works for people with Asperger Syndrome are jobs where they can handle their work relationships and responsibilities on their own, and contribute meaningfully to society. Everyone has a place in the world of work. People with Asperger Syndrome have much to offer their communities. They just need some help to reach their potential.

> Including differently-abled people benefits society on many levels.

The modern world has progressed because of innovation and invention in response to the need to overcome obstacles or the passion for a special interest or vision. These are the particular gifts of people with Asperger Syndrome. Through their unique abilities, they have made extraordinary contributions to research, manufacturing, medicine, technology, and the arts.

Many famous people have exhibited traits associated with Asperger Syndrome. (This does not mean to say they had it, but to demonstrate that such behavior has been familiar throughout history.) One famous contemporary person is Glenn Gould, a pianist born in Toronto, Canada. He became a renowned recording artist, particularly of works by Bach, and was known for his innovative radio documentaries, television shows, and occasional writings. When he was just twenty-two and not well known outside his own country, his performance of Bach's "Goldberg Variations" made him a star, and then a legend. After his death, it was speculated that Gould had Asperger Syndrome. This might have explained his wearing heavy coats and scarves in the middle of July. He would also constantly hum when he played, something he apparently couldn't help. Engineers were left to try to remove the humming from his recordings. Reportedly his behavior could sometimes be off-putting. Nevertheless he was a well-spoken, refined, and a highly intelligent man.

> The world also needs to learn greater tolerance, and one way to do this
> is to offer our communities a positive experience of people who are
> different.

Finally, enabling people to contribute to society improves productivity overall because it reduces the stress on the family and professionals, such as doctors, teachers, counselors, and the social workers, who support them.

This book is geared to this group. Give a man a fish, and you help one person. Teach a man to fish, and he can help his entire community.

1.4 The rewards

Whether you are a family member, a professional, an employer, or someone with Asperger Syndrome, you will find many rewards in this process. You will meet many people who will want to help you in your quest and you will experience the positive impact your work has on others.

It is gratifying to help someone gain greater self-awareness, to support him in building a foundation of skill, and to point him in the right direction and help him to succeed.

> Anything is possible when approached with an open mind and a drive to thrive.

There are thousands of employers out there who will benefit from having an employee with Asperger Syndrome on their payroll. Many are searching for new talent pools to tap to help fill the gap as the wave of retiring baby boomers hits the market. They have no idea of the potential available to them in the Asperger Syndrome population.

People with Asperger Syndrome can contribute significantly to their communities with the proper training and guidance. They make wonderful, if not superior, employees when matched with the right job and the right employer. However, employers will not hire them if they cannot do the job. Like any other candidate for a job, people with Asperger Syndrome must be qualified, prepared, and ready to work. This book walks you step by step through a proven process to get people with Asperger Syndrome into the workplace and help keep them there.

1.5 A proven process

Finding work that works for someone with Asperger Syndrome is more complex than just making a good match. That is why conventional vocational support services for people with disabilities are frequently inappropriate or ineffective for them.

One needs to understand the disability, assess the work skills of the candidate, target the right jobs and the right employers, and develop the right support to help them transition into the workplace.

1.5.1 Understanding Asperger Syndrome

By its very nature, Asperger Syndrome manifests very differently in different people. The challenges shift with each individual's level of functioning and personality. That is why it is so important for you to work with the individual and not the disability.

1.5.2 Assessing the individual

Assessing the strengths and challenges of the candidate involves a number of steps, taking the time to really get to know: the person you are working with; how he reacts to various situations and environments; how he learns; what triggers anxiety, frustration or anger in him; and how aware he is of himself and others. You need to learn his level of independence, productivity, and ability to follow instruction and understand and convey information. You want to be able to predict ahead of time how he will react in various situations. Anything that makes him stand out negatively provides an opportunity for you to help him adapt and be successful while still preserving his individuality.

1.5.3 The right employer

Finding work that works also involves connecting with the right employer. You want to find employers who are willing to take the time to appreciate how an employee with Asperger Syndrome can contribute to their companies. You might be surprised how many of them there are. It will also be part of your job to understand the employer, his needs, tolerances, and motivation. The relationship you build with the employer is equally important to the one you develop with the candidate.

1.5.4 The right support

People with Asperger Syndrome are unique. They think differently, process information differently, respond differently and see the world differently. Because of their unique challenges, they require unique strategies and teaching methods. Understanding who they are makes all the difference in working with them effectively.

Individualizing your approach to finding work that works will give you the insight you require to help the candidate reach his potential in the workplace. *How to Find Work that Works for People with Asperger Syndrome* is designed with this individualized approach in mind. Each method, strategy, and tool in this book takes into consideration that each person with Asperger Syndrome is a unique individual. You'll find it easy to choose and customize an approach appropriate for *your* Asperger friend.

I have taken all the strategies, methods, and lessons I have learned and developed over the years and developed them into a system that makes finding work that works achievable. I have made it easy to assess the employment skills of a candidate with Asperger Syndrome and develop short- and long-term strategies to help him gain and maintain employment. You will learn how to identify realistic career directions based upon interest, skill, education, and aptitude, balanced with the person's challenges and the current market. You will develop your own unique way of talking about Asperger Syndrome to friends, colleagues, professionals, and employers. Beyond this, you will learn how to help the candidate develop a way of talking about his own disability that will instill confidence and dispel fear.

> The more you know about how to support people with Asperger Syndrome, the better equipped you are to help them reach their potential in the workplace and in life.

1.6 Finding work for someone else is easier than finding it for yourself

The reason entertainers have managers and authors have publicists is because it always sounds more interesting and credible when someone else boasts about you. The same applies to finding work. It is easier to promote someone else than it is to promote yourself.

1.7 How this book will help you

This book is designed as a comprehensive guide for family members and professionals, although many people with Asperger Syndrome will also find it useful. It covers everything you need to know to help candidates with Asperger Syndrome get into the workplace and stay there, including:

- the roles people play when finding work that works
- knowing what employers want and how to give it to them
- understanding what competitive employment really is
- effective teaching strategies for adults with Asperger Syndrome

- assessing work readiness
- identifying workplace challenges
- addressing workplace challenges
- building a foundation of skills for the workplace
- choosing appropriate career directions
- how to find the right employers
- how to conduct an effective job search
- how to educate employers
- disclosing the disability
- how to transition into the job
- how to keep the job.

After reading this book, you will be an expert on finding work that works for people with Asperger Syndrome. You will be able to talk intelligently to employers and contacts about the disorder and you will be equipped with the tools to make a difference. People will find what you have to share compelling and interesting. This will be particularly beneficial when you are speaking with potential employers. The knowledge and skills you gain from this book will make finding a job for the candidates easier than finding one for yourself.

Understanding the roles of each of the players that contribute to making a successful work experience for someone with Asperger Syndrome will equip you for the journey ahead. As a family member or professional, you will be challenged to examine your own role in the process. The insights you gain about yourself may surprise you! What I have learned from my clients has helped me to improve my employment program, its strategies and methods, and has ultimately led hundreds of people with Asperger Syndrome to enjoy successful, meaningful work experiences. As a person with Asperger Syndrome, this guide can serve as a map to understanding your role in the process better as well as offer you valuable insight into the trials and tribulations you and the other players face while supporting you. You can use this information to help you help yourself and the people helping you.

By the time you finish this book, you will have gained the knowledge you need to help your Asperger friends find and keep meaningful work. You will be armed with two very powerful tools: knowledge and hope. Perhaps most important, you will experience the reward of helping someone with Asperger Syndrome reach his potential.

2 The employer

Generosity is a gift that comes full circle.

Irene owns a small retail distributing company that supplies retail outlets with all the accessories they need to display and sell their products. She started her company in the early 1990s, selling bags to retail stores out of her home office in her basement. Her business expanded to include hangers and tissue paper and then boxes and coat racks. Before she knew it, she was shipping products across the country and she had exceeded the storage space her basement could offer. She rented a small warehouse in an industrial part of the city and set up shop. At this point she was looking for some help in her warehouse. What a win–win situation for candidates with Asperger Syndrome!

Irene was willing to give someone with Asperger Syndrome a try but she was honest that hers was a small company and if employees were unable to be productive, she could not afford to keep them on. I placed two people with her in a job-share situation. Joel would work the morning shift and Ted the afternoon. By splitting the shift, there was a chance that things would work out for at least one of the two. Joel and Ted were in their early twenties and this was the first job for both of them. They were interested in working in a warehouse and both were eager to prove that they could do it. Job coaches worked with Ted and Joel for two weeks, helping them learn their job and organize their schedules so that they would be most productive. The job coaches also worked with Irene to show her how best to communicate with Ted and Joel.

Both young men worked really hard learning the entire warehouse and the product codes, of which there were hundreds. They had to learn safety procedures and routines. The job was also physically challenging for both of them as neither was used to lifting or standing on his feet for hours at a time. At the end of their shifts, Ted and Joel were exhausted.

To Irene's surprise and delight, both Ted and Joel learned their jobs quickly. Ted was much more outgoing than Joel but both were great workers and before long were working independently. Although the two young men did not work together on the same shift, they would see each other on the overlap at lunch time. They would acknowledge each other but other than that did not have much cause to interact.

When Irene and I sat down a couple of months later to discuss long-term employment for Ted and Joel, I was thrilled when she told me that she wanted to hire both of them as full-time, permanent employees. Irene told me that it was really hard to find good workers in her industry. When she did find good workers, they were hard to keep. Joel and Ted were her solution. Both were always on time, rarely sick, and very detailed when picking the orders. Irene knew that Ted and Joel were not perfect but she said that she would take Joel or Ted's problems any day over the problems of some of her past employees. "If Ted is working too slowly, all I need to do is ask him to work a bit faster and he does. He doesn't get upset or talk badly behind my back. He just does his best. Even when Joel can't lift some of the boxes, I don't mind because he makes up for it in other areas. Both of the guys are polite and easy to get along with. But mostly they work hard and I know that they are always trying their best." Irene went on to say, "What you see is what you get with these guys. I never have to worry about them causing trouble, taking smoke breaks, or lazing off. If I see one of them not working, it's not because they are being lazy, it's because they are finished what they were working on and just forgot to tell me that they needed something else to do. I can think of worse problems and, besides, they are getting better with that issue, too."

Before Irene met Ted and Joel, she had never worked with anyone with a disability. She told me that she would keep an open mind. Today, Irene is one of our biggest supporters. She tells everyone about how well these young men have done. She takes great pride in them and their success. This is a true success story about an employer with an open mind and a problem to solve.

Today, Irene is starting another company and has already contacted me to make sure I'll have some employees for her.

2.1 Understanding the employer

Part of finding work that works involves understanding the employer. This is important because employers have their own specific set of needs. Employers tell me that they appreciate it when someone who approaches them has an understanding of the following:

2.1.1 What motivates an employer

There are many things that motivate employers but perhaps the most basic is that they need to make a profit. After all, an employer is in business to make money and it is usually this bottom line that tips the decision-making in the process of hiring. Even employers with the biggest of hearts need to make fiscally responsible decisions.

> An employer with a big heart is wonderful. One with the payroll to back it up is much better.

The majority of employers are good corporate citizens. Most employers, within their means, want to contribute to their communities. You see this all the time when they sponsor sports such as little league baseball – for instance, "Joe's Meat Market Sluggers." This being said, an employer will not hire anyone who cannot pull his weight. The profit/loss factor cannot be ignored. Employers need to know that whomever they hire will contribute something to the company. This could range from crunching numbers in the finance department to an entry-level position such as pushing grocery buggies into the corrals or cleaning the parking lot. It has to be worth the employer's while on the bottom line in order for him to justify hiring anyone.

2.1.2 What employers fear

People tend to "fear" the unknown. If one doesn't understand something or something is completely out of one's experience, then it is more likely that one will be wary of it. Employers who have never been exposed to people who are cognitively different may be more nervous about hiring them. Knowing this ahead of time is important as it allows you to prepare for a variety of reactions. Think about how it might feel to an employer to experience Asperger Syndrome for the first time. Candidates with Asperger Syndrome tend to avoid eye contact, they might not say a lot to the employer or understand his questions, they might blurt out something inappropriate or they may have some odd behaviors. These differences can be intimidating to anyone who is not sure how to respond. I once accompanied a client to an interview and the client blurted out "Hey, you talk like Forrest Gump," to the interviewer. The employer was taken aback and was not sure how to react.

One of the best ways to combat fear is education. With knowledge comes understanding, which reduces fear and misconceptions. Once an employer understands what to expect from an employee who is different, then he is usually open to hearing about what that person can do, even if that contribution might be limited.

2.1.3 Why employers hire

Employers hire for a variety of reasons. Why employers hire and whom they hire will vary depending upon the size and needs of the company and the company culture. The top reasons employers hire fall into three main categories:

- politics
- to meet specific labor needs
- corporate responsibility.

2.1.3.1 POLITICS

Companies who do a lot of work with their government may be required to meet certain hiring requirements in order to maintain their contracts. For example, the Canadian federal government has an employment equity program called "Federal Contractor Requirements." There are also requirements for those companies that do business with provincially based governments. Under these contracts, employers are required to reflect their communities in their hiring practices. This means that a percentage of their workforce must include people with disabilities. Countries that have similar programs include Germany, Japan, Egypt, and Poland.

Other political incentives to hiring people with disabilities include various wage subsidy and tax incentive programs. These programs offer a subsidy or a tax reduction to employers for hiring a person with special needs. Some of the countries that offer these incentives include the United

States, Canada, Australia, New Zealand, the United Kingdom, Israel, and the Netherlands.

Although these types of political incentives do not solve the employment equity issues that permeate society, they can offer opportunities in the job-finding process. Companies or employers who are watching their bottom line may welcome a wage subsidy or tax break. This can tip the scale in their decision-making process. One caution, however, when discussing government money or incentives with employers: Ensure that the employer is serious about hiring the candidate and is not just after the incentive. The latter could be a disastrous set-up for the new employee, who is going to be putting a great deal of energy into the job. Most employers are quite genuine when hiring people with special needs, regardless of any incentive that may be offered, but it is prudent to check this out.

2.1.3.2 TO MEET SPECIFIC LABOR NEEDS

Millions of new job opportunities will be opening up over the next decade. Studies have shown that historically, hiring trends of people with disabilities follow those of the general population. This means that employers will be doing a lot of hiring in the years to come. In addition, the baby boom generation is aging and will be entering into retirement over the next decade. This will present opportunities for younger generations to fill those positions.

This is good news for job-seekers, and particularly good news for people with Asperger Syndrome who were often getting passed over, not necessarily due to their lack of skill or ability, but because of fears and misconceptions. Employers who face a hiring shortfall will be more motivated to look into different talent pools in order to meet their hiring needs. Combine that need with education and a solid support strategy and this can place people with Asperger Syndrome in an excellent position.

> An employer who is open to learning how to accommodate a worker with Asperger Syndrome, in order to reap the long-term gains of having a good employee, is a good employer to know.

The needs of the labor market simply help employers to open their eyes more easily to alternate possibilities of which they were perhaps unaware in the past.

2.1.3.3 CORPORATE SOCIAL RESPONSIBILITY PROGRAMS

Many companies today place a high priority on giving back to their communities. They will often have corporate or social responsibility programs. Firms and individuals look for evidence of good corporate citizenship when choosing whether or not to do business with or accept a position within a company. The company culture and philosophy also influence employee retention, something that holds great value for employers. Many employers and governments have developed "best practices" initiatives to support the hiring and training of people with special needs. For example, The Royal Bank Financial Group in Canada has created an Employees with Disabilities Advisory Council which has researched how the bank can be an employer of choice for people with disabilities. They have implemented several initiatives and programs to support workplace accommodation and hiring practices. They have been held up as a model to the corporate community and many other financial institutions have followed their lead by implementing similar initiatives.

"Social marketing" is becoming a new concept in the corporate world. Corporations are beginning to recognize that monetary, in-kind, and voluntary-based contributions that support increased employability of people with disabilities are excellent marketing practices. Microsoft, for example, proactively recruits people with disabilities as part of their hiring practice. The company highlighted its leadership in this area when it founded the Able to Work Consortium in October 1999 together with the National Business and Disability Council. Able to Work is an independent business consortium of more than 20 companies dedicated to increasing employment opportunities for people with disabilities by providing information and generating awareness. Microsoft has also implemented scholarships for students with disabilities at both the high school and college levels. Clearly, they understand the value in this untapped labor force. Microsoft also appears to have a vested interest in autism spectrum disorders. They have become the first national American corporation to provide coverage for Applied Behavioral Analysis (ABA) for the treatment of autism for their employees.

2.2 Competitive employment

This book is geared to helping you find *competitive* work that works. Before you begin looking for work for the candidate with Asperger Syndrome, you need to understand clearly the meaning of competitive employment.

Employers need their employees to be productive and to earn their wage because most companies cannot afford to keep them otherwise. Employers will hire people with disabilities and even make some accommodation for their special needs but only if, at the end of the day, the employee earns her keep. Competitive employment means equal work for equal pay. When you are finding work that works for candidates with Asperger Syndrome, you must keep this in mind. They must have a basic foundation of skill in order for an employer to consider them seriously as candidates for competitive jobs.

Let's take a look at the different types of employment:

- *Competitive employment* includes any activity carried out for pay or profit.

- *Full-time employment* refers to people who usually work thirty or more hours per week.

- *Part-time employment* refers to people who usually work less than thirty hours each week.

- *Permanent employment* means any job that does not have a specific termination date.

- *Short-term jobs* are classified as temporary.

- *Seasonal jobs*, such as construction, fishing, and farming, are still considered permanent and often require long hours during their active season.

- *Self-employment* is becoming more and more prevalent with people providing services on a contract basis, producing goods, and selling someone else's product as examples. Self-employed people rely on their own initiative and skills to generate income.

2.2.1 What is considered competitive?

It is required that employees have a basic level of skill in order to be considered competitive. The minimum requirements will fluctuate from one employer to another depending upon the needs of the company and the demands of the job. However, there are basic expectations that employers agree make an employee competitive in the workplace. An employer will look at two main areas when hiring: skills and attributes. *Skills* are the actual ability to do the job; for example, computer skills, written communication skills, the physical ability to lift a product. *Attributes* refer more to the qualities or character of an individual; for example, easygoing, creative, a self-starter.

There is no question that some job accommodations will be necessary for most employees with Asperger Syndrome. Employers will need to understand that employees with Asperger Syndrome may require greater supervision or might need a little longer to build up their speed on a job. Even with this understanding, the employer still requires such employees to have a basic level of skill and to fit into the company's corporate culture.

These are the top ten skills and attributes employers were seeking in 2003, based upon Job Outlook 2003, US National Association of Colleges and Employers (Bureau of Labor Statistics, US Department of Labor, www.bls.gov):

1. Communication (oral and written)

2. Honesty/integrity

3. Teamwork (works with others)

4. Interpersonal skills (relates well to others)

5. Motivation/initiative

6. Strong work ethic

7. Analytical skills

8. Flexibility/adaptability

9. Computer skills

10. Time management/organizational skills

2.2.1.1 COMMUNICATION SKILLS

Employers expect employees to be able to show they can both listen and convey information orally and in writing. Being able to communicate is important to employers because they need to know what their employees are thinking and trust that employees can articulate their thoughts about work. This helps the employer produce quality work. Communication skills also include non-verbal messages that are conveyed to others. Communication skills in general are challenging for people with Asperger Syndrome and non-verbal communication skills are particularly challenging.

2.2.1.2 HONESTY/INTEGRITY

Employers need to be able to trust their employees. This trust includes knowing that their employees will produce work on time and in a manner that is acceptable to the employer or their client, as the case may be. Employers need to know that their employees will be punctual and put in the hours that they are paying them for. This is an area in which employees with Asperger Syndrome can excel. They are often extremely trustworthy, honest, and reliable.

2.2.1.3 TEAMWORK

It is often necessary for employees to work together whether on a project or to cooperate with one another regularly on general assignments. Employers want to know that their employees can work together, that they have the skills to be cooperative and productive in a team environment. Although this may not be a *forte* for candidates with Asperger Syndrome, they are capable of participating in a team environment, particularly when the team is small and consistent. To facilitate teamwork, it is often an asset to the employee with Asperger Syndrome to have one primary contact on the team.

2.2.1.4 INTERPERSONAL SKILLS

While teamwork generally refers to *working* well with others, interpersonal skills refer to *relating* well to others. This means having empathy, compassion, and understanding of what others are feeling and thinking. This is a challenge for the employee with Asperger Syndrome who, just by the nature of the disorder, tend to be egocentric and self-focused. It is most likely that you will have to address aspects of this challenge when you are helping the candidate build a foundation of skill (Part 2 of this book).

2.2.1.5 MOTIVATION/INITIATIVE

Having a motivated employee is crucial to an employer. An employee who lacks motivation will not be as productive or as reliable. An employer is more likely to keep an employee who is motivated over one who is not, even if the motivated employee has fewer skills. If the employee is motivated, then she will likely take it upon herself to learn or upgrade skills to be better at the job. Many candidates with Asperger Syndrome are highly motivated to work. They will do whatever is necessary and within their power to please the employer and do a good job. A person who is not motivated is difficult to prepare for getting a job, let alone keeping it. The motivation needs to come from within the individual.

All employers and supervisors to some extent have to motivate their employees. It is part of the employer/supervisor's job to help employees pull together as a team and to support overall goals and strategies. But employers should not have to *battle* to motivate an employee. If the employee lacks self-motivation, it can be an impediment to the employer.

Employers also want employees who are able to take initiative, which means that they are capable of doing things without being told to do them. This can be a challenge for some people with Asperger Syndrome because it often involves the use of judgment and observation skills. Asperger Syndrome tends to interfere with some elements of judgment, so it is harder for the candidate to know what jobs need to be done before being asked to do them. This can be accommodated by helping the candidate develop a list of jobs to do when she is not otherwise occupied. This is often enough to satisfy an employer's basic requirement.

2.2.1.6 STRONG WORK ETHIC

Finding employees with a strong work ethic can be difficult for employers today, which is why they find this so important in a new employee. A strong work ethic includes reliability, punctuality, willingness to work overtime when required, and doing more than what is expected. Employers highly value these qualities in an employee. Employees with Asperger Syndrome often have an excellent work ethic and they can shine in this area.

2.2.1.7 ANALYTICAL SKILLS

Many jobs require analytical skills, such as the ability to think critically and draw conclusions based upon information that is provided. Often, candidates with Asperger Syndrome have good analytical skills and can analyze information quickly, particularly if it is technical in nature, for example in accounting, engineering, or computer programming.

2.2.1.8 FLEXIBILITY/ADAPTABILITY

Employers want people on their staff who can go with the flow. Change is a regular part of most job environments and employers want to know that their employees can shift easily and quickly with new ideas, technologies and cultural changes. A willingness to be flexible and to compromise will make a person a more valued and desirable employee. People with Asperger

Syndrome are known to struggle with flexibility, but that does not mean that they are incapable of it. With effort and some solid strategies in place, they can usually meet a level of flexibility that the employer will find satisfactory.

2.2.1.9 COMPUTER SKILLS

There are few jobs left today that do not require at least minimal computer skills. If a person does not have adequate computer skills, she drastically narrows her employment options. Most employers want to see at least a basic knowledge and experience level in computers, which should include word processing, email, and Internet. Many more employers today will want to see a more advanced knowledge base that will include presentations, spreadsheet knowledge and possibly some basic programming and/or web knowledge.

2.2.1.10 TIME MANAGEMENT/ORGANIZATIONAL SKILLS

Employers want employees to have good organizational and time management skills, because these enable them to work more effectively, be less stressed and distracted, and achieve more. While some candidates with Asperger Syndrome have excellent skills in this area, others struggle with time management and require solid strategies to compensate. The use of checklists, day-timers, and electronic schedulers can be useful in addressing issues in this area. It is possible for candidates to improve their time management and organizational skills to a level that an employer will find acceptable.

2.2.1.11 PERSONAL ATTRIBUTES

Personal attributes are the qualities or characteristics you have as a person. These attributes can affect the way you work independently or with colleagues. Employers are interested in employees who have helpful personal attributes such as:

- creativity
- attention to detail
- self-confidence
- a friendly, outgoing personality
- tactfulness

- good manners and courtesy

- a good sense of humor.

In this area, the candidate can make up for any shortcomings. An employer is more likely to hire a really friendly, likable person who is motivated and driven to do her best over someone who is super-qualified but miserable to be around. Although people with Asperger Syndrome are not necessarily known for their tact, their innate honesty and work ethic often make up for this.

Once employees with Asperger Syndrome get comfortable with their surroundings, they often begin to blossom, and their unique charm and personality solidify their position in the company. It is the personal attributes of an employee that sometimes saves his or her job and motivates employers and staff to support him or her above and beyond.

2.2.2 How does someone with Asperger Syndrome compete?

Studies show that communication skills top the list of the personal qualities and skills that employers seek in new hires. Honesty/integrity, teamwork skills, interpersonal skills, and motivation/initiative closely follow. The "perfect" candidate also has some type of relevant work experience to offer. Today's workplace increasingly requires employees to work in teams, interact effectively with coworkers and customers, and manage job responsibilities without close supervision.

It seems that many of the qualities that employers value are the very things with which many candidates with Asperger Syndrome struggle most. The fact is that people with Asperger Syndrome will have a greater challenge competing with the general public for employment opportunities. They are a different type of employee and they will require at least minimal accommodation from their employer. Nonetheless, they *can* compete and they *can* succeed by finding their niche and selling themselves on their many positive attributes.

It is a reality that a certain part of finding work that works for candidates with Asperger Syndrome relies on finding an understanding employer. Regardless of how skilled the candidate is, it is likely that she will encounter some difficulty, at some point, due to her challenges. With education and support, the candidate can work at a competitive level and be a valued employee. Ironically, it is often the candidate's differences that will provide her with the opportunity to get a foot in the door. This is discussed in greater detail in Chapter 13.

2.2.3 Work accommodation

Work accommodation is the added support an employer gives to employees to enable them to be productive in their job. For people who have a physical disability, that might mean building a wheelchair ramp or modifying a workstation. For employees with Asperger Syndrome, that might mean accommodating a longer learning curve, breaking assignments into smaller, more manageable steps, answering a few more questions than usual, learning how to communicate more clearly, allowing the employee to build up to full-time hours, writing out directions, or adapting to some behavioral anomalies.

How much an employer is willing to accommodate an employee depends on the employer, and his needs and motivation to hire the individual. If it appears that the new employee will end up being productive and staying with the employer after the initial cost of training, he is more likely to be open to accommodation. Ultimately there must be some incentive for any employer to hire someone who needs accommodation. Often this incentive will be a financial benefit to the employer, either in the short term, as in the case of a wage subsidy, or in the long term, as in the case of filling high turnover positions with long-term employees. In either scenario, the employer has the incentive to hire because it will positively impact his bottom line and help the company to grow and prosper.

2.3 Who hires someone with Asperger Syndrome?

The world is made up of a wide variety of people who are motivated by many different things. This is one reason the world is so exciting, and also so frustrating at times. There are very specific reasons why employers will hire employees with Asperger Syndrome, or any other disability for that matter. Getting a feel for who will hire and why they hire will be vital to your success in finding work that works. First, you need to have a willing employer who is motivated for the right reasons. There is one thing that is always important to business people and you should continually keep this in mind. They want value for their money. It does not make sense to hire someone who can't do the job. But to get a good employee, employers are usually willing to make job accommodations.

Who hires someone with Asperger Syndrome will usually be a person who is motivated by one or more of the following:

- they have a very specific need that must be met

- they want to reduce their staff turnover in certain positions

- they have a personal reason, for example, they have a relative or friend with a disability.

2.3.1 Someone with a very specific need

There are many candidates with Asperger Syndrome that are skilled in something that is either unique or highly desired. There was a fellow who was a talented painter. He had great difficulty keeping employed in more typical jobs, but he excelled in painting and became well known for his skill and creativity. He honed his talent and today his paintings sell for hundreds of dollars. He was able to use his unique skill to pay his bills and build an independent life.

The right person with Asperger Syndrome may have the particular qualification, skill, or the unique experience that meets the needs of an employer. In the right situation, with the proper set-up, this can be a fantastic fit. For example, when a certain city was looking for someone to design the computer programs that would run all the traffic lights in the community, they needed an employee who had a talent in analytical, mathematical, and problem-solving skills. The person they hired did such an excellent job on this project that other cities sought to purchase the software. The employee they hired had Asperger Syndrome. He had the skills, the focus, the fascination and the talent to get the job done.

Not every employer will have unique needs like the one mentioned above, yet this comes up surprisingly often. Take note of the gifts and special talents the candidate has and keep an open mind and a watchful eye. You never know when an opportunity might come along to make an exceptional match.

2.3.2 High turnover positions

Employers who have a high staff turnover benefit from hiring employees who are willing to stay in a position for a longer period. Every time an employer hires an employee and trains that person, it is an investment. Hiring and training takes time and money. Losing that employee, that investment, within a short time is costly to employers. There are quite a few people with Asperger Syndrome who thrive in high turnover jobs. They can manage the level of skill required for the job and can often do the job far longer and better than other employees and still enjoy it. Although at some point they might tire of the job because it lacks the variety they would ultimately like, they often do well in such jobs and will stay for an extended time in that position. This is a wonderful way for the candidate to build employment experience so he or she can move to another, more exciting position.

There are various reasons why high turnover positions exist within companies. For example, people in entry-level jobs upon obtaining experience may move to a higher-level position. Some positions are very repetitive and this does not appeal to everyone who initially takes such jobs. High turnover positions create a continuous need for employers to hire. This can create opportunities for some candidates with Asperger Syndrome.

2.3.3 Personal reasons

Many people in the world are motivated by good will. Most of these people work for a living and some are employers. They can be very helpful in the quest to find work that works. People who have had positive previous experience with employees with disabilities will tend to be less concerned with hiring someone with Asperger Syndrome. In fact, they are often motivated to do so because they understand the value of people who are "different." They know that hiring a person with a disability may require special accommodation and understanding, but they also recognize the positive value that hiring someone with a disability can bring to a work environment. Employers who are altruistic (do something for more than the money), employers who have a relative with a disability, employers who themselves have a challenge, and employers who have supported people with disabilities in the past, intrinsically "get it." These employers transform the workplace. They make excellent contacts when finding work that works.

Summary

- Employers are in business to make money. They can only afford to hire people who will produce. People with Asperger Syndrome can be productive employees when set up for success.

- Education dispels fear and misconceptions and opens the doors to opportunity.

- Employers always need good employees who are productive and reliable, and they are willing to make job accommodations to get and keep them.

- Take advantage of the incentives/programs your government offers employers to hire people with disabilities.

- Learn which companies in your community have social or corporate responsibility programs. They are often more open to the concept of accommodation and usually willing to hire people with disabilities.

- Take the time to understand what an employer values in an employee. Then help the candidate build those skills.

- It is always the people behind the company that make the decisions to hire. Keep in mind that it is the personal relationship you have with the individual in the company that will likely clinch the deal of hiring the candidate. People may be motivated to hire for a variety of reasons, but the decision always comes down to someone's personal judgment. Understanding employers, what motivates them and what their needs are, helps in your approach to finding work that works.

3 The job coach

To become our best, all of us need a little coaching.

Michael Jordan, Muhammad Ali, Venus Williams, and Tiger Woods all used coaches to help them achieve their potential and be successful. But coaches are not just for athletes. Increasingly in today's fast-paced work environments, people of all abilities are seeking support from personal trainers and business coaches to help them get over hurdles that might otherwise hold them back. People with disabilities need to know that they are not the only ones in the workplace who need support from time to time.

A coach is a professional who can provide support, perspective, advice, and training to help another person be the best he can. A *job* coach plays a vital role in the overall success of work that works for people with Asperger Syndrome. This is accomplished by supporting both the person with Asperger Syndrome and the people who interact directly with him in the workplace.

A job coach sets the tone in the first few weeks before the Asperger employee comes into the work environment. The coach educates the employer and staff, helps to calm concerns and misconceptions, and outlines what the most effective processes are for the employee. Virtually anyone can become a good job coach if the effort is put into learning effective coaching methods. For example, when a young man named Josh was placed in a job at a large bank, he was hired to work three half-days a week helping out with some of the back-office jobs at one of the main branches. Before he began his job, the job coach learned that there was to be a big staff meeting at the branch. Josh's job coach took this opportunity to be placed on the agenda. With his permission, at the meeting the coach spoke to the branch staff about Josh, about Asperger Syndrome and about what the staff could expect from Josh during his transition into his new job. She also explained to the staff how they could interact effectively with Josh. This was a wonderful opportunity to tell some success stories that would endear Josh to the staff, even before they had met him. After the meeting there was overwhelming enthusiasm about Josh coming on board as part of the team. The staff had a better understanding of what they could expect from Josh, how they needed to communicate with him and what his capabilities were. The job coach challenged everyone at the branch to start thinking about jobs in their departments that would be appropriate for Josh and at the same time alleviate some of their own workload. This challenge eventually resulted in Josh getting more variety in his duties and later led to an increase in his hours.

Because the job coach had spoken at that meeting, the staff recognized her as part of Josh's support team. This set the stage for them to approach the coach if they had any questions or concerns. It was thrilling for everyone to learn that on Josh's first day many of the staff remembered his name and made an effort to say hello and help him feel comfortable. Josh grew to be an important member of the branch staff. As it turned out, very few questions or problems arose with Josh, but the staff knew that they had outside support in the job coach, should anything go wrong. All of these factors came together to help Josh be successful in his job.

> People with Asperger Syndrome can really do well in the workplace when they are set up for success. The job coach plays a vital role in doing this.

3.1 The importance of a job coach

Having support on the job is fundamental to helping people with Asperger Syndrome find work and keep it. The job coach is like a translator, teacher, social worker, advocate, and supervisor, all wrapped into one. A good job coach knows how to develop the lines of communication and foster the appropriate relationships that smooth the employee's transition into a new job. Although employees with Asperger Syndrome are ultimately responsible for their own success, the job coach plays a vital role in setting the stage for them to learn the job and realize their potential.

A job coach is important in three main ways. He:

- is an impartial representative for the employee with Asperger Syndrome

- provides a link between the employer, the employee, and the employee's family

- dramatically increases the chances for long-term success.

3.1.1 Impartial representative for the employee with Asperger Syndrome

When we love someone, it is hard to be impartial. We support them, regardless of their foibles and idiosyncrasies. But to help someone with Asperger Syndrome find and keep a job, it is critical to be impartial in order to see his challenges clearly and to support all sides involved in the placement process. Such objectivity is easier for someone who does not have a pre-existing relationship or emotional attachment to the prospective employee. This is where a job coach steps in.

The job coach is able to represent the employee with Asperger Syndrome pragmatically. He promotes the talents and skills of the employee while diplomatically explaining the challenges they pose, and the strategies necessary to overcome them. By being an impartial representative, the job coach is able to help both the employer and employee overcome challenges that could otherwise impede success.

3.1.2 Provides a link

Family members are often uncomfortable negotiating with an employer around issues regarding their relative with Asperger Syndrome. It is difficult for them to be unbiased simply because they love their relative. From the employer's side, it can be uncomfortable to listen to family members because all too often they do not clearly understand what goes on in the workplace. The employer will not want to offend the family member and might "sugar-coat" the situation. This discomfort can lead to a variety of negative situations. This will not happen every time, of course; still, both the employer and family members prefer to speak with someone neutral.

Jim was a young man in danger of losing his job after three years with a company. His family had never involved outside support and for three years things had seemed to be going well until one day the employer called and asked the family to pick their son up from work. Apparently Jim was having temper tantrums on the job. The employer didn't know what to do, so he tried his best to calm Jim down. The temper tantrums increased in volume and intensity to the point that Jim became so disruptive that the employer was forced to take drastic action. He called the family to take Jim home and told them if they were unable to correct the problem, he would have no choice but to fire Jim.

Jim's family was in shock. There had been minor incidents on the job in the past but nothing that indicated to them that the situation was serious. Yet the employer felt he had tried to explain the situation to the family and felt the family was not taking it seriously because they thought, "Well this behavior never amounts to anything." They were used to Jim's tantrums.

The question was what could be done to solve the problem. The answer was to bring in a neutral third party who quickly found that half the problem was the miscommunication between the family and the employer. Too many unclear messages were flying back and forth. It took some mediation, a good solid strategy, and some job coaching to resolve the situation. Jim is now tantrum-free, back at work, and doing well.

The employer needed to speak with a neutral party to express his frustration and so did the family. It was so much easier for them not to have to speak with each other because they were emotionally involved. Being neutral, the third party, in this case the job coach, was in a position to hear clearly what everyone's concerns were and, therefore, to act appropriately.

> Good job coaches know how to be effective mediators. They are able to relay clear information, remain objective, and take appropriate action to support the process for everyone involved.

3.1.3 Dramatically increases chances for long-term success

Having a job coach involved in a job placement increases the prospects for long-term employment. By establishing the appropriate lines of communication, setting up expectations, mediating, and supporting everyone involved, the job coach establishes the groundwork for success. This does not imply that the job coach needs to hover over anyone or control the entire situation. A good job coach knows how to provide the appropriate amount and type of support in each situation. This will vary considerably from one situation to the next, depending on the circumstances and the abilities of the candidate. Some may require intensive one-on-one support, while others will manage well with weekly check-ins.

3.2 Role of the job coach

Employees must prove themselves in any job. Ultimately, they are responsible for their own success. The job coach paves the way for that success by coaching the employee, supporting the employer, and phasing out his support role.

Each of those three primary roles involves several steps:

1.   Coach the employee

     ○   define the expectations of each job responsibility
     ○   clearly explain the expectations to the new employee and ensure they are understood
     ○   break each job responsibility down into manageable steps
     ○   effectively teach each job responsibility
     ○   facilitate communication.

2.   Support the employer

     ○   establish rapport with the manager/supervisor and key coworkers
     ○   educate key staff members
     ○   create the Professional Binder (see page 295)
     ○   problem-solve issues as they arise.

3.   Phase out support

     ○   build natural supports
     ○   conduct regular off-site check-ins
     ○   be available to provide support as needed.

3.2.1 Coaching the employee

Coaching the prospective employee is a limited-time engagement, not a lifetime support. The coach is not there to do the job, but to help the employee become able to handle the job independently.

The job coach's role as a coach in a work setting is to clarify the expectations of the job and to map them out in a way that will be easily absorbed by the employee with Asperger Syndrome. It is up to the job coach to learn in detail how the employer wants a particular job done, and to support the employee in learning that job and retaining the information. The job coach should be able to estimate how long the employee will need assistance, how intensive the support should be, and how quickly the support should be phased out.

The job coach plays a significant role in helping the employee and the employer learn how to work together, communicate with each other and build a relationship. The job coach can interpret information to help the two understand each other, but should ensure that the communication remains direct between the employee and the employer at all times. After all, *they* are the ones who need to be talking!

3.2.2 Supporting the employer

Only part of the job coach's role is to support the employee with Asperger Syndrome. It is equally important to support the employer. Too often, the emphasis is put solely on coaching the employee. But the employer is half of the employment equation. In fact, the job coach's job is to support *all* parties in the placement process.

A supported employer is more likely to go the extra mile to make things work with an employee who has Asperger Syndrome. The good job coach engages the employer and fosters a direct line of communication between employer and employee. This personal connection is key to the success of a placement. When an employer takes personal interest in a project (in this case, an employee), he is more likely to make it work. In fact, he will bend over backwards to make it work because a failure becomes a personal failure. The good job coach knows this and works hard to foster in the employer a personal relationship with and investment in the new employee.

3.2.3 Educating the employer

The job coach must take the lead in educating the employer and coworkers about how to work with someone with Asperger Syndrome. The new employee and job coach will decide together what will be disclosed with regard to the disability. (For in-depth information on disclosing a disability, see Chapter 12.) The job coach will then map out what education the employer should have in preparation for working with the new employee. All three – employer, employee, and coach – should be involved in deciding which staff should also be educated.

It is important that the employer know how to communicate effectively with the employee with Asperger Syndrome so that the employee can function independently in the job. To support this, the job coach can review with the employer these general tips on how to work with someone with Asperger Syndrome.

3.2.3.1 HOW TO WORK WITH AN EMPLOYEE WHO HAS ASPERGER SYNDROME

- Give verbal instructions a little more slowly and break them down into individual steps.

- Be direct and clear in your instruction and try to keep it brief and to the point.

- Ask the individual to repeat what you have asked him to do. You may have to repeat instruction before the employee completely understands what is expected.

- Write down instructions if you can. This will help the employee to perform the task with fewer questions and reminders.

- People with Asperger Syndrome work best if there is a routine or system involved in the job. This is not always possible but even *some* routine is better than none. For example, maybe the employee can do the same thing every morning upon arrival, or have a coffee/lunch break at the same time every day, or do a certain task every day at the end of the shift.

- It is difficult for most people with Asperger Syndrome to handle multiple tasks. If you can have them focus on one thing at a time, performance will be much better.

- Although employees with Asperger Syndrome *are* cognitively different, resist the temptation to treat them differently. For example, they are accountable and responsible for their work. Expect them to be on time and to live up to the requirements of their position. If they fall short of expectations, you may wish to review whether they understood the job clearly, whether they were distracted by something, or whether something out of the usual happened that day. This may help the two of you solve the problem and develop ways to deal with situations that may arise in the future. If you are having difficulty getting the results you want, call the job coach. He should be able to resolve most issues quickly.

- Judgment and decision-making are often a challenge for people with Asperger Syndrome. When you are giving an assignment, keep this in mind. If a particular job requires the employee to make decisions, try to outline the type of answers you want beforehand so that the employee can do the job effectively and give you the result you want.

- Stating the obvious is usually useful when working with employees with Asperger Syndrome. What is obvious to you may not be to them.

- People with Asperger Syndrome often have a wonderful sense of humor once you get to know them. Allow some time for them to adjust to their new environment and you will start to see their personality come out.

The employer should keep a copy of these tips on file for future reference.

3.3 When and how to phase out support

The objective of job coaching is to help the new employee learn the job and work independently. Phasing out support is a key step in that process. It is also one of the most difficult things for a job coach to determine. The amount and type of support will vary with each employee, employer and job situation. If the job coach provides too much support, people can get the impression that the new employee is not capable of doing the job. If the job coach provides too little support, the employee can flounder.

3.3.1 Too much support

Too much support can trigger a dangerous backlash. The employer and coworkers may begin to think that this new employee is not capable of performing the job effectively. They start to rely on the job coach and believe that he is actually responsible for any success that the new employee is having. They see any mistakes that arise where the employee is working as being the fault of the new employee if the job coach is not there assisting. When the job coach finally phases out, the employee with Asperger Syndrome is set up to take the blame for things that may not be even remotely related to his performance. The employee becomes an easy target for scapegoating by coworkers.

As you might imagine, this is a volatile situation. The Asperger employee, with poor social skills and little comprehension of the situation, is often left defenseless. A situation like this can create enormous frustration in the employee. Eventually, the employee lashes out inappropriately because he has no idea how to handle it. Frustration leads to inappropriate behavior, which leads to negative consequences. The person that is on the receiving end of those consequences is usually the employee with Asperger Syndrome.

Unfortunately, this domino effect is seen often enough for one to be particularly wary of giving too much support.

3.3.2 Too little support

At the other end of the spectrum, too little support can leave the employee with Asperger Syndrome stranded. This is what I refer to as the "hope and a prayer" technique. The new employee enters a job with so little support in place that he does not understand, or misunderstands, the expectations of the position. The employee is often isolated because he has no idea how to build positive working relationships, or may misinterpret situations and act oddly. Even if the employer knows that the employee has Asperger Syndrome, it is unlikely that the employer possesses knowledge and understanding to deal with problems.

In this situation, the frustration builds up in the employee, the employer, and the coworkers. Even when everyone around that new employee has a heart of gold and wants to see success, the situation can become a disaster. There are many stories from people with Asperger Syndrome who have lost their jobs because of too little or no support. The work environment has been soured because of poor relationship building, poor communication and, sometimes, poor performance. If a job coach does not provide enough appropriate support, the new employee is set up for failure and scapegoating.

How and when to phase out coaching will depend on the employee and the employer. The general rule is to phase the coaching out as soon as possible and move into off-site support, such as drop-ins and telephone check-ins. The coach remains available for on-the-job support as needed.

Before moving to off-site support, the coach needs to feel confident that the new employee is ready to work independently. Then the coach should speak with the employer to make sure he is comfortable with the phasing out. Usually, employers are quite aware of how well their new employees are progressing. They want them to be independent as soon as possible, yet are willing to take the time to ensure that the employee has adjusted and the job is being done well. As long as the employer is comfortable, he will be happy to see the employee working without a job coach. It is at this point that the job coach should move to off-site support.

The coach should check in regularly with the employer and the employee to make sure everything is going well. The coach should ask the employer such questions as "Is Joe meeting his targets?" and "Have there been any unusual behaviors?" Whatever the challenges are for the employee in the workplace, the coach should be checking in about them with the employer. That enables the coach to catch problems or issues as they arise and address them rapidly. If the coach does not ask specific questions, he risks overlooking some serious issues. By the time the employer mentions anything, it has often become a much bigger problem and subsequently more difficult to handle.

> The right *amount* of support is just as important as the right *type* of support.

3.3.3 Building natural supports

Every employee needs some support in a job. The employer provides that, either formally, through such things as job training, job shadowing, and mentoring, or informally, through management or coworkers. As he phases out, the job coach will begin to shift the support previously provided over to those natural supports.

Generally, employees ask their supervisor for help and direction or go to a coworker to get support. Since people with Asperger Syndrome have difficulty developing those relationships, the job coach should identify three key people: The manager or supervisor, and two coworkers who are willing to act as mentors to the employee. The coach will introduce the employee to these people and make sure that he knows that if there are any questions or problems, he can speak to any one of them. The coworkers should be able to solve most problems or make a judgment call as to what should happen next. If neither of the coworkers is available, the employee may go directly to the manager/supervisor.

Establishing natural supports accomplishes two things. First, it helps the Asperger employee build relationships by identifying the people he is to connect with regularly. Second, it ensures that the manager/supervisor is not being bothered with minor problems. In addition, the coworkers will frequently take a personal interest in helping the employee succeed. When people make something personal, they want to see it be successful because it reflects well on them. Thus, they will often go out of their way to support the employee who has Asperger Syndrome.

It is important that the employee makes sure he does not rely too heavily on a coworker, because if too much of that person's time is taken, then this interferes with the coworker doing his own job. It is also an indication that the employee with Asperger Syndrome does not understand his own job. In that case, the coworkers should be instructed to call the job coach. Boundaries are very important when setting a job up for success. The employee with Asperger Syndrome must understand what is expected with regard to productivity as well as socially.

The job coach will also teach the new employee the protocol of the office so he will know to whom questions are to be addressed, even when the main contact is not available, and to whom to speak with regard to specific work issues. For example, when time off is needed for a doctor's appointment, the employee should know to whom the request for time off should be directed.

3.4 What to look for in a job coach

A good job coach is a combination of teacher, mentor, social worker, and supervisor. Each of those roles requires skill and a natural talent to understand how people behave. The job coach has enormous influence in setting up a job placement so that it succeeds for everyone involved. It is important when choosing a job coach to look for the following qualities:

- knowledge of Asperger Syndrome
- experience
- natural teaching ability
- professional image
- confidence
- creativity.

3.4.1 Knowledge

It is essential for the job coach to be familiar with Asperger Syndrome in order to be able to read the candidate accurately, to devise effective coaching strategies that address the challenges and problems, and to educate others. If the coach does not have this full knowledge, then a scripted presentation should be included as part of an orientation package before he begins working with a person with Asperger Syndrome.

3.4.2 Experience

It is always preferable to look for a job coach who has experience, particularly in coaching people with Asperger Syndrome. That, however, may be a challenge because there are limited numbers of job coaches with experience in this field. This is primarily due to the lack of specialized training available for job coaches in methods and strategies appropriate for people with Asperger Syndrome. Short of this specialized experience, you should look for someone experienced either in coaching people with cognitive disabilities or, preferably, in working with very high-functioning individuals.

3.4.3 Natural teaching ability

Not all people are created equal when it comes to teaching. There are those who teach well naturally and those who don't. You want a job coach who is a gifted and natural teacher. This will make a difference when he is teaching a person with Asperger Syndrome because it will be natural for him to mold the teaching style to the style of the person who is being taught. This is not always an easy task. If the coach is a good, natural teacher, he should be able to quickly identify and adapt to the learning style of a person with Asperger Syndrome.

One way to determine whether someone is a good teacher is to have him teach you something during the interview. "Describe for me how you would teach me to tie my shoelace." Since there is pressure to perform well during the interview, this will also give you insight into how the coach functions under pressure.

3.4.4 Professional image

The job coach is a role model for the new employee and also represents the employee to the employer. He must present well physically and intellectually in a professional manner that fits into the work environment. The job coach will be judged by the employer on his presentation and competence even though the candidate with Asperger Syndrome will be the new employee. If you are a relative or a friend of someone with Asperger Syndrome then, when interviewing prospective job coaches, pay close attention to how they present at the interview. Do they show up in sandals and T-shirt or do they present as if they are heading out for a day at the office? This makes all the difference to them setting the stage for success at a later date for the new employee.

3.4.5 Confidence

During the interview, you will have an opportunity to determine the coaches' level of confidence. Do they appear comfortable with themselves? Do they seem to know what they are talking about? Be prepared with a question or two that tests the confidence and competence of each applicant, for example:

- How would you handle a situation where the person you are coaching is acting inappropriately?

- How would you work with parents whom you feel are controlling?

3.4.6 Creativity

Creativity is an important quality in a job coach. It is particularly valuable when working with people with Asperger Syndrome because of the unique way they process information. In order for the coach to be effective, he will need to be able to think quickly and come up with unusual, often unorthodox methods of teaching so that the lesson will get across. Experienced coaches say that one of the qualities they draw upon most is their creativity.

3.5 A guide to job coaching

The goal of the job coach is to support the Asperger employee to be independent and productive in the workplace. There are seven initial steps that promote a positive experience for all involved:

1. Establishing a relationship with the employee.

2. Establishing a relationship with the employer.

3. Facilitating the relationship between the employer and employee.

4. Learning the expectations of the job.

5. Identifying challenges.

6.   Providing the tools to help manage challenges.

7.   Establishing norms for judging competitive employment.

3.5.1 Establishing a relationship with the employee

If the job coach has not worked with the employee before there will be a need to establish rapport quickly with the employee. In order to do this, the job coach should be friendly and supportive but at the same time establish himself as an authority. There is a need to distinguish clearly between being a friend and being a boss. The coach needs the employee to listen, respect, and act on what is said. If this relationship with the employee is not established immediately, it likely will not occur at all.

3.5.2 Establishing a relationship with the employer

From the first moment the job coach has contact with an employer, he should begin building a relationship of trust, competency, and responsibility. The job coach should not underestimate the influence that he has in this role. The coach's relationship with the employer may make or break the placement for the candidate. An employer will look to the job coach for guidance and support when it comes to matters regarding the employee with Asperger Syndrome. If the coach projects an image of someone who is competent, reliable, and effective, the employer will work harder to make things work. If the coach is successful at establishing this relationship, he can also expect the employer to make contact as soon as an obstacle arises. This early warning may give the job coach the opportunity to help save the employee's job!

3.5.3 Facilitating the relationship between the employer and the employee

It is important for the job coach to facilitate the relationship between the employee and the employer from the outset. The job coach may do this by encouraging the employer to speak to the employee directly when giving instruction. The reverse should also be encouraged when the employee has something to say. A natural and effective way of facilitating this relationship is for the job coach to stand behind or beside the employer when the employer is speaking with the employee. This more or less forces the employer to address the employee but the job coach is right there if clarification is required. This not only supports the employer but also helps the employee identify the authority figure, something that can be difficult for some people with Asperger Syndrome.

3.5.4 Learning the expectations of the job

Expectations and job responsibilities should be the first thing that the job coach establishes at the work site, if they have not been provided beforehand. With job description in hand, the job coach should go over each job responsibility with the employer in detail and make notes. The coach should learn about any "unwritten" or "hidden" expectations there may be of the employee, for example, dress code, how people at the workplace like to be addressed, break schedules, or routines. He will want to prepare the employee by going over the expectations of the job as early as possible.

It is helpful for people with Asperger Syndrome to have an established set of procedures for the job. That means identifying the steps involved in assignments, writing down routines, listing jobs that he can do that will show initiative. It is a good idea to create a binder for the position and add information as it is learned. This gives the employee a tool to which he can refer when there is no one around to ask for assistance, and it may help him to avoid asking someone the question in the first place.

> Learning what will be expected of the employee will make moving into the job easier for everyone.

3.5.5 Identifying challenges

It is important for the job coach quickly to identify any challenges that might impede the employee from keeping the new job. He needs to identify the job accommodation needs of the employee so that arrangements can be made with the employer and to begin arranging the job coaching strategy.

The job coach should watch closely for any jobs that require skills that might be beyond the employee's level. These might include jobs that require decision-making, multi-tasking, interpersonal skills, and so on. Close attention should be paid to how the employee is interacting with coworkers. This will alert the job coach to any potential behavioral or social problems. The coach must watch the employee closely on the job, allowing the individual to interact independently and then assess what types of supports should be put in place that will be effective based upon the employee's learning style.

When watching for challenges, the job coach should try looking at the employee through the eyes of the employer. He should listen to personal instincts and natural reactions. The coach should make a note if he feels bothered, annoyed or concerned. Chances are if the coach feels it, the employer will also. Keep the old adage "an ounce of prevention is worth a pound of cure" in mind. A good job coach can anticipate many challenges simply by using a trained eye and put preventative measures in place to avoid trouble.

The following three-step process helps the job coach determine the need for and type of job accommodation the employee with Asperger Syndrome may require.

- *Step 1* Gather information about the type of work. Researching job postings, contacting human resource personnel, and talking with employees currently performing the job should accomplish this. Ideally this information is gathered during the career direction process rather than being left until the employee is transitioning into the job. The following are examples of the types of questions to ask: What is the purpose of the job? What are the essential job responsibilities? What are the most important skills that would make someone successful in the job? How much judgment and multi-tasking does this job require? How is productivity measured?

- *Step 2* The job coach now needs to use the information gathered in the previous step and combine it with his knowledge of the employee; for example, learning style and challenges. The coach can now identify potential difficulties and functional limitations that may impact the potential for success on the job.

- *Step 3* Armed with the knowledge of what the problem areas might be, the job coach can now plan an accommodation strategy. The Strategy Guide in Chapter 10 can be used to assist in this process. Beyond this, the job coach can look at creative ways of solving potential problems. For example, if there is an aspect of the job that the coach knows will be a challenge for the employee, such as the employee having to take over telephone reception duties during lunch, can this responsibility be traded for another, less problematic one?

The job coach also needs to be able to anticipate how many job-coaching hours will be necessary to support the employee to full independence. This will help the coach to prepare both the employee and the employer when it is time to phase the job coaching out.

3.5.6 Providing the tools to help manage challenges

Once the challenges are identified, it will be important to provide the employee and the employer with tools to help manage specific obstacles. For example, if the employee is struggling with productivity, the job coach can put a speed and accuracy scale in place and teach the employer how to implement it. Part 2 of this book covers the process of identifying and teaching effective strategies for many of the challenges people with Asperger Syndrome face in the workplace. In fact, The Strategy Guide in Chapter 10 is an excellent resource for the job coach and can also be shared with the employer at the appropriate time.

Without such tools, the employer will be left alone to try to work with any obstacles. That may leave him feeling unsupported and frustrated and may put the employee's job at risk.

3.5.7 Establishing norms for judging competitive employment

When the employee is learning a new task, the job coach should try doing the job himself. Assessing how long it takes to become proficient at the job as a beginner and then using that information to help measure the employee's progress is valuable. The job coach should also observe other staff to see how well the "experts" do the job and then set the ultimate goal somewhere between the two. The goal should be to help the employee achieve an acceptable level of performance without a lot of additional attention from the employer.

Summary

- The job coach is fundamental to helping the employee with Asperger Syndrome maintain a job.

- A good job coach wears many hats. He must be a good teacher, mentor, advocate, and mediator.

- Take the time to find a job coach who is knowledgeable, experienced, professional, creative, and confident.

- Become familiar with the job coach role so that you know what to expect and how to get it.

4 The candidate
The employee with Asperger Syndrome

Finding work that works for a person with Asperger Syndrome is like climbing a mountain in bare feet. When you place your feet carefully and thoughtfully, you get to the top.

In human resources, the person who is seeking employment is called the *candidate*. The candidate in this book is your Asperger friend or relative and is the star of the show when finding work that works. Understanding Asperger Syndrome and in particular your Asperger friend is a very important part of finding work that works. The more you know about the syndrome and the person, the better equipped you will be to bring all the pieces together to support a successful work placement. This chapter will give you insight into the struggles and the battles your Asperger friend has within himself. This is important because you will need to support your friend in making some very important decisions before the two of you embark together on the journey of finding employment.

First, I think that it is important to explain that I am not a clinical expert on Asperger Syndrome. My knowledge comes predominately from first-hand experience working with hundreds of people with Asperger Syndrome. There is a lot of clinical literature available on Asperger Syndrome if you wish to learn more about it from a medical perspective. But for the purposes of finding work, I think that it is important to keep things at a basic level. After all, you will be speaking mainly with people who have never heard of Asperger Syndrome and you will want to be able to talk about it using language that is easy for them to understand.

I want to review the basics of the disorder and then talk about how it affects the individual when making decisions about her life and career. As you will read later in this chapter, there are some pretty important decisions that your Asperger friend needs to make and you need to be in a position to explain the options and choices clearly. This chapter will prepare you to sit down with your Asperger friend and explain the facts about what she needs to do if she is serious about finding work that works. In reading this book and particularly this chapter, the candidate with Asperger Syndrome will personally gain insight into the choices and challenges she may face in seeking employment.

4.1 Asperger Syndrome 101

Hans Asperger, a pediatrician from Vienna, first named Asperger Syndrome in 1944. Like autism, Asperger Syndrome has a spectrum of severity. Asperger Syndrome is something that people are born with and cannot be cured of. Many people with Asperger Syndrome have no wish to be "cured" and are content living their lifestyle.

Statistics are hard to nail down because there have been very few population studies on Asperger Syndrome. Unofficially, there could be as many as 48 million people with autism spectrum disorder (including Asperger Syndrome) living in the world today. A study by Stephan Ehlers and Christopher Gillberg in 1993 estimated that 36 out of every 10,000 people had Asperger Syndrome and another 36 out of 10,000 had social impairments that could have been Asperger Syndrome. That equates to over 160,000 adults with Asperger Syndrome living in the United Kingdom alone. There has been an explosion of autism spectrum diagnosis in the world that has received much attention. There is only speculation as to the reasons for this. Contributing factors include greater public awareness and widening of the diagnostic criteria. Some people believe that environmental factors or vaccines are contributors. Social demands have shifted over the past couple of decades, which has caused there to be a greater demand for interpersonal, social, and communication skills in the workforce. This draws greater attention to people who lack these skills, which may also be a contributing factor to the increase in diagnosis.

Asperger Syndrome tends to make individuals loners who get a reputation for being odd, eccentric, or misfits because of unusual behavior, lack of social skills, and unique special interests. These individuals have a difficult time relating to others and building relationships primarily because they have difficulty ascertaining how others are feeling or what they are thinking. This lack of empathy makes it really hard for them to carry on conversation because of difficulty anticipating what the other person is going to say or do. Also, their reactions to what other people do or say may not be appropriate. So they tend to either dominate conversations or not participate in them at all.

There has been a lot of media coverage on the "special interests" that many people with Asperger Syndrome possess. The public seems to be captivated by the savant aspect of Asperger Syndrome. These fixations and gifts can be wonderful if they are used to help the individual develop, learn and broaden her skills. The danger of these special interests is that they can also be a serious preoccupation that interferes with the person learning anything else. In conversation, fascinations will often dominate as the candidate may go on about a subject in finite detail. It is interesting to watch someone with Asperger Syndrome masterfully maneuver a conversation back to her favorite topic. Although this may be an impressive novelty to witness the first time it happens, after a while the novelty wears off and there is the potential for some to avoid interacting with the candidate. This will contribute to the candidate's isolation if she is unaware that other people are not sharing her interest in the topic.

People with Asperger Syndrome have to make a deliberate effort to "fit in" to the "neuro-typical" world. They need to learn social rules and expectations one step at a time and then make a conscious decision to act in accordance. This does not come naturally for most people who have Asperger Syndrome. In fact, it is much like acting like someone else completely different. It is not surprising, therefore, that some people who have a diagnosis that falls on the autism spectrum refer to having "Wrong Planet Syndrome." Perhaps the benefit of this is that they are not as concerned about what others think or with being popular or cool. They are truly individuals and walk to the beat of their own drummer. Unfortunately, this also makes them stand out and can draw negative attention that may result in hurtful actions from others.

In order to learn social rules, people with Asperger Syndrome need to create an enormous internal database of information so that they can determine what action or reaction is appropriate for every situation encountered. This poor understanding of social rules makes interaction difficult. They want to connect with people but lack the skills to do so. Because people with Asperger Syndrome tend not to relate easily to what others are thinking or feeling, they have a hard time building relationships with peers. They can also have difficulty maintaining eye contact, which can make them come across as a little unusual or suspicious to those who do not understand their discomfort.

Having Asperger Syndrome presents an obstacle to reading non-verbal cues, and thus individuals tend to miss a great deal of what is going on around them. For example, they may not recognize when someone they wish to speak to is busy, preoccupied, or is ready to leave the room, because they miss the messages sent through body language. They might misinterpret something because they did not understand the sarcasm or the double meaning. It is important to make a conscious effort to be clear and not use innuendo, idioms, or clichés when talking to a person who has Asperger Syndrome because these are often taken literally. Also make sure to explain humor if you think that it is something that has not registered. Every joke and humorous mishap is an opportunity to teach about the unwritten rules of social culture.

When people with Asperger Syndrome speak, the message is frequently very direct. They say exactly what they mean candidly, which can sometimes offend others who do not understand. Choice of language is usually precise and formal. Some people with Asperger Syndrome are extremely gifted with language and exhibit a keen wit. You may also notice that their voices tend to be either louder or quieter than average and may have a flat tonal quality. This is a trait of Asperger Syndrome. Some of the behaviors associated with Asperger Syndrome are misunderstood and misinterpreted as rude, arrogant, self-focused, or dismissive. Often these characteristics overshadow the positive attributes that many people with Asperger Syndrome have. It takes a longer time to get to know someone with Asperger Syndrome and a willingness to see beyond the surface. Anyone who has made this effort though, finds the person well worth it!

Children with Asperger Syndrome often experience ruthless bullying and teasing in school. They may be alienated and isolated by their peers. This can leave them scared, bitter and angry, and these emotions follow them into their adult life resulting in issues including depression, aggression, low self-esteem, negativity, and hopelessness. All of which impact their ability to fit into mainstream society, further complicating their lives.

Quite a number of people with Asperger Syndrome graduate from high school and continue to post-secondary education. They may get married, have children, and a career. It is also possible for some to go their entire life with never being diagnosed with Asperger Syndrome. It is only when differences are so pronounced that they impede one's ability to function normally that there is cause for concern. A diagnosis often comes as a relief in such cases because there is finally some understanding about why things have been so difficult.

> I may now have social interaction down to a science. However, there is one thing I must make an effort never to forget and that is what it's like to suffer from Asperger syndrome. (Marc Segar, *The Battles of an Autistic Thinker*)

Many of the challenges people with Asperger Syndrome face in life present obstacles for them in employment. The following is a list of some of the workplace behaviors with which many people with Asperger Syndrome may struggle:

- belief that her way is the best way
- odd or unusual behavior such as talking to herself
- difficulty beginning projects – unsure where to start
- difficulty empathizing with others' thoughts and feelings
- difficulty relating to and interacting with authority figures
- difficulty interacting in a team environment
- difficulty multi-tasking
- difficulty seeing the full scope of a project
- difficulty with unstructured time
- difficulty writing reports
- exaggerated or overly sensitive reactions to feedback
- low motivation to perform tasks of no immediate personal interest
- asking excessive questions, or the same question repeatedly

- perfectionism
- poor judgment and decision-making skills
- poor manners
- reluctance to ask for help or seek advice
- resistant to change
- sarcasm, negativism, criticism
- slower productivity/performance
- stress, frustration and anger reaction to change or interruptions
- struggle to take initiative
- higher anxiety levels particularly when meeting new people or encountering change or new situations
- abrupt manner in expressing thoughts, ideas, or opinions
- single-mindedness, unwilling to see the viewpoint of others.

Part 2 of this book addresses how to assess and address many of these workplace challenges. For now, I want to balance the above list with a list of some of the many positive attributes of Asperger Syndrome:

- excellent rote memory
- easy absorption of facts
- generally good performance in math and science
- often good language skills (but they may have limited language content and poor social understanding)
- honesty
- rules-oriented, which frequently results in an excellent work ethic
- conscientious
- detail-oriented
- hard working
- focused (when within area of interest)

- intelligent
- kind hearted.

4.1.1 Theory of mind

Theory of mind is a relatively new hypothesis in the field of autism spectrum disorders. It is included here because I believe it to be relevant to understanding Asperger Syndrome. *Theory of mind* refers to the concept that people with autism spectrum disorder do not understand that other people have different viewpoints, ideas, plans, or thoughts and that they have great difficulty understanding the beliefs, attitudes, and emotions of others. This makes it very difficult for some people with Asperger Syndrome to be empathetic to the feelings of others. An example would be that if someone lacks theory of mind they would assume that what they are feeling, you also must feel. They would also have trouble recognizing dishonesty in others because they themselves are very honest. For example, the candidate with Asperger Syndrome may have difficulty understanding that her coworkers and peers *even have* thoughts and feelings. This may make the candidate appear arrogant, self-centered, or indifferent.

As you get to know a person with Asperger Syndrome, you may find that many of her underlying problems relate to limited theory of mind. It may also help you understand why the candidate acts the way she does and says the things she says. If a person lacks theory of mind, it explains why there is such difficulty relating to and communicating with others.

4.1.2 Self-esteem, confidence, and depression

People with Asperger Syndrome are at a higher risk of suffering from low self-esteem, confidence, and depression because of the struggles they experience in their daily lives. Some of the contributing factors to these issues are rigid ways of thinking; limited insight into challenges; a low tolerance to stress, anger and frustration; negativism; and often a poor understanding of themselves as a whole. Being alienated and excluded from activities because they are different may also contribute to their feelings of self-loathing and hopelessness. Depression differs from sadness or grieving because it is a chemical reaction in the brain. Although it is highly treatable, depression affects the way someone sees the world as well as the way she acts and feels. It is not uncommon for those who suffer from depression to do poorly in their jobs, turn to alcohol or drugs, isolate themselves or, in extreme cases, take their own lives in an attempt to stop their hurt.

Sometimes you cannot begin addressing employment challenges with someone with Asperger Syndrome until some of these underlying issues have been addressed. Learning to recognize the symptoms of depression will help you differentiate it from Asperger Syndrome. Here is a list of symptoms that should alert you that someone may be feeling depressed:

- continued sadness and feelings of hopelessness

- increased anger, irritability, agitation

- changes in eating or sleeping habits

- forgetfulness

- guilty feelings and low self-esteem

- lack of enthusiasm, poor motivation, and low energy

- abuse of drugs or alcohol

- suicide threats.

One of the most effective methods of dealing with these challenges is to build upon an individual's strengths. Get the person into an environment where she will be valued and supported and set clear boundaries and expectations. Everyone needs to have positive experiences to help build confidence and self-esteem. Once someone is able to see that she can do things well, it generally follows that the person feels better and has a better self-perception, and depression is often alleviated.

Some types of depression require medical intervention. Many of the anti-depressants on the market today work well for people with Asperger Syndrome in treating depression and anxiety. However, it is important to note that medications are prescribed for the treatment of specific symptoms, and not to treat the disorder as a whole.

4.1.3 Memory

Long-term memory is truly an impressive attribute that most people with Asperger Syndrome share. They may have the ability to memorize large amounts of data such as telephone numbers, addresses, dates, license plates, directions, and any other number of facts that fascinate them. Even those who appear not to have some of these more exceptional memories will often remember intricate details of the past quite vividly. This memory for detail is something that the average person sees as very desirable. Indeed, it is an enviable skill. This memory factor is something that can impress a potential employer and can, of course, be very useful in many jobs.

4.1.4 Attention to detail

Many people with Asperger Syndrome are detail-oriented. This is an attribute for employers. While employers do not have the time to wait for something to be perfect, they greatly value and appreciate the time and attention paid to detail. The challenge for many people with Asperger Syndrome is to maintain their level of detail at a competitive level of speed, which is the other side of the coin. Perfectionism is also a trait of Asperger Syndrome. The drive for perfection can be so overwhelming for some people that it hinders their ability to finish an assignment in a timely fashion. This makes it an obstacle to employment.

Depending upon the severity of the compulsion, the flexibility of the individual and the extent of the behavior, the perfectionism may be diminished. If, however, the compulsion is severe, the candidate may require support from a behavioral therapist.

4.1.5 Judgment and common sense

Without exception, every client with Asperger Syndrome I have worked with has struggled with judgment and aspects of "common sense." This is a characteristic of Asperger Syndrome.

As you might imagine, this is a significant challenge for people who are seeking employment. I recall a situation of a young man with Asperger Syndrome who was working in a hardware store. He was asked to take some shelving down because the owner of the store was having the walls behind the shelves painted. Doing exactly as he was told, the young employee got out his screwdriver and disassembled the shelves – with everything still on them! You can visualize the mess, and the emotional state of the owner when he came running from the back of the store upon hearing the thunder of crashing paint cans, brushes, and rollers. It had not occurred to the young employee that he should remove the products from the shelves. The employer never said anything about that part of the assignment! Common sense would dictate that the employee would know to remove the products before taking the shelving down. Not necessarily so for the employee with Asperger Syndrome!

Although there are some strategies you can implement to diminish this challenge, it cannot be totally eliminated. Depending upon the prominence of this challenge, you may find that you will need to modify job goals to work around this problem.

It is paramount to keep this judgment and common-sense challenge in mind when finding work for candidates with Asperger Syndrome.

4.2 The candidate's role in finding work that works

On the surface finding work seems pretty clear-cut. One decides what job one wants and goes out and gets it.

Unfortunately, it is not that simple for anybody, let alone someone with challenges. There are some important factors for someone with Asperger Syndrome to consider that will quite likely change the course of her life. Helping the candidate understand her role in finding work that works is a very important part of the job finding process because without full cooperation, there is little point in proceeding. It all boils down to this: What the individual puts into the process, the individual will get out of it.

4.2.1 Committing to finding work that works

Anyone with Asperger Syndrome is going to be faced with a decision before embarking on finding work that works. This decision will impact how things unfold in life from this point forward. A candidate must decide how committed she is to finding and keeping work and how much effort she is willing to put into being successful. This may seem like a straightforward question to some people. But in my experience, most candidates with Asperger Syndrome have never really examined the depth of commitment they must make to be successful in the workplace. You see, if the candidate chooses not to put heart and soul into finding work that works, it is unlikely that true potential will be reached, regardless of how much support and guidance are offered. *There are certain things that only the candidate can do.*

To help you understand the extent of commitment the candidate must make, I have created the following scenario:

> Imagine for a moment that it is the future. You live on a planet where there is no work for you, and there never will be because the planet has been drained of its resources. You have been offered a ticket to travel to

another galaxy where there are good jobs but you are told upfront that your life will be difficult. You are also told, however, that if you work hard and assimilate, you can be very successful. You understand that if you go to this galaxy you will be thrown into a completely different culture and need to learn a new language, customs, laws, and social rules. It will be a very steep learning curve and some people will be prejudiced against you. It is even possible that some people may treat you poorly. You know that you will have to work harder than everyone else in order to be treated equally. The people in this galaxy will have very little understanding of your culture and customs and will find your behavior odd and unusual. There will be some people who will take an interest in you, see your potential and offer you opportunities. Ultimately, though, it will be up to you to make something of yourself in this new place.

Going to this new galaxy is a huge commitment and it will impact the way you live your life from this point forward. You will have to alter many things about yourself including how you interact with people, how you think and how you look at yourself. What would you decide?

When you ask your Asperger friend if she is ready to commit to finding work, this is a much deeper question than it appears to be on the surface. You are asking the candidate to be fully exposed to a world that she does not understand and that is also not very understanding. For the candidate, it will be like moving her life to the galaxy I described earlier. The individual will be exposed to things that are in many ways foreign and will have to decide if she is ready to do what it takes to make it.

The candidate's commitment will require learning the unwritten rules of social culture, basically by rote. One by one, she must add each to a database of information so she can try to say and do the appropriate things at the appropriate times. This is a huge undertaking, and not something every person with Asperger Syndrome wants to do.

There was a man with Asperger Syndrome who very much resented having to "play the game" that was necessary for him to fit into the business world. He felt that he should be accepted for his differences. He made a valid point and, in a perfect world, few would disagree. Nevertheless, it was pointed out to him that by choosing not to "play the game" of the "neuro-typicals" he would have a hard time keeping a job. In fact, this point had been proven many times over because he had not been able to maintain employment. This was not because he had Asperger Syndrome but rather because he chose not to address the issues that it presented, maintaining that people should accept him for who he is. So, this fellow had a decision to make. He could commit to addressing his issues and "play the game" as he put it, or he could stay where he was and basically stay in a self-defeating cycle. This was a difficult choice for him because it went against what he believed.

Being born with Asperger Syndrome is unfair, but who said life is fair?

In order for him to succeed in his field he had to conform to certain behaviors and standards. It was suggested that he strike a compromise and "play the game" during business hours and be himself the rest of the time. It was also brought to his attention the fact that everyone has to play the game once in a while and that perhaps every now and again, playing the game is not always so bad. For example, people dress up for job interviews because they want to create a good first impression. In effect, this is "playing the game" because if they did not come dressed appropriately they would most certainly be eliminated from the competition. Even *he* dressed up for an interview so, in essence, was already playing the game. Although this did not completely satisfy him, he appreciated the logic and agreed that it was worth a try.

You will need to talk to the candidate about the true commitment involved in finding work. Being committed to the process is part of the candidate's role, because without full commitment it will be hard for her to reach full potential.

4.2.2 Self-acceptance

Many children with Asperger Syndrome have experienced ridicule, teasing and bullying in school because they were different. So severe has this experience been for some people that the symptoms have been likened to post-traumatic stress disorder. I recall one day working with a client who in front of my very eyes regressed into a childhood memory as we sat in my office. He was telling me about something that happened to him in school. As he got into the story, I noticed his body tensing. His voice became loud and aggressive and within two seconds he was up on his feet and screaming at me as if I were his fifth-grade teacher. So traumatized was this man by his childhood experiences that even talking about an incident caused him to relive it.

It is no wonder then that many adults with Asperger Syndrome suffer from low self-esteem and lack confidence. But if they want to move forward, beyond the trauma of their childhood, they need to learn to accept themselves.

Three areas of self-acceptance that candidates should consider if they want to move forward in their life are:

- accepting differences and celebrating uniqueness

- accepting the diagnosis

- accepting the challenges.

4.2.2.1 ACCEPTING DIFFERENCES AND CELEBRATING UNIQUENESS

Perhaps the most important ingredient of self-acceptance for people with Asperger Syndrome is for them to acknowledge their strengths, gifts, and uniqueness. The contribution people with Asperger Syndrome can make in this world should not be overshadowed by the challenges they face. They should be known for who they are as individuals, not by their disorder.

Innovative, creative, genius, gifted, brilliant, and *intelligent* are words often associated with Asperger Syndrome. Many famous people who have made important contributions to the world have displayed characteristics of Asperger Syndrome, people such as Albert Einstein, Ludwig van Beethoven, Alexander Graham Bell, Henry Ford, Vincent Van Gogh, and Howard Hughes. These people are not only known for their eccentricities but celebrated. In some ways, it is unfortunate that these folks were not around to get an official diagnosis of Asperger Syndrome because this would most certainly have changed the way society views the disorder.

Ironically, I think that the general public already appreciates Asperger Syndrome because they celebrate many of the characteristics of the disorder in pop-culture. Look at the characters Dr. Spock and Data from "Star Trek," and "Star Trek: The Next Generation." They definitely displayed traits of Asperger Syndrome with their precise language, above average intelligence and eccentric mannerisms. Andy Warhol, for example, might be considered synonymous with pop-culture and he clearly showed the unconventional features that are often associated with Asperger Syndrome.

Hollywood jumped on board as well with the movie "Rain Man" where Dustan Hoffman plays an autistic savant. The movie did extremely well at the box office. So did "As Good as it Gets" starring Jack Nicholson as a man with obsessive-compulsive disorder.

The point is that, given the opportunity and the right association, people are willing to accept the differences of people with Asperger Syndrome. More important is the requirement that people with Asperger Syndrome themselves need to accept and appreciate their uniqueness and differences.

> Every person with Asperger Syndrome needs to hear this message: Having Asperger Syndrome is not bad, it simply creates a difference.

There are people in the world who strive to be "different." Being different can be highly rewarding and can even bring fame and fortune. Look at, for example, fashion designers who create a "whole new" look to differentiate themselves from other designers, and musicians who come up with a "different" sound. Being different means being unique and, to some people, this is desirable. If people with Asperger Syndrome can view their differences in this positive manner, and diminish the negatives, good things can happen in their lives.

4.2.2.2 ACCEPTING THE DIAGNOSIS

Having a diagnosis of Asperger Syndrome means being cognitively different. This is not a choice; it is a fact and one can choose to accept this or not. The advantage of accepting the diagnosis is that it can provide insight into challenges and therefore opportunity to progress and find strategies to be successful.

Some people accept their diagnosis. Some people go into denial. While denial is understandable, it can preclude progress. This can be very frustrating to the people who want to help someone be successful. Denial stops people from learning from mistakes because they are unable to see their role in what went wrong. Sometimes the family is in denial as well. This makes it even more challenging for someone with Asperger Syndrome to accept her own differences because trusting, supporting family members "do not exist" to help her see reality. Of course, it also makes it difficult to get professional help and support when someone will not accept a diagnosis.

You cannot force someone to accept that she has Asperger Syndrome. This is something the individual must come to terms with independently. All you can do is provide that person with information and help in understanding the advantages of acceptance. Although a diagnosis may be difficult to accept, it will help a person to have greater self-understanding as well as her role in life. With this understanding comes insight and direction. Perhaps for the first time in her life, the individual will be in a position to make choices that will positively impact the future because she will no longer be blind to personal challenges. She can then choose to do something about them.

4.2.2.3 ACCEPTING THE CHALLENGES

Dr. Temple Grandin is an excellent example of someone who has taken ownership of her autism. She tells her story in her autobiography *Thinking in Pictures*. Here is a person who has accepted her challenges in life and used them to help herself become successful. At the same time, she has not attempted to be someone she is not. Accepting herself and taking responsibility for her challenges has allowed her to find new ways of solving problems that have made a humanitarian difference in the world.

Even if candidates do not accept a diagnosis, they can choose to accept that they have personal challenges. This insight may not come easily for some people with Asperger Syndrome who lack self-awareness but, with help, they can learn to see themselves more clearly. In fact, awareness is half the battle to achieving success. Once candidates become aware of their challenges, they are in a position to do something about them. With guidance, some solid strategies and a concerted effort on their part, people with Asperger Syndrome can reach full potential.

You can support someone with Asperger Syndrome to be more self-aware by verbally reflecting their behavior back to them (see section 8.10). When you see the person do something inappropriate that makes her stand out, make it known. The more you do this, the more opportunity she will have to understand and explore himself.

> Accepting one's challenges results in greater awareness...and with this awareness comes learning and growth.

A large part of the work I do with people with Asperger Syndrome involves helping them be more self-aware so they can acknowledge and address their challenges. Candidates respond exceedingly well to honest, direct feedback. They are often extremely interested in how they are perceived by others but rarely get the opportunity to understand it. The story of Lucas is a good example. Whenever Lucas spoke to someone, he would stare at the person's chest. His behavior was completely innocent but, until it was brought to his attention, he had never understood the impression this behavior might leave with others, particularly with women. He was grateful to have this feedback and once he understood the potential consequences of this behavior, he was motivated to change it. He very much wanted to be accepted, yet if no one told him what he was doing that was considered odd or inappropriate, how could he possibly know?

The more receptive one is to seeing personal challenges and accepting them as part of oneself, the more opportunity there is for growth.

4.2.3 Self-responsibility

Self-responsibility is an attitude and it must come from within the individual. It cannot be given to someone, just as self-esteem cannot. Like anyone else, those with Asperger Syndrome are the only people who can take responsibility for themselves. They may attribute their happiness or unhappiness to things that happen around them; in other words, they might blame external factors for a life situation. But, in the workplace, if employees do not take responsibility for their actions they may suffer harsh consequences, including reprimands or dismissals. To be successful, they need to realize that their lives are the way they are because of the choices they make, including how they choose to behave. This is based upon the concept of cause and effect. For example, if you choose put your hand in fire, you will get burned. If you choose to jump in a lake, you will get wet. If an employee chooses to yell at coworkers, she puts her job in jeopardy.

When candidates choose not to take responsibility for their actions, reactions, and behavior, they rob themselves of the opportunity to learn. When people do not learn from their mistakes, they do not change the way they do things and this means that they will repeat the same mistakes. This is a vicious cycle that is easy for anyone to get into if they do not learn self-responsibility.

Learning self-responsibility is perhaps more difficult for people with Asperger Syndrome because they do not learn as well by example. They may have trouble relating their behavior to the consequence and need support to learn the lesson. Self-responsibility is usually learned best when it is modeled in childhood; however, it is also possible to learn it as an adult although it may take a more determined effort.

There are two ways that self-responsibility can be taught to your Asperger friend:

- by example
- by requirement.

4.2.3.1 BY EXAMPLE

Modeling self-responsibility in the workplace is part of teaching it. An employee with Asperger Syndrome is unlikely to learn self-responsibility from people who are passive, self-pitying, and prone to blaming their life circumstances on the basis of someone else's actions or on "the system." If this is something that has been modeled in childhood, she will have a harder time learning self-responsibility.

If the candidate has grown up amongst adults who hold themselves accountable for their actions, acknowledge their mistakes, and work for what they want in life, there is a good probability that she will act self-responsibly in her own life. This is not only because the behavior is modeled and taught but also because it is encouraged and nurtured.

4.2.3.2 BY REQUIREMENT

The second element of teaching self-responsibility is to expect and require it of the person. People tend to live up to expectations when they understand that it is a requirement. For example, if the employee is not dressing appropriately for work, you can present her with a choice. She can arrive at work dressed appropriately or go home and change, return to work and then make up for the lost time. If the next day the employee arrives at work not dressed appropriately, you send her home to change and again make up the lost time. If the day after this, the employee arrives at work dressed appropriately and you say, "You look very nice today. Let's get to work." The employee learns that doing what is required or expected has a positive outcome. By doing this you are helping the employee understand that there are choices and that her actions have consequences.

People with Asperger Syndrome need expectations outlined clearly. They need to know what is required of them beforehand because they are not likely to know unless told. If you are not consistent in following through on consequences the lesson will be lost. This process is the most effective way of teaching a candidate self-responsibility.

Now, using the ideas presented to you, it is a fair question to ask, "Is the candidate ready to begin the process of finding work that works?"

How do you know? Use the Work Readiness Checklist.

4.3 The Work Readiness Checklist

I have created a simple tool called the Work Readiness Checklist to make it easy for you and your Asperger friend or relative to determine if she is truly ready for the process of finding work that works. If she is not ready, the checklist makes it clear what area/s need to improve or change for her to become ready. Many of the items on this list have been discussed in this chapter. It is recommended that you have a discussion with your Asperger friend or relative and clearly outline what her role will be in finding work. Use this checklist to guide you through the discussion. You want to make sure that your friend is fully prepared for the road ahead.

☐   **Wants to work?**

This should be the first question you ask because it is really the most important one. It may seem a bit ridiculous to have this item on the checklist; nevertheless it is an important question because there will be people who simply do not want to work. If they don't want to work then it is very hard to force them to do so. Finding work for someone who does not want to work is a tiring venture and one that will cause both of you endless frustration.

You might be surprised to learn how often I get a client in my office who has never been asked this question. They have simply followed what their family, school and society have expected of them. You might get a half answer to the question, such as they want to make money but they really don't want to work. Although it is not necessarily for the reasons you would prefer, you can at least work with this answer. Many people are motivated by money and if this gets the candidate to a place of happiness and success, then that is all that really matters.

If the candidate really wants to work, then you can check the box.

☐   **Motivated to learn new skills?**

Part of the commitment of preparing for employment means being motivated to learn new skills. In the case of someone with Asperger Syndrome this will include social and communication skills.

If the candidate is prepared to expand her knowledge base and wants to learn, you can check this box.

☐   Open to constructive feedback?

An important element of finding work for a person with Asperger Syndrome will involve building a foundation of basic social and communication skills. The candidate will have to participate in an assessment that will identify workplace challenges as they pertain to her Asperger Syndrome. Any challenges will be brought to her attention. This may be hard for some people who are really sensitive. They might get defensive or angry when getting the feedback, even when it is presented gently. The candidate needs to understand that feedback is part of the process of finding work and without identifying challenges it is difficult to help her be successful in a job. Therefore, being open to examining challenges and listening to constructive feedback will be important to how she progresses.

If the candidate understands the importance of the feedback and is open to receiving it, then you can check this box.

☐   Willing to take responsibility for their actions, reactions and behavior?

Discussed earlier in this chapter was the importance of self-responsibility. It is not necessary that the candidate be self-responsible right now, but he must be willing to take responsibility when things are pointed out.

If the candidate is willing to take responsibility or willing to learn how to take responsibility for himself, you can check this box.

☐   Willing to work on issues that arise?

Some candidates will actually refuse to try strategies that address their workplace challenges. It is futile to put strategies in place if they are not going to be used. It also negates the entire process of building a foundation of appropriate work skills. The candidate must be willing to try strategies and offer feedback as to their effectiveness. A willingness to work on issues as they arise is fundamental to the process of self-development and learning how to be successful in the workplace.

If the candidate is willing to try strategies and work on issues that arise, you can check this box.

☐   Committed to being on time?

Unless there is a reasonable explanation, employers expect employees to be at work on time. If they are going to be late for some reason, they are expected to call and let the employer know ahead of time.

If the candidate is committed to arriving at work on time every day, then you can check this box.

☐   Committed to doing their best in everything they do?

No one is expected to be perfect. However, employees should be prepared to do their best at all times. This is all anyone can ask.

If the candidate is committed to doing her best, check this box.

☐   Willing to make sacrifices?

Working for a living requires making sacrifices. The candidate must be prepared to make sacrifices if she is going to be successful in finding and keeping a job. Things such as getting up earlier and practicing proper hygiene will be expected and the candidate may not be accustomed to doing this. This will require a commitment on her behalf.

If the candidate is willing to make the necessary sacrifices that are required to work, then you can check this box.

☐   Able and willing to reduce and control any aggressive behavior?

There is no room for aggression or violent behavior in the workplace. This includes verbal aggression such as swearing, yelling, and name calling, as well as physical aggression such as causing damage to a person or property.

For a variety of reasons, the candidate may harbor anger. The consequences of aggressive behavior in the workplace may be extreme. If the candidate has any violent tendencies or has been violent in the recent past, it is recommended that these issues be addressed before placing the candidate in a work situation.

If the candidate does not display aggressive behavior, or is willing and able to control it, then you can check this box.

☐ **Able to handle a reasonable amount of stress?**

In the job search, you will probably target jobs that are lower on the stress scale for the candidate with Asperger Syndrome. With this in mind, all jobs will have some amount of pressure and stress and the candidate must be able to tolerate a moderate amount without going into an anxiety attack or meltdown.

If the candidate is capable of handling moderate stress, then you can check this box.

☐ **Willing to disclose challenges to an employer?**

The importance of disclosure and disclosure options are discussed at some length in Chapter 12 of this book. At this point, the candidate needs to understand that if she requires accommodation and support to get and keep a job, she will have to disclose something to the employer. A willingness to share information about challenges with the employer to get the employer's support is necessary in helping the candidate reach her potential. This is very important to the overall success of a work placement.

If the candidate is willing to disclose challenges, then you can check this box.

Summary

- Understanding Asperger Syndrome is key to supporting the process of finding work that works.

- The candidate is the only person who ultimately controls her destiny.

- Understanding the depth of the commitment one must make to prepare for, gain and maintain a job is crucial before embarking on the road to employment.

- The candidate should walk away with four things from this chapter: that being different is good, and the importance of self-awareness, self-responsibility, and self-acceptance.

5 Family

Family should be like good advice: It's there if you need it but you shouldn't be bound by it.

I was inspired by a poem by the humorist Erma Bombeck, which appeared in her book *If Life is a Bowl of Cherries – What am I doing in the Pits?* She sums up the child-rearing process by comparing children to kites on a day with little wind. Mom and Dad run down the road pulling the colorful nylon triangle at the end of a string. It drags along the ground and shows no inclination toward going up into the air. But with enough effort, the kite makes a leap and lifts ten feet, it hovers and then climbs to fifteen feet. But it is too close to dangerous electrical lines and trees. The scared Mom and Dad quickly navigate the kite away from the danger. Then an unexpected gust of wind swoops the kite upward. Mom and Dad frantically try to unravel the string to give it more room to fly but it is difficult to hang on to. Inevitably, they reach the end of the string but the kite is demanding more freedom. It wants to fly higher. Dad stretches to accommodate the tugging kite. Mom wants the kite reeled in where it is safer but the string releases from their hands. The kite soars into the beautiful blue sky while Mom and Dad watch with a mixture of sadness, wonder and pride. The kite they built together is flying better than expected and it takes off into the wild blue yonder. They feel proud because they see how well their kite is doing as it flies toward the sun, but they miss holding onto it.

Unlike the kite, children will return home. But the relationship amongst the family members has changed. When family members nurture and encourage their relative with Asperger Syndrome to grow and learn, the relative will take off like the kite in the story. He may not always fly all the way to the sun on his own, but he can go far on a long string.

When finding work that works for people with Asperger Syndrome, the family plays a crucial role. It can either be the pillar that supports and holds the family member up, or the anchor that pins him down in the process. This is significant because it is often what takes place at home that either supports or defeats what happens at work. The family must go through a transition from seeing their relative as a dependant child to seeing him as an independent and capable adult. This is not always easy when the relative has Asperger Syndrome and is more vulnerable and susceptible to harm. It takes a real effort to create an environment and attitude of constant learning and positive reinforcement for the relative. Cultivating self-esteem and independence in a relative who lacks social and communication skills and self-awareness takes patience and endurance.

As the relative grows into adulthood, the roles of family will shift and change. This too can be a difficult process for families because it can be hard to know exactly what role they should be playing and how much they should be participating. Issues such as knowing when and how to let go, who to trust in the community, and how to support their relative appropriately as an adult, weigh on their minds. This can be complicated by established family dynamics, which blur boundaries and create obstacles for development and growth. An enormous transition takes place for a family when a relative with Asperger Syndrome begins to become independent and self-reliant. For some, this transition will be uncomfortable. For others it will be simply a progression. Regardless of how many bumps are on the road ahead, the journey is worth the effort.

The purpose of this chapter is to:

- define the role of family in the process of finding work that works and outline how it can support the process

- provide insight into the challenges often created by the family during the process of finding work for a relative with Asperger Syndrome, so these challenges can be avoided

- answer some of the frequently asked questions that families have about the job-finding process.

First, an examination of the role of the family.

5.1 Family roles

Family members play many roles over the lifespan of their relative with Asperger Syndrome. It is often the parents or siblings that get the most involved, but aunts, uncles, and grandparents can also be primary supports. Regardless of their relationship to the relative, the role they play in regard to the job-finding process will be the same.

When finding work, there are three significant roles for family to play:

- at-home support system
- team player
- advocate/educator.

5.1.1 At-home support

There is a lot that the family can do on the home front to support a relative with Asperger Syndrome in accomplishing his goal of finding employment. "Home front" refers to wherever the relative lives, which may be in the family home or on his own. The family has a unique relationship with their relative with Asperger Syndrome and usually has terrific influence. Their support is powerful because it can either help the relative achieve goals or hold him back.

Most, if not all, families want the best for their relatives with Asperger Syndrome. They are motivated to provide support in any way that will help the relative reach full potential. It can be difficult, however, if they are not sure how to go about doing this. For this reason, the following is a list of five ways for the family to support the process of finding work that works:

- to uphold consistency
- to promote self-responsibility
- to encourage self-awareness (education)
- to foster and support independence
- to keep an open line of communication.

5.1.1.1 TO UPHOLD CONSISTENCY

In Chapter 7, I refer to consistency as the glue that bonds the Four Pillar Teaching Technique together. Consistency in strategies, expectations, lessons, and consequences must be maintained across the board. This means that whatever is put in place at the work site must be reinforced on the home front. For example, if Sheila is being taught to improve her table manners at work by keeping her mouth closed while eating, this must also be required at home. Altering or shifting behavior in people requires repetition. This helps create new habits to replace the old. If the strategy is not consistent or reinforced at home, Sheila will get mixed messages and be confused, and this will slow her progress in altering the behavior. The family must be consistent with the other players in both choice of strategies and how they are applied.

5.1.1.2 TO PROMOTE SELF-RESPONSIBILITY

Self-responsibility is something that is learned. The individual with Asperger Syndrome will not be born with it. People first learn self-responsibility as children at home. The environment that the family creates in the home can do a great deal to encourage this or stifle it. Parents who model responsible behavior usually rear children who become responsible adults. This is perhaps a more difficult task for parents with a child with Asperger Syndrome, but how they choose to teach that child will have an enormous impact on the way that child chooses to look at life and take responsibility as an adult.

The family can begin by helping their relative to learn to be responsible for his possessions, money, and decisions. This will also help to nurture independence as the child grows and becomes an adult. Teaching problem-solving is another great way to foster self-responsibility. When the relative with Asperger Syndrome comes to the family with a problem, they should resist the temptation to solve the problem. Rather, they should discuss the problem and support their relative in deciding how he should best handle it. Asking questions about the nature and frequency of the problem, brainstorming possible solutions, and listing the pros and cons of each solution can do this. This helps the relative with Asperger Syndrome to take responsibility for his own situations, and recognize that choices are available to solve them.

Promoting self-responsibility begins with helping a person be aware that he *is* responsible for his actions and that there *are* choices. This will transfer to the workplace if it is supported and taught on the home front.

5.1.1.3 TO ENCOURAGE SELF-AWARENESS

For people with Asperger Syndrome who lack awareness of themselves and others, it is extremely important for the family to encourage and teach it at home. With increasing awareness the ability to carry responsibility also increases. In many ways the two go together. It should be an everyday part of the family support strategy to encourage awareness by describing to their relative how his behavior may be perceived by others. This supports the relative to be more aware of his own behavior as well as bringing awareness to how others may view it and react. This should be done in a gentle, informative way with no judgment. It is less important to tell him that the behavior is "wrong" than it is to point out how it could be done differently. Indeed, simply stating what they see as an observation and then discussing how others might react or feel about a situation is often a very non-threatening and effective approach to helping the relative with Asperger Syndrome learn awareness.

Another important role the family can play in helping a relative to be more self-aware is to teach them what Asperger Syndrome is. Many adults with Asperger Syndrome are unable to describe the disorder or explain the impact it has on his life. Exploring the disorder together, and then pointing out which behaviors can be attributed to it, really help to build the relative's self-awareness and knowledge base.

5.1.1.4 TO FOSTER AND SUPPORT INDEPENDENCE

In our society we all have the right to personal freedom. This means the right to make our own life choices about education, work, religion, relationships, and so on. We also believe that a person should be given opportunities to succeed to the extent of his abilities and desires. Unfortunately, people who are different are not always offered this right or are held back from fully experiencing it.

People with Asperger Syndrome may struggle to gain all the skills required to live a fully independent life. But, given the right support and tools, they are capable of at least greater independence. Fostering and supporting independence is part of the family's role on the home front. They can do this by providing love, support, encouragement, and opportunity to their relative. Allowing the relative to make choices and experience the outcomes helps him explore abilities and expand knowledge. As he learns and experiences more, the relative will be more willing and able to try new things. This not only supports independence, it also helps overcome fears and anxieties.

By fostering independence, the family instills confidence in the relative and sets him up to be successful in the workplace. He will have a more positive self-image and be more likely to explore challenging options, thereby opening doors to greater opportunity.

5.1.1.5 TO KEEP AN OPEN LINE OF COMMUNICATION

The family has the advantage of an established relationship with their Asperger relative. This means that they will be in a position to observe subtle shifts in mood, behavior, and attitude. They will also know if there is any change in sleep or eating patterns or if medication has been adjusted. This is important information that needs to be communicated to the involved professionals and the job coach.

Keeping an open line of communication is a vital role that the family plays to staying on track in the process of finding work. If the relative with Asperger Syndrome comes home from work one day upset, the family needs to explore the reasons and then inform the appropriate people or person; in this case the job coach. A plan of action can then be discussed and decided upon between them.

5.1.2 Team player

Part of the family role is being an integral part of the support team that is dedicated to helping their relative find work. Even if it is a small team, made up of a parent, the job coach, the employee, and the employer, the process of finding work is still a team effort.

Like any good team there must be excellent communication and cooperation. The family is an invaluable source of information because they are more often than not experts on their relative, even if they are not experts on Asperger Syndrome itself. They often know what situations or things trigger their relative, what he is afraid of, what he is really good at and what his limitations are. The family can contribute immensely to the team and they need to be valued for their contribution. At the same time, the family must regard the opinions and recommendations of the other players. The other players will have different perspectives because they will see the Asperger relative in different situations and from another viewpoint. This too, is valuable to the process.

This is what teamwork is about: People working together to achieve a common goal.

As a central part of the team, another role the family will play is to connect the other players to one another. The family should make sure that the other players on the team are not only aware of each other but also keeping each other informed.

5.1.3 Advocate/educator

An advocate is someone who speaks on behalf of and supports others to help them get through a system or process. The role of advocate is a very important one for the family and one that they often have little choice in taking on if they want services for their relative with Asperger Syndrome. It is likely that some member of the family has been playing this role for quite some time already. It was probably a family member who found the doctor to make the diagnosis of Asperger Syndrome. It was probably a family member who went to the school and spoke to the teacher about their relative's unique challenges, and it was probably a member of the family who helped their relative get into the local college and helped them get student supports. This is a role that will continue through the process of finding work. Family will need to continue advocating for their relative to connect them with professionals and, depending upon the situation, even with employers.

Many support professionals have heavy workloads. Also, there is so much for professionals to know that they cannot possibly be familiar with it all. It is often left to a member of the family to educate and inform the people involved in their relative's life about Asperger Syndrome and how to interact with their relative.

Once the family begins mentioning that their relative has Asperger Syndrome, they will discover that people want to know what it is. If they are not already prepared to educate people about Asperger Syndrome, I suggest that they write a script. I like the term "elevator speech" because the script is short and sweet and to the point. It gives people an introduction without boring them with clinical details in which they may have no interest. Later, if someone is interested in hearing more, he will make this known and then a decision can be made about how to proceed. As part of the support role, each member of the family should become familiar enough with Asperger Syndrome to describe it, if it ever comes up in conversation. In this capacity, family members can confidently educate people who express interest.

An "elevator speech" is a thirty- or sixty-second blurb that gets right to the point. Imagine that you are on an elevator and you have a minute or less to explain to someone, whom you have never met, what Asperger Syndrome is. If you can accomplish this, then you are on your way. Here is an example:

> You've probably never heard of Asperger Syndrome, so let me explain. It's a neurological disorder that people are born with and it interferes with the way the person reads social cues and understands language. People with Asperger Syndrome tend to be very literal and are likely to view things in terms of black and white. They need support understanding the gray areas. They are sort of like a computer in a way because they are really good at storing and analyzing data but they don't relate well to people – not unless they are intentionally programmed to do so.

The point of the comparison with a computer is to draw the listener in, pique interest and offer something to which he can relate. By no means is it intended to objectify the person with Asperger Syndrome. Speaking in terms to which people can relate is key to educating them. Engaging their interest entices them to learn more. Since Asperger Syndrome can be a very difficult concept for people to grasp, it is important to speak in everyday terms. Stay away from clinical jargon. It sounds antiseptic and can scare people off.

It is important that everyone chooses their own language and ideas for writing their elevator speech because they will have their own ideas about what Asperger Syndrome is, and how it impacts their relative. The main point is that in supporting the process of finding work for their relative with Asperger Syndrome, they need to be putting a positive image of this disorder into the minds of the public. Playing the roles of advocate and educator, family members are in a unique position to do this.

5.2 Family challenges

Working with hundreds of people with Asperger Syndrome, I have had the opportunity to witness many family dynamics. Two things that every family has in common is a love for their family member with Asperger Syndrome, and the best intentions. Families are complex and each has its own method of dealing with the issues that come with the territory of having a relative with Asperger Syndrome.

There have been several challenges that I have seen repeatedly over the years in my role as a professional. These are actually "pitfalls" because they impede the process of the family member with Asperger Syndrome moving forward and becoming self-reliant. I refer to these challenges as "pitfalls" and "parent traps" because they are never intended to hold the relative back. The intention is always good but the result is not always in keeping with that intention. It is important to point out these pitfalls so that they may be recognized early and their course altered.

As in anything that is worthwhile, it takes work to accomplish this. The pitfalls about to be discussed will be easier for outsiders to spot and most likely very difficult for the people involved in the challenge to recognize on their own, at least not without a lot of self-awareness and introspection. It can be very hard to look honestly at one's behavior and trace it back to the cause. There are often very sensitive issues and fears underlying behavior and these may be difficult for many to own up to. Nonetheless, if these issues are impeding the relative from growing and realizing his potential, they should be brought to the attention of the family member concerned. Perhaps simply being aware that these pitfalls exist will be enough for families to circumvent them.

There are four pitfalls that I believe to be the greatest stumbling blocks for families. These are the challenges presented by the family that most frequently bar the relative with Asperger Syndrome from realizing his full potential in the finding-work process:

- letting go
- over-protection (smothering *vs.* nurturing)
- sabotage
- unrealistic expectations.

5.2.1 Letting go

Part of helping the relative with Asperger Syndrome find work is encouraging him to take on more of an adult role. This requires letting the relative have greater independence and allowing that individual to experience life without watching his every move. Although this seems natural and in theory not problematic, I have seen many families struggle to allow this natural process to take place for their relative with Asperger Syndrome. By unintentionally hindering this process, they block the relative from reaching his full potential because, in essence, he is not allowed to grow up. This makes it very challenging for the relative to become a fully responsible adult and act accordingly in the workplace.

Perhaps you have heard of the "empty nest" syndrome. It is the name given to the grouping of feelings some parents have when their last or only child leaves home, and they no longer have a baby "chick" in their nest. It is a very difficult stage for some parents but perhaps more difficult for parents with a special needs child. In the case of finding work for a relative with Asperger Syndrome, letting go may not always refer to the relative leaving the family home. More often it refers to the process of mentally and emotionally letting go of the relative so that he can become a complete, independent adult. Whether the relative is physically leaving the home or not, this can be a difficult stage for some parents. During this stage it is normal to experience feelings of loss, sadness, depression, and fear. It is absolutely normal to experience a grieving process because letting go involves change. The very nature of change means that one is leaving something to move on to something else, whether or not by choice, whether positive or negative. It is natural to grieve when leaving something significant behind and this is a healthy and necessary stage of the letting-go process.

One of the best pieces of advice I was given when experiencing emotional pain was not to fight my emotions. As uncomfortable, even unbearable as those feelings were at times, I learned that I always survived them. Actually, by not fighting my emotions, I found that I went through them more quickly, which was a real bonus. Experiencing change repeatedly over the years has given me confidence that I will come out on the other side not only alive but, more often than not, a better, wiser person.

Kids with Asperger Syndrome are naturally more dependant on their families because of their disorder. They are in greater danger of being manipulated, bullied, and isolated because they are more vulnerable and naive than other children. They lack many of the skills, such as judgment, decision-making, and common sense, that are necessary to help them be safe in the world. So it is understandable that family members have the urge to fight the letting-go process. However, this is the pitfall for families.

When the family fights letting go, one of two things can occur. The family can lose the fight and their relative with Asperger Syndrome rebels and leaves. The relative with Asperger Syndrome is then left to his own devices choosing not to accept family support. This can place the relative at a disadvantage and may also put him in physical danger without the support to fall back on if needed. I have seen this happen and it is very unfortunate.

The other possibility when the family fights the process of letting go is that they stifle the relative and force him to continue being dependant on the family. In this case, the family unintentionally robs the relative with Asperger Syndrome of the right to be independent and he may never fully reach his full capacity to be self-reliant.

The people who have the most difficulty letting go of their relative with Asperger Syndrome are those who have difficulty with separation and change and those who feel their relative is not ready to leave home. These people are generally more inclined to encourage dependence with controlling behavior, such as making decisions for the relative, not allowing the relative to make mistakes, using guilt to manipulate outcomes, and deciding what the relative is allowed to experience. This is usually done unconsciously and for reasons that have little to do with the relative with Asperger Syndrome. The good news is that families who are able to recognize these behaviors in themselves are in the best position to change it.

Letting a young adult with Asperger Syndrome leave the nest may be very daunting, but it is necessary. Without the encouragement and support to be independent, the young adult will not fully transition into adulthood. The family can either assist this process or resist it. If they assist the process then they will encourage and teach the family member with Asperger Syndrome to experience things for himself. Remembering that the family member with Asperger Syndrome will require far greater support in absorbing the lessons of life is important to this end. He will need help to understand what the mistake is, why it is a mistake, what the consequence is, and what the consequences might be in the future. Assistance will also be required in expanding the lesson to other situations and the relative may have to experience the lesson repeatedly before fully absorbing it.

It is not uncommon for it to take much longer than average for a person with Asperger Syndrome to make this transition. However, the transition can be made. There are adults with Asperger Syndrome who live independently, earn a living, are married, and have children. Granted, this is not the case for all people with Asperger Syndrome; but all of them can reach some level of independence if encouraged and supported to do so. Anything is possible!

5.2.1.1 LETTING-GO STRATEGIES

- Teach the family member with Asperger Syndrome how to do household chores, including cooking, to help him become more self-sufficient.

- Make the family member with Asperger Syndrome responsible for his own spending money and give him a bank account.

- Resist the urge to "rescue" the family member when things go wrong. Instead, use the situation to teach a life lesson. Remember, while others can learn from the experience, the person with Asperger Syndrome requires an explanation.

- Support the decision-making process and do not make decisions on behalf of the relative with Asperger Syndrome. Encourage the development of making personal choices.

- Monitor your own behavior and reasons for your actions. Are you stifling or encouraging?

- Live your own life. When family members are consumed with their relative with Asperger Syndrome, it makes letting go more difficult.

5.2.2 Over-protection – smothering vs. nurturing

No family member wants to see someone they love struggle and get knocked off his feet repeatedly. Part of the family's job is to protect their relatives, to set them up for success in life, and then to sit back hopefully and watch them prosper. When they have a family member who has Asperger Syndrome, it is more difficult to get to the place where they can sit back and relax. It is a constant effort to move forward and it can be very painful for them to stand on the sidelines. Their instincts tell them to jump in and protect their relative, but this becomes complicated when the relative is an adult. The family struggles to know how to guide and support their adult relative while still honoring and nurturing his independence.

The second pitfall I see families fall into frequently in my practice is being over-protective of the relative with Asperger Syndrome. I have heard this referred to in the social services professions as smothering, suffocating, and stifling. The underlying agenda of smothering is criticism and judgment. The "smotherer" thinks of the person as a piece of property to be molded. Of course, this is usually an unconscious thought. The smotherer makes all the decisions for the relative with Asperger Syndrome, essentially taking away his voice.

Typical acts of smothering include continually watching and commenting on the relative's behavior. The smotherer anticipates every move the relative makes, and then prevents the relative from initiating action. The relative is reprimanded in front of other people and is not allowed to disagree or sometimes even speak. This may be shocking for some of you to read. Unfortunately this is not uncommon. I have had meetings with families where the adult relative with Asperger Syndrome is not allowed to say a word. I will ask questions directly to the person with Asperger Syndrome, and a parent or sibling will answer every single time, knowing full well that I am not addressing them.

Generally speaking, the smotherer does not trace the behavior back to his own control issues. This blocks the smotherer from seeing the smothering behavior and thus seeing the need to change it. Herein lies the problem. The relative with Asperger Syndrome, by not being allowed to express who he is, does not develop an individual identity and grows up without knowing who he really is. The relative with Asperger Syndrome is therefore unable to cultivate the tools necessary to adequately grow and reach his full potential.

When I work with clients who either have been or are being smothered, it is very challenging because it can be difficult to decipher what it is that he wants in life. This complicates the job-finding process because a great deal of time is spent trying to build up the self-esteem and confidence of the person so that he will think about his *own* wants and needs. This is difficult for the candidate because the family, or a member of it, has always defined who he is. In addition, the person may blossom in my program but then regress after spending a weekend at home. It is a slow process of two steps forward, one step back. In addition, if the smotherer is feeling particularly threatened, there is a risk that he may sabotage the entire process. I will talk about this in more detail in the next section.

On the opposite end of smothering is nurturing. When the family nurtures their relative with Asperger Syndrome, they love, teach, honor, and listen to their relative's individuality. They do not embarrass their relative but rather encourage him to experience and learn from mistakes and decisions. When this happens, the relative feels confident and trusted and is in a better position to explore himself and grow. Chances are that when the relative feels nurtured rather than smothered, he will not rebel, simply because there is no need. The relative feels in control of his own life, rather than feeling helpless and dependant.

5.2.2.1 STRATEGIES FOR NURTURING

- Encourage and celebrate the individuality and differences of the relative with Asperger Syndrome.

- Avoid imposing guilt.

- Encourage self-expression.

- Teach and explain the cause and effect of situations as they occur.

5.2.3 Sabotage

One of the most painful experiences for a professional to experience is watching a client have a job sabotaged by a family member. "Sabotage" may sound harsh, but it is true and it happens more often then one might believe. Look at the situation of Craig, a twenty-three-year-old man with Asperger Syndrome who went through an employment program and came out ready to work. He was motivated and willing to try anything to gain experience. He ended up working in a local business counting inventory. The job was right up his alley as he was great with numbers. He was also a very responsible young man and could handle the job with some initial coaching and support. But his mother was not so sure. She expressed concern that the job might be too challenging. Then she expressed that the job did not pay enough. Then the dilemma was that the shift Craig had to work went on too late and then that he had to work Saturdays. There always seemed to be something wrong with the job.

The job coach kept running into interference between Mom, Craig, and the employer. Craig was doing great in the job but he was getting very agitated about his mother's negativity. Throughout his entire life, Craig had not left his mother's side. He was the perfect son, he went to the store for her when she was sick, he made dinner for her when she was late coming home, and he helped with filing and data entry when she needed extra help in her office. Now he had his big dream coming true and it was clear to him that he was not pleasing his mother. While his siblings were supportive of Craig, his mother made it clear that this job was both *not good enough* for Craig and *too difficult* for him. Craig came into work one day and quit his job.

One should not dispute that Craig's mom wanted the best for Craig. This is not the issue. The issue really was that Craig's mom seemingly put her own needs higher than her son's. Perhaps it was too scary for her to be without her son and she felt threatened with his newfound independence and success. For her, this possibly was just the beginning. If Craig was successful in his job, he might get promoted to a better, higher-paying job. Then Craig might want to get his own apartment. Maybe it was easier to let Craig down now than to have him taste success and then fail. Although Craig quit the job, his mother influenced the decision. Ironically, Craig's mother put him in a program in which the goal was to find employment, but once this was accomplished, it appeared as if she sabotaged the job.

When a family sabotages the success of their relative with Asperger Syndrome, they are doing so for a variety of reasons, and almost always sub-consciously. However, the most common underlying reason for sabotage is fear: Fear of the relative *not being successful* and not wanting to see failure. The second fear is of the relative *being successful* and thus changing the family dynamic. Sabotage is rarely ever because of the reasons that are being stated.

People tend to live up to or down to expectations. When family members expect their relative with Asperger Syndrome not to succeed, they will sometimes "manipulate" situations to ensure this outcome. They will find ways to make it impossible for the relative to succeed.

They will hide behind the reason that the relative is not capable of self-reliance or independence. Then they make sure that the relative does not have the opportunity to become so. This is sabotage. They will hide behind excuses, such as the job is too difficult or not good enough. They may also point a finger in the direction of the service provider (agencies who provide services–employment or otherwise–to people with special needs), who is working with the relative toward the goal of independence and employment and is therefore a threat. They will sabotage the relationship by saying negative and unsupportive things about the service provider to the relative in an effort to damage the trust and shake the confidence of both parties. The family's own fear and need is so great that it supercedes the relative's right to freedom and independence.

Sabotage can be circumvented if the family is able to identify:

1.   that they are sabotaging

2.   why they are sabotaging, and

3.   that their relative deserves the opportunity to be successful and that if he or she fails, it is an opportunity to grow and learn.

Families who sabotage do not do so maliciously. In fact, they believe that their love is so strong that they must protect the relative with Asperger Syndrome from both the world and himself. They believe that they are acting in the best interests of their relative.

The bottom line is: One needs to discover and resolve the emotional issues affecting a relative working or leaving the family in order to break the cycle and allow him to be independent and successful. *Being aware is the first step in prevention.*

5.2.3.1 STRATEGIES TO PREVENT SABOTAGE

- Family members can ask themselves:
  - What is scary about the relative getting a job?
  - What are the payoffs for keeping him at home?
  - If the relative gets a job, how will this alter *your* life?
  - Does the relative deserve to be successful?

- Allow the relative to choose his own work options and trust in the process.

- Trust that service providers have the relative's best interest in mind and want to see him succeed.

- Do not say negative things about the job to the relative.

- Show how proud you are that the relative is out doing his best to be successful.

5.2.4 Unrealistic expectations

What the family expects from their relative with Asperger Syndrome can sometimes be a hindrance to the relative as well as to the process of finding work, when the expectations are unrealistic. This can happen when the family over- or underestimates the ability of the relative. Either way, it sets the relative up to fail.

It is very important that family takes the time to develop realistic expectations so they may play a supporting rather than a defeating role in the life of their relative. It is often difficult for family members to negotiate between hope and reality when supporting their relative. They may only see challenges and limitations. Conversely, they may be blinded by their love and only see their relative's strengths and not his limitations. Although this is understandable, it can create pressure on the relative to achieve things that are beyond his ability. This is not to say that the relative should be limited, but expectations should be attainable and there is no reason why expectations cannot change and grow as the relative also grows and develops.

The family also should remember to keep expectations in check in relation to what the labor market and employers are able to deliver. For example, it is not realistic that a person with high school education and no work experience will get a twenty-dollar-an-hour managerial job. This may sound ridiculous but it is not rare to encounter a family with unrealistic expectations such as this. They may also expect that their relative should get a nine-to-five job in a large company and receive full benefits. They do not take into account that their relative, like anyone entering the labor force, has to pay his dues. This may mean that the relative has to work shifts, part-time hours, and two jobs, or simply start off in a lower position and climb the ladder like anyone else.

The relative with Asperger Syndrome is not immune to the same processes that every other person looking for work must face. The fact that their relative is considered to have a disability does not mean that he should get preferential treatment. Workplace accommodation is a level of support, not the key to "special treatment."

5.2.4.1 STRATEGIES FOR MAINTAINING REALISTIC EXPECTATIONS

- Listen to the recommendations of unbiased players such as job coaches and professionals to help gauge what is and is not realistic for the relative.

- Expect that the relative will have to work his way into a job and that this may mean starting at an entry level and going from there.

- Keep expectations attainable.

- Check in with the relative to get a feeling about what he thinks of the expectation. If he or she thinks the expectation is not realistic or attainable, you may need to make an adjustment.

5.3 Working with professionals

It is important that family and professionals work together when finding work that works. While professionals will use their experience and training to make recommendations about the relative's career options, the family will have unique knowledge about the relative's needs and abilities.

Here are some guidelines to help the family work with professionals:

- *Be equipped.* Be prepared for meetings with employment specialists, counselors, employers, and job coaches. Write down your questions and concerns, and then note the answers.

- *Be organized.* Keep a file with all reports and assessments so that you can readily access information. You will find that as you go through the system, service providers may want to repeat services when this isn't necessary. If you can have the documentation handy, this may be avoided and save valuable time and energy.

- *Be knowledgeable.* Learn as much as you can about Asperger Syndrome so you can be an active participant in the process of finding work. Learn about the labor market and what jobs are appropriate for your relative.

- *Communicate.* It's important to keep open dialogue – both positive and negative. If you don't agree with a professional's recommendation for example, say why you don't and be specific. Then listen and get clarification if you do not understand something.

5.4 There is light at the end of the tunnel

I think that it is extremely important that the family understand how feasible it is for their relative to learn the necessary skills to become independent, successful, and happy. It may be a long journey to get to this place, but it is a journey that many have taken and they have arrived at a destination of triumph. The family can be a wonderful contributor to this process and can revel in their accomplishment and joy when they see their relative come home from his first day on the job or when he gets honored at the company luncheon. These are moments of victory for both the relative with Asperger Syndrome and the family.

Rest assured that there is light at the end of the tunnel. Keep your eyes on the prize and reach for the stars!

6 Professionals
(Educational, medical, and employment professionals)

People who devote their lives to others are the wealthiest people on earth. Nothing in the world guarantees a greater return on this investment than the human heart.

Eight o'clock in the morning and the telephone rings in my office. It is a guidance counselor from a local community college who is researching support services for a student with Asperger Syndrome. The student is in culinary arts and is having enormous difficulty adapting to the stress of the course load, which has resulted in her having devastating anxiety. The anxiety has caused the student to pick at her hands, creating open sores that are a health concern in the classroom. If the student is not able to get this under control, she will be expelled from the program. The counselor is desperate for resources but does not have a clue as to where to begin. It was a fluke that she happened upon my web site as she was searching for help.

On the phone the counselor tells me how frustrating it has been for her to find professionals who can provide help for this student because so few of them have even heard of Asperger Syndrome, let alone know how to work with a student who has it. She herself had never heard of it before this student walked into her office. Luckily, this student was pretty knowledgeable about his disorder and was able to tell the counselor the problems it was creating for him. She was relieved to find a local professional who could understand the situation and had the experience and knowledge base to do something to help.

Professionals play a role in connecting people with Asperger Syndrome to the appropriate resources, guiding them toward realistic, attainable goals, and listening to their needs. However, if they do not recognize the disorder or know little or nothing about it, they can easily, and unintentionally, mislead a person. This can result in long drawn-out, frustrating experiences for the individual with Asperger Syndrome, which may impede her progress in reaching her potential and gaining meaningful employment.

6.1 What professionals need to know

In order for professionals to do their job effectively, they need to be able to recognize, understand, and communicate with their clients, patients, and students with Asperger Syndrome. It is most important that professionals take the time to learn background information on Asperger Syndrome because this knowledge makes an enormous difference in how they proceed in working with that individual. The first step is learning how to recognize the signs of Asperger Syndrome.

6.1.1 Recognizing characteristics

Many people have never met a person with Asperger Syndrome, or at least they do not know if they have. This is as true for professionals as it is for everyone else. Once someone is introduced to Asperger Syndrome and begins understanding what it is, he or she is much more likely to distinguish it from other disorders. In fact, it is often the case that when Asperger Syndrome is described to a group someone will say, "I know someone who acts like that." Or "I have an uncle who is just that way!" When you are familiar with something or your attention is drawn to it, you begin noticing it.

Recognizing the predominant characteristics of Asperger Syndrome is important to the role of professionals. There are so many diagnoses in the world that there is no way professionals can be familiar with them all. However, they can learn many characteristics that will tip them off that something is not quite right and point them in the right direction. Frequently it is the professional or a family member who flags something that is not right, which creates a domino effect resulting in a diagnosis. For some people a diagnosis is just the thing that helps them make sense of their life and gets them on the right track.

In Chapter 4 there is a description of Asperger Syndrome and a list of the characteristics. Reading that description will be helpful to professionals and will offer them a better than average understanding of the disorder. However, a list of symptoms can be cumbersome to remember when professionals have so much to remember about so many other disorders. To simplify things, note that there are three main problem areas which, when combined together, should trigger the professional to suspect Asperger Syndrome. These three areas are poor or impaired interpersonal skills, poor motor coordination, and well-developed language skills. It is the combination of these three characteristics that separates Asperger Syndrome from other disorders.

Once professionals suspect that an individual has Asperger Syndrome, they are in a position to help them. It is often the "not knowing" that is half the battle for many people with Asperger Syndrome. They can feel discouraged and hopeless because they cannot figure out why they are having such difficulty in life. Having someone identify key traits in them and then assist them in connecting with appropriate resources can sometimes be all that is needed to break a cycle of hopelessness.

6.1.2 Triggers and stresses

Beyond recognizing Asperger Syndrome, professionals benefit from understanding what things trigger and cause stress for people with Asperger Syndrome. Having this knowledge helps the professional create or direct the individual with Asperger Syndrome to more appropriate environments and situations. It also empowers the professional to help the individual with Asperger Syndrome to recognize what creates anxiety so that she can be proactive in life choices.

Here is a list of things that generally trigger or cause stress/anxiety for people with Asperger Syndrome:

- being misunderstood
- crowds
- noise
- confusion/chaos
- unstructured time

- social situations

- change

- distractions such as a busy environment.

Stress causes the body to react chemically, causing the person to have feelings of failure, despair, anxiety, and depression. It may also result in hyperactivity. Feelings of suicide are not uncommon, particularly for people with Asperger Syndrome in their twenties. Professionals should be in tuned to the serious impact that stress may have on individuals with Asperger Syndrome.

The best way for anyone to deal with stress is to try to eliminate the source. This is not always possible. If, for example, the noise level at work is causing stress for an employee with Asperger Syndrome, it may not be sensible for her to quit the job. But it may be reasonable for the employee to wear earplugs to reduce the sensory overload. A professional can be very helpful in identifying the causes of stress and finding solutions, but only if the professional is aware of the things that trigger people with Asperger Syndrome.

Some effective methods that people with Asperger Syndrome have used for coping with stress include meditations and yoga, listening to relaxing music, having a quiet place to which they can retreat, exercise, and relaxation exercises such as breathing and visualization. Spending time on a special interest may also be calming for some people with Asperger Syndrome.

6.1.3 Communicating

Professionals who take the time to learn how to communicate effectively with people with Asperger Syndrome will have greater success in supporting them. The key to communication when speaking with people with Asperger Syndrome is to be clear and direct. In other words, say exactly what you mean. If you want a person with Asperger Syndrome to do something, then tell her what you want and avoid posing it as a question. When you pose your need as a question and then do not get the desired response, you must either accept the response or go back to what you asked. For example, let's say that you ask, "Do you want to go home now?" when you really mean, "It's time to go home now." If the response to your question is "No," you must either decide to accept this decision or go back to the person and say, "Well actually, I want you to go home now." The person with Asperger Syndrome is likely to wonder why you asked the question if you did not really want her answer.

It is also important for professionals to articulate what they expect from someone with Asperger Syndrome because she is unlikely to know otherwise. An example would be, "I expect you to be in my office for your appointment at five minutes to three." Or, "I expect you to send me a copy of your resumé tomorrow." If it is unclear whether the message got through, the person can be asked to repeat the professional's expectation. Outlining expectations and setting clear boundaries are necessary for effective communication with people with Asperger Syndrome (see Chapter 7).

6.2 Who are the professionals?

Remember a children's television show called "Mr. Rogers?" He would sing a song called "Who are the people in your neighborhood," and then would list people such as police, firefighter, construction worker, and so on. One might easily change the song lyrics to "Who are the professionals in your neighborhood." For candidates with Asperger Syndrome seeking employment, these people could be divided into three categories, educational professionals, medical professionals, and employment professionals.

The following is a general list of the professionals who fall within each of these categories, with a description of their professional role. Also provided is specific information to guide each category of professionals in how they can play a role in helping people with Asperger Syndrome.

6.2.1 Educational professionals

Educational professionals are faced today with large classes, stretched resources, and limited support when teaching students with different needs in mainstream classes. They do not have the time or the means to become an expert on each challenge that their students may face. This being said, most educational professionals are extremely devoted and interested in helping their students reach their full potential. They are eager to utilize information to help them develop more effective teaching methods for their students with different needs, including those with Asperger Syndrome.

It is useful for educational professionals to understand that students with Asperger Syndrome are not deliberately behaving badly or being difficult. Teachers and their assistants can help their students with Asperger

Syndrome by providing support and assistance with social skills by helping them to learn how to react to social situations and to read social cues.

While students with Asperger Syndrome may appear capable and have a good memory for facts, they may have poor comprehension and be rigid in their thought process. Teachers should try to build upon the student's strengths and motivate her by using the student's unique special interests to help her develop talents and broaden her knowledge and skill base.

During the elementary years, behavioral problems may be the greatest challenge for teachers who have students with Asperger Syndrome in their classrooms. Academically, however, students with Asperger Syndrome often do quite well. The students' ability to memorize information, do mathematical calculations, and focus intensely on subjects of interest serves them well. Difficulties with social skills, language, and obsessive behaviors usually become more challenging as the student moves through the school system. This can result in the student being bullied and teased by her peers.

Let's take a look at who is included in the category of educational professionals and what their typical roles are.

Educational professionals will include:

- *Elementary school teachers* – Elementary school teachers play a vital role in the development of children. They introduce children to numbers, language, science, and social studies.

- *Secondary school teachers* – Secondary school teachers help students delve more deeply into subjects introduced in elementary school and expose them to more information about the world. Vocational education teachers instruct and train students to work in a wide variety of fields. They often teach courses that are in high demand among local employers, for example bookkeeping, computer programming, and auto mechanics.

- *Teacher's aides/classroom/educational assistants* – Teacher's aides/classroom/educational assistants provide instructional and clerical support for classroom teachers, allowing teachers more time for lesson planning and teaching. Many teacher's assistants work extensively with special education students. As schools are now integrating special education students into general education classrooms, teacher assistants increasingly assist students with disabilities in this setting.

- *Guidance counselors* – Guidance counselors in elementary, secondary, and post-secondary schools help students evaluate their abilities, interests, talents, and personality characteristics in order to develop realistic academic and career goals.

- *Cooperative education teachers* – Cooperative education teachers usually teach at the secondary-school level. Their job is to place students into an appropriate job situation where credits are earned and which count toward the student's graduation diploma.

- *Principals and assistant principals* – Principals and assistant principals manage elementary and secondary schools. They hire, evaluate, and help improve the skills of teachers and other staff. They visit classrooms, observe teaching methods, review instructional objectives, and examine learning materials. Many principals and assistant principals develop school-to-work transition programs for students. Increasingly, principals must be sensitive to the needs of the rising number of students with special needs in order to accommodate their unique learning styles.

- *Special education teachers* – Special education teachers, like any other teacher, teach regular subjects as well as valuable life skills such as how to tie a shoe lace and how to tell the time. They often work one on one with students with special learning needs.

- *School psychologists/psychometrists* – A school psychologist/psychometrist conducts individual psychological assessments; assists teachers in developing effective educational, social-emotional, adaptive, and behavior management programs for the classroom; coordinates referrals to community agencies and provides short-term counseling interventions.

6.2.1.1 WHAT THEY CAN DO TO HELP

There are limited programs available that have been designed specifically for students with Asperger Syndrome. Teachers may have to rely on teaching methods that have been designed for higher functioning people with autism to help them cope. Applied Behavioral Analysis (ABA) may be useful for teachers to learn about. It is based on the concept that behavior that is positively reinforced will be repeated. In other words, rewarding positive behavior is more likely to increase it.

Educational professionals may also find it helpful to use visual aides when working with students with Asperger Syndrome. Aides, such as charts and pictures, convey more information and increase the likelihood of information being absorbed. Teachers may reduce problems with students who have Asperger Syndrome by preparing them in advance for changes that may occur in the classroom. People with Asperger Syndrome struggle with change, but if they have time to prepare and adjust beforehand, they handle situations much better.

When finding work that works for people with Asperger Syndrome, educational professionals have a significant impact. They are often the first professionals to see the strengths, challenges, and potential of the student with Asperger Syndrome. Teachers, guidance counselors, and cooperative education teachers can have an enormous influence on the student with Asperger Syndrome by encouraging the student to pursue special interests that might lead to a career in the future. They can also use the student's unique gifts to direct her into broadening her knowledge and skill base. For example, if a student is fascinated with computers, the teacher might encourage her to learn computer programming.

Educational professionals can also be involved in the set up of cooperative educational programs that place students in work environments. This is an opportunity for the educational professional to design a positive work experience for the student with Asperger Syndrome, who so often gets negative reactions. The teacher who thoughtfully selects placements that are in keeping with the abilities and interests of the student with Asperger Syndrome sets the student up for a successful experience. The educational professional who is informed about Asperger Syndrome is able to prepare and educate employers and help establish work routines that can result in a positive experience for all involved.

Educational professionals can also act as advocates to help the student with Asperger Syndrome navigate the school system. This might include supporting the student in choosing appropriate post-secondary direction, knowing that the student with Asperger Syndrome requires more practical, hands on approaches to learning, often found in community college and apprenticeship programs. When educational professionals are aware of the triggers and stresses of a student with Asperger Syndrome, they are in a position to guide the student toward appropriate career avenues. They can also provide students with a "reality check" if they are interested in careers that may be particularly challenging for them because of their Asperger Syndrome. This supports the students in making good, informed decisions.

6.2.2 Medical professionals

Medical professionals play a key role in diagnosing disabilities and educating families, in addition to ensuring that there are no underlying medical reasons for challenges. Family practitioners, for example, will also check on the psychosocial development of their young patients by checking developmental targets and asking questions about school. When they discover information that is a red flag – for example, that it takes their patient three hours to complete a thirty-minute homework assignment – the family practitioner may act as an advocate to look at all the possible diagnoses.

Medical professionals and their roles will include, but not be limited to:

- *Family practitioner* – A family practitioner is a medical doctor/primary care physician who provides general medical care to adults and children and specializes in family practice. She is often the first point of contact for a family seeking medical resources.

- *Psychiatrist* – A psychiatrist is a medical doctor trained in the medical, psychological, and social components of mental, emotional, and behavioral disorders. She helps patients and their families cope with stress and crises. Psychiatrists often consult with family practitioners and psychotherapists, such as psychologists and social workers.

- *Clinical psychologist* – A clinical psychologist specializes in understanding the nature and impact of developmental disabilities, including Asperger Syndrome. She may perform psychological assessments and tests and may help with behavior modification and social skills training.

- *Social worker* – A social worker provides counseling services or acts as a case manager helping to arrange services.

- *Psychoanalyst/therapist* – A psychoanalyst/therapist is an experienced, licensed mental health professional (e.g. psychiatrist, psychologist, social worker, counselor, or clinical nurse specialist) who has completed advanced training at a psychoanalytic institute. A psychoanalyst/therapist provides an atmosphere of acceptance and support where a client can explore her problems.

- *Occupational therapist* – An occupational therapist focuses on developing practical, self-help skills with the client that will assist in daily living, such as dressing, eating; she may work on sensory integration, coordination of movement, and fine motor skills.

- *Speech/language therapist* – A speech/language therapist is involved in the improvement of communication skills, primarily speech and language.

- *Physical therapist* – A physical therapist helps to improve the use of bones, muscles, joints, and nerves to develop muscle strength, coordination, and motor skills.

6.2.2.1 WHAT THEY CAN DO TO HELP

Knowing the early warning signs of Asperger Syndrome is key to early diagnosis and intervention. This allows for the proper strategies, support, and teaching techniques to be introduced early in the child's development, which will contribute to her self-esteem and understanding, and pave the road to greater success.

A few of the key warning signs for Asperger Syndrome that medical professionals should become familiar with are:

- significant impairment in social interaction, including impaired non-verbal behaviors such as eye contact and facial expression

- poor development of peer relationships

- lack of shared interests or spontaneous reciprocal social interaction

- significant preoccupations with interests, activities, and patterns of behavior that are abnormal in intensity or focus

- hand or finger flapping, repetitive motor mannerisms

- no significant delay in language or cognitive development.

Listening to the family when they bring up concerns regarding their relative. The family has the greatest exposure to the relative with Asperger Syndrome and is often the first to detect early signals that something is wrong.

Referring the patient to an appropriate specialist is important if the medical professional suspects Asperger Syndrome. Early intervention is crucial to the patient's development. Referring the patient to a psychologist, for example, might be the very thing that puts them on the road to victory.

Coordinating treatment and support with educational and employment professionals is important to the overall well-being of the person with Asperger Syndrome. It is this coordinated effort and sharing of information with all of the players that supports the process of finding work that works and speeds the process.

Being sensitive to the needs and feelings of the person with Asperger Syndrome helps medical professionals build trust and places them in a position where they can help. People with Asperger Syndrome have the same feelings and needs as others and should be treated with the same respect. They can sense when they are not being treated equally or if they are not being regarded as the intelligent, sensitive individuals which they are.

Refer families and patients with Asperger Syndrome to local or national resources such as Asperger or autism chapters/societies for information and to help them connect with other resources (the resources section of this book has some pointers). Pointing the patient in the direction of appropriate government resources for funding and vocational support is also extremely useful.

6.2.3 Employment professionals

People who are in the business of helping others find and keep employment may play the most significant role of all the professionals in finding work that works for people with Asperger Syndrome. They can be found in community agencies such as Goodwill Industries, government employment centers and offices such as Vocational Rehabilitation Centers, and sometimes community centers. There may be private services and agencies that provide employment services for people with disabilities as well. It is part of the role of the employment professional to work directly with clients or, when she herself is not the best resource, to connect them to employment services that are appropriate to the clients' needs.

Although there may be a frustrating lack of employment resources specific to the needs of people with Asperger Syndrome, employment professionals are still the best line of contact for individuals with different needs who are seeking employment. It is employment professionals who will be most connected with local programs and services. Unfortunately, an inherently challenging dilemma for employment professionals is the lack of information available to them on specialized services. There often is not a general resource index that lists professionals, agencies, and services for their community and, if there is, it may not be comprehensive enough. It takes some research and digging on the part of the employment professional to come up with specific resources appropriate for her client. This is not only frustrating to families and other professionals but also a source of great frustration for employment professionals who want to connect their clients to appropriate resources as rapidly as possible.

One of the stumbling blocks that employment professionals face in their job, one which often causes them great anguish, is the unrealistic expectations placed upon them by their clients. Clients often look to the employment professional to solve their problems; to hand them the perfect job on a platter. Employment professionals are meant to be a support system and guide for their clients, not magicians who can produce a magic pill to make everything all better. The employment professional often spends a great deal of time helping a client take responsibility and participate in the process of finding work.

For the employment professional there are generally two types of clients. There are the clients who are resistant to the process, make excuses and blame others for everything that is not right in their life. These clients might be referred to as the "Yeah, but…" clients. Then there are the clients who are receptive and motivated, who implement ideas and strategies, take responsibility and participate in the job-finding process. These could be called the "Yes, and…" clients. Each type of client faces similar challenges in the workplace; however, the "Yes, and…" client will usually reach her potential and find employment sooner. It is very difficult for employment professionals to work with the "Yeah, but…" clients because of the resistance they bring to the process. It is often an uphill battle that results in the client resenting the professional for not "fixing" the problem or delivering the solution.

In fairness, there will always be personal differences and personality conflicts. In truth, everybody can't like everybody. If the client and the professional do not hit it off, the client should not hesitate to move on to another professional where the mix of personalities is better.

The employment professional must wear a number of hats when working with clients. She plays the roles of employment or career counselor, social worker, mentor, advocate, educator, job developer, and trainer regardless of her official capacity. Employment professionals must be well versed in all aspects of the job-finding process in order to support and help the client. They are usually well trained, talented with people, and good at their jobs. The challenges for employment professionals when finding work that works for people with Asperger Syndrome is their lack of knowledge regarding this disorder and how specifically they should work with these individuals. As this book is geared to this process, it will provide the necessary tools to resolve this dilemma.

Employment professionals and their roles include:

- *Career counselor* – A career counselor is a person who gives information and helpful suggestions to people seeking a first career or who wish to change to a new career. This might include information on training and further education options as well as resumé-writing and interview skills. The career counselor helps map out career routes, but the decision rests with the individual.

- *Vocational rehabilitation counselor* – A vocational rehabilitation counselor is trained to work with people who are disabled, physically, intellectually, or socially. She has the training, experience, and knowledge to work with many disabilities.

- *Job coach/trainer* – A job coach is a person who is called into the workplace when an employee is new to a job or has difficulty learning new skills.

- *Employment specialist* – An employment specialist is a liaison between the individual receiving services, the employer, family, public agency representatives, and the community. An employment specialist is a special type of rehabilitation counselor who focuses on helping people gain employment.

- *Supports coordinator* – A supports coordinator is a professional who coordinates services and connects professionals, and can often act as an advocate for the individual with Asperger Syndrome.

- *Personal support worker* – A personal support worker is a person hired by an agency or a family to work one to one with the individual with Asperger Syndrome. She may connect the individual with recreational and community programs to support a more well-rounded quality of life.

- *Transit trainer* – A transit trainer is a person trained to teach people with disabilities how to travel on public transit with the goal of assisting the individual to become independent.

- *Mentor* – A mentor is someone who takes a special interest in helping another person develop into a successful employee. An effective mentoring relationship is characterized by mutual respect, trust, understanding, and empathy. Good mentors are able to share life experiences and wisdom, as well as technical expertise. They are good listeners, good observers, and good problem-solvers.

- *Advocate* – An advocate is a person who acts or speaks on behalf of another individual to resolve issues and help that person navigate complicated programs and/or services.

6.2.3.1 WHAT THEY CAN DO TO HELP

Connect with local associations that specialize in autism spectrum disorders to find out what is available locally for clients.

Develop a list of medical professionals who are familiar with Asperger Syndrome in or around the community.

Learn to recognize the characteristics of Asperger Syndrome.

Read first-person accounts of Asperger Syndrome. These provide wonderful insights into how people with Asperger Syndrome function and view the world, which is invaluable when working with them.

Understand what environments are best suited to clients with Asperger Syndrome so that the job search is appropriately targeted.

Read this book!

6.3 Finding local resources

Professionals spend a great deal of time looking for local resources. It is an arduous task and even more difficult when one does not know where to begin. There are several avenues available to people wishing to find local resources for people with Asperger Syndrome. Understand upfront that resources specific to Asperger Syndrome are likely to be very limited and even more limited for adults with Asperger Syndrome seeking employment services. You may have to broaden the search to more general resources and then "educate" the professionals involved.

Here are five common avenues to investigate when searching for local resources:

- the Internet – key words, search terms
- *Yellow Pages*
- public agencies – schools, employment offices, vocational rehabilitation centers
- local libraries
- networking.

6.3.1 The Internet

As the World Wide Web has become a common marketplace, more and more organizations are using it for exposure and have comprehensive web sites. This is a terrific place to begin researching resources. Some of the key words you can use that are helpful in narrowing resources are:

- Asperger Syndrome + employment + [your city/region/state/province/country]
- autism + employment + [your city/region/state/province/country]
- employment services + disabilities + [your city/region/state/province/country]
- vocational rehabilitation services + [your city/region/state/province/country]
- disability services + [your city/region/state/province/country]

- job coach + disability + [your city/region/state/province/country]

- employment specialist + [your city/region/state/province/country]

- supported employment programs + [your city/region/state/province/country].

6.3.2 The *Yellow Pages*

The *Yellow Pages* are still a wonderful place for finding local resources. Some of the headings you might find services under are:

- rehabilitation services

- employment services

- social services

- job training and vocational rehabilitation

- job counseling services

- job training and related services

- vocational rehabilitation agencies

- vocational training agencies

- youth centers.

6.3.3 Public agencies

Public agencies are also a good place to begin researching. These include schools and government agencies and offices. Special education teachers are often familiar with local resources and may be able to point you in the right direction. Dropping into your local employment office that is run by the government is another avenue that might reveal resources. Community colleges have student service departments that usually are able to advise and connect students with special needs to local resources. You may be able to access region-wide resource guides through public agencies.

6.3.4 Local libraries

Your local library will likely have information of local government programs and services. The libraries may also have resource guides and indexes that are local, regional, and national.

6.3.5 Networking

Regardless of where you begin to locate resources, you will eventually need to make a few calls and talk to people. Don't be afraid to talk to people and ask them who they know. It is generally through networking that you get the contacts you require.

Professionals are incredibly dedicated people. They usually go above and beyond the call of duty to help people. Although they may struggle with many of the same issues and frustrations in the system that the other players do when helping people with Asperger Syndrome find work that works, they still pull on their resources and creativity to contribute to solutions. It is by learning to recognize the characteristics of Asperger Syndrome, understanding the unique challenges being faced, and helping these important individuals to help themselves, that professionals often break the cycle of hopelessness.

Summary

All of the players involved in finding work that works for people with Asperger Syndrome contribute to altering the public's perception of people who are differently-abled. They play a role in projecting a positive image of how people with Asperger Syndrome can contribute to their workplace and their communities through education, outreach, and exposure. The power of each of the players lies in their common desire to be successful. Working together, they become their own super power, capable of making dreams a reality!

Part 2
The foundation

7 The Four Pillar Teaching Technique

A foolproof method for teaching people with Asperger Syndrome

When helping someone with Asperger Syndrome learn, it is helpful to look at situations as if you are a foreigner trying to learn something in another culture. If you have ever been in a foreign country where you did not speak the language and did not know the customs, then you know how challenging it can be to do the simplest things, such as ask for a glass of water or even say hello to someone. It's also true that what might be considered a polite gesture in one culture could be interpreted as something rude in another. When I was traveling in South America in the 1990s, I fell into conversation with a local woman in a town I was visiting. As we talked about our families, I described my niece as being about this high, motioning with my hand to waist level. The woman looked at me oddly when I did this but, since I didn't know any better, I just continued on with the conversation. Later, I learned that in that culture the gesture for describing a person is made with the hand out, palm facing sideways. I had motioned with my palm facing down, which is how they describe an animal. In other words, I had just described my niece as being a dog that stood about waist high. No wonder the woman looked at me oddly! If no one tells you what is appropriate, you will never know when you are doing something inappropriate. Once someone shares with you what is expected, then you try to do it differently the next time.

People with Asperger Syndrome have told me that this is what life is like every day for them. They go through life simply doing their best to fit in with what they know, not always aware of what is acceptable and what is not. They also need to have things pointed out to them, whereas someone without Asperger Syndrome will often pick up cues naturally without needing them explained.

Working with hundreds of people with Asperger Syndrome has taught me to be systematic in my approach to teaching. I learned early on that if I wanted my clients to learn from me, then I needed to be the one to adapt if I was going to be effective. I am about to share with you my "foolproof" method for helping people with Asperger Syndrome learn. If you follow this strategy and apply it to all your teachings, you will find that your lessons will come across clearly. As with any system, it takes time to perfect your skill and it is normal to expect some trial and error. If you make a mistake or two along the way, remember to be kind to yourself. Wisdom often comes in the form of mistakes. If you stick with the system, you will succeed in getting your message across.

The system is called the *Four Pillar Teaching Technique* because each pillar holds up a different, yet equally important part of a lesson. If one or more pillars are missing, then the lesson falls down, leaving behind only a fragment of information that can be left up to misinterpretation! Not something you want to do when you are working with people with Asperger Syndrome.

The Four Pillars are:

1.   effective communication

2.   clear expectations

3.   clear consequences

4.   consistency.

7.1 Pillar 1: Effective communication

Say what you mean and mean what you say…but do it in fifteen words or less.

The secret to communicating effectively with your Asperger friends is to be clear about what you are saying and how you are saying it. The four key steps to communicating effectively with people who have Asperger Syndrome are:

- don't make assumptions
- plan your lessons ahead of time
- be direct
- use detail.

7.1.1 Don't make assumptions

The first step in communicating clearly with a person who has Asperger Syndrome is: Don't *assume* they know things that everyone else knows.

All of us make assumptions in our daily interactions with people. We often assume that we know what someone is thinking or what he is going to do next. Have you ever noticed that when you make assumptions, you often get it wrong? People can wind up feeling hurt or getting angry about something they don't even know is true. Making assumptions is always dangerous! It can be even more dangerous when you are making assumptions about what someone with Asperger Syndrome thinks, knows, or understands because Asperger Syndrome makes people see the world differently. You can be setting others and yourself up for disaster if you make assumptions.

> People with Asperger Syndrome often know more than we think they know and sometimes understand less than we think they do.

Brenda, a bright young woman with Asperger Syndrome, had an experience that illustrates the point of assumptions *versus* non-assumptions. One day, during a break, she and her job coach decided to go for a walk together. The coach noticed right away that rather than walking with her, Brenda always walked several steps ahead. At this point the coach could have assumed a number of things:

- Had she offended Brenda?
- Was she walking too slowly?
- Was Brenda being rude?
- Did Brenda not like her?
- Was Brenda acting superior?

This was the coach's opportunity to apply her training and not make an assumption. Making an assumption could have led her into teaching the wrong lesson. So the job coach brought Brenda's attention to the behavior and asked why she was walking ahead.

Brenda was shocked by the question. It had never occurred to her that she should walk alongside people. Brenda had no idea that people might perceive this behavior as unusual. She turned to the coach and said, "Thank you for telling me. All these years I have been walking ahead of people and no one has pointed it out to me!" They continued to talk about how people might interpret her walking ahead of them and discussed what was going on in her mind when she was doing this. "Essentially," she told the coach, "I was just walking."

Making assumptions is dangerous when you are in a teaching role. If you notice something unusual or odd about your Asperger friend's behavior, bring it to his attention and talk about how it might be perceived. Asking questions rather than making assumptions allows you to keep your lessons on target.

7.1.2 Plan your lessons ahead of time

Have you ever learned how to do something and then had someone come and tell you to do it in a completely different way? Doesn't it always seem harder to re-learn something than it did to learn it the first time? You in effect have to "unlearn" and then learn again.

Re-learning is challenging for everyone and even more so for people with Asperger Syndrome because the syndrome makes them more rigid in their thinking and routines. Once they have developed a method or system, they like to stick to it. It is always important to plan ahead when teaching. It is crucial to plan ahead when helping people with Asperger Syndrome learn because if they are not taught the right thing at the right time, it may be necessary to go through the challenging unlearn/re-learn process all over again. This is unnecessarily painful for everybody. People with Asperger Syndrome tend to do well in a structured environment. Whenever possible, they like to know beforehand what, when, where, why, and how. Once they've got something in their head, it can be challenging to change it. Plan ahead!

> Teaching it right the first time will save you tons of time, and your Asperger friend oodles of frustration.

If you want to get it right the first time, then I suggest doing a bit of homework before you plan your lessons. If you are in a work environment and you are teaching an employee with Asperger Syndrome a new assignment, take some time to plan. Find out how the employer wants the task done. Ask coworkers if they have any helpful tricks or tips for getting the task completed more efficiently. If the task is something new to you, try it out yourself to get a feel for it. Once you have done all these things, plan out your lesson step by step. Run the lesson by the supervisor to see if everything you are teaching is correct and make any necessary adjustments and then get a final approval. This may seem like a lot of preparation but in reality it doesn't take that long. Doing this will save you enormous time that you might otherwise have to invest later, should you find out you made a mistake and have to do it differently.

Planning ahead does not mean that you have to forgo being spontaneous. It is often necessary to be spontaneous when you are teaching. In fact, being creative and spontaneous can be the difference between a good teacher and an amazing one. The amazing teachers make spontaneity look easy and natural. What looks like spontaneity is, in fact, the teacher rapidly planning ahead. Before acting, he is thinking about the approach, the method, and its impact on the individual, at the speed of lightning. It is this rapid processing that makes you look as if you are being spontaneous and helps you to go with the flow.

There will be times when you are teaching something on the job that is not crucial. You do not have to do extensive planning with everything you teach; use your judgment. If the task is a crucial part of the job and one that may put the job in jeopardy if performed improperly, then it is vital that you do your homework and plan your strategy. Remember, it is always easier to teach than to re-teach.

7.1.3 Be direct

Have you ever been in a conversation with someone and mid-way through, thought to yourself, "I don't have a clue what this person is talking about?" Imagine having a communication disorder such as Asperger Syndrome and trying to understand that same conversation.

Many people are not good communicators. Here are just some of the reasons why:

- they don't choose appropriate vocabulary
- they don't seek feedback to identify what is being absorbed
- they don't use directive or clear language

- they don't speak clearly
- they don't want to offend anyone so they "sugar coat" their meaning.

Keep in mind:

Put sugar on donuts – not on words.

You would be surprised how many managers do not know how to be direct and clear in their approach. If you want to get a message across to someone with Asperger Syndrome, it is vital that you *speak in direct terms* and *be specific*. Being direct means saying exactly what you mean and identifying exactly what you want. People have expressed to me a concern that being direct can sound rude. This does not have to be the case. If you are worried that a direct statement may sound rude, then it's easy to put the word *please* in front of it or behind it. This changes the feel of the statement. For example, say, "Fill up the photocopier." Now say, "Please fill up the photocopier." It makes a difference, doesn't it? Being direct does not mean being impolite.

If you want your Asperger friends to understand you clearly, then you need to think about how you communicate with them. Keep in mind that Asperger Syndrome makes the mind process information differently and interpret things more literally. Avoid saying things with implied meanings, clichés, and idioms. Having Asperger Syndrome makes deciphering these things more difficult.

Statements with implied meanings	Directive statements
Are you going to work on the database assignment?	I want you to work on the database assignment.
Brian, you're the last one leaving today.	Please put the alarm on because you are the last to leave the office.
I feel like lunch.	I'm hungry, let's go out for lunch.
We are behind schedule on the Jacob's job.	You are going to have to stay late to meet the deadline.

Figure 7.1 Statements with implied meanings/directive statements

Let's take a look at implied meanings (see Figure 7.1). It is common in our culture to say one thing and really mean something else. People who do not have Asperger Syndrome usually understand that there is an implied meaning. For example:

People with Asperger Syndrome will not always register an implied meaning and if they miss the connotation, they will usually not take the appropriate next step. When this happens it leaves their coworkers and supervisors confused and causes trouble for themselves as employees. The employee with Asperger Syndrome misses the point innocently and without any knowledge that anything is awry. But this can have serious repercussions in a working environment where deadlines need to be met and time is costly to the employer. Figure 7.1 shows how obscure implied meanings can be. However, once put in a directive format, the meaning becomes crystal clear. Clarity is the language people with Asperger Syndrome understand.

A cliché is an expression that has become completely predictable. Clichés say one thing yet often mean something else. People with Asperger Syndrome often take things literally. Imagine the list of clichés below being taken literally. What messages are getting across?

- There are plenty more fish in the sea.
- All's fair in love and war.
- Behind the clouds, the sun is shining.
- Every cloud has a silver lining.
- Shake a leg.
- The sharper the berry, the sweeter the wine.

How often do you use clichés? Fill in the missing half of these clichés to see if you are guilty of using them yourself.

Animal clichés

Bald as _____

Busy as _____

Blind as _____

Clean as _____

Drunk as _____

Do the same for these food clichés

    American as _____

    Thick as _____

    Flat as _____

Idioms are quite similar to clichés. They are an expression that is particular to itself and cannot be understood from the individual meanings of its elements, for example:

"To pull an all-nighter"

Definition: To not go to bed in order to finish some important task.

Usage: Usually used in reference to school, university or work.

Example: "I pulled an all-nighter to get the report finished on time."

In summary:

Avoiding any indirect pattern of speech will dramatically improve communication with your Asperger friends.

7.1.4 Use detail

A common mistake many people make when helping people with Asperger Syndrome learn is that they don't give enough information. When people have Asperger Syndrome, they require a great deal of information before they are able to generalize. Spelling things out in detail helps the person with Asperger Syndrome understand what is required of him, which ultimately increases his ratio for success. The more detail you can provide, the better he will understand and the happier everyone will be with the results.

A number of years ago, the mother of one of my higher needs clients came to me because her son was giving his money away to people begging on the streets. If a beggar asked for spare change, Rob would either give it to them or say that he only had a twenty-dollar bill. Of course, the beggar said that that would be fine, and Rob would kindly hand over the money. Rob's mom had asked him not to give his money away but it hadn't worked because sometimes the beggar would ask for a quarter, lunch, or maybe a juice or coffee. Rob was not able to generalize "don't give your money away" to incorporate all the various ways a person on the street could beg.

This put Rob in a dangerous position. He became a target because the people on the street knew he could be easily manipulated and sometimes they bullied him out of his money. To correct the problem, I invited all of his coworkers at the music store where he worked to assist in making a list of every possible phrase that a beggar might use to solicit something from Rob. I then asked the staff to pretend to "beg" from Rob every time they saw him over a period of a week.

Meanwhile, I spoke to Rob and told him what we were doing and why. I scripted one response phrase for him to use whenever someone was begging from him. The phrase was "No, I'm sorry." This phrase was chosen because it was to the point, general enough to address different requests, did not invite dialogue, and would not incite anger. I instructed Rob to use this phrase and then to walk away.

After the week, Rob had been exposed repeatedly to over a hundred different ways of begging. When he didn't respond with the correct phrase, his coworkers corrected him.

By hearing a large variety of phrases, Rob was able to understand that he was not to give beggars anything, regardless of what they asked for. Providing enough detail was the key to helping Rob absorb this lesson. Today, Rob keeps his money in his pockets and feels safer walking down the street.

7.2 Pillar 2: Clear expectations

> If Charles Dickens had a character with Asperger Syndrome in his book *Great Expectations*, he would have had to change the title to *Clear Expectations*.

This is how important this next pillar is to helping people with Asperger Syndrome learn.

It is human nature to have expectations. You expect certain behaviors and certain outcomes for different situations. In business, companies call expectations *rules*, *mandates*, or *ethics* and outline them in a manual. For example, a financial institution might identify a dress code that is appropriate for its environment. There is nothing wrong with having expectations, unless you fail to communicate them to the people involved. There are three main rules to follow when applying expectations in the Four Pillar Teaching Technique:

- weigh the expectation

- state the expectation

- show how to meet the expectation.

7.2.1 Weigh the expectation

If you have ever had an unrealistic expectation put on you, then you know how unfair it feels. Setting someone up for success means being *realistic* about your expectations. Being realistic is not only important, it is fair; and a good teacher must be fair. In order to set fair expectations, you need to weigh them by examining whether or not they are attainable.

When you are examining expectations, consider these questions.

- Is what I'm expecting reasonable?

- Can it be accomplished in the time frame I have in mind?

- Does my Asperger friend have the skill and ability to meet the expectation?

Adjust your expectation so that you can answer "yes" to all three questions. You do not have to remove the challenge from the expectation; it's okay to set the bar reasonably high. Just ensure that the bar is manageable and that the expectation is attainable. The goal, after all, is to help people succeed.

7.2.2 State the expectation

Once you have decided what your expectation is, then you need to state it clearly. This may seem obvious but it is surprising how often people forget to state an expectation. All too often I hear direction given with the expectation left out. This is like having a sandwich without the bread. You have the filling but nothing to contain it or to tell you where it begins and ends. Directions and instructions need to have a beginning and an end when you are teaching them to anyone but this is extremely beneficial for someone with Asperger Syndrome. For example, let's say you want the candidate with Asperger Syndrome to work on a data-processing assignment. To ensure that the task gets completed properly and within the appropriate time frame, you need to tell the candidate what the expectations are. In other words, you should state the parameters: "I expect to have the first draft of this assignment by 1 p.m. tomorrow. It has to be in electronic format so that I can check it and get it back to you for revisions."

Here are some examples of expectations that need to be identified:

- Deadlines – time frames, schedules, etc.

- Outcomes – what they look like, format, etc.

- Behavior – dress, hygiene, appropriate conversation, manners, etc.

Once you have stated the expectation, you can make sure that your Asperger friend knows how to meet it.

7.2.3 Show how to meet the expectation

Stating an expectation is not much good if someone does not know how to meet it. After establishing the expectation, you want to ensure that your Asperger friend has the tools and skills to meet it. By applying the techniques discussed in the first pillar, you can plan a strategy that will help your friend learn the necessary skills required to meet the expectation if he does not already have them.

Become gifted at stating the obvious.

A great tip when helping someone with Asperger Syndrome meet an expectation is to remember to express the obvious. It's easy to overlook teaching something that you assume everyone already knows. When you are working with someone with Asperger Syndrome, it is prudent to cover every important aspect of your lesson. Do not assume what they know or do not know. If you are unsure, then ask them. If someone already knows something, they will tell you. If they do not know something, but tell you they do, it will become apparent soon enough. Asking questions such as, "Do you understand how to accomplish this?" or having the candidate show you what he already knows will tell you exactly where you need to pick up your lesson. From this point you may continue to teach the skills necessary for the candidate to meet the expectation.

Upon occasion you can strike a sensitive note with the candidate and get an answer like "Of course I know that!" when you are showing him or her how to meet an expectation. You can often tell if this is true or not but, either way, I suggest that you honor the answer given. If someone doesn't understand something, you will find out soon enough and it is more important at this point to build trust than it is to engage in a battle of wills. If it is revealed that the candidate didn't know how to do something after all, you can simply teach it later. The trust you establish when helping someone learn is often as important as the lesson itself.

In summary, when you are teaching someone with Asperger Syndrome, always make note of your expectations, make sure that they are realistic and attainable, and state them clearly. Determine that your Asperger friend knows how to meet the expectation and teach him any skills he may not have while being sensitive to what he already knows.

7.3 Pillar 3: Clear consequences

Consequences are natural...punishment is not.

The law of cause and effect is that every action has a consequence. It is as natural as nature itself. Some people call this law "what goes around comes around," or "the Golden Rule." Behaviorists call it "behavior/consequence" and it is an important part of the Four Pillar Teaching Technique. Unfortunately, people often misunderstand the meaning of the word "consequence." They may think that it is synonymous with punishment. This is not the case. "Punishment" refers to a *penalty* for an offence or action. "Consequence" refers to the *result* or *effect* of an action. This is an important distinction. You should be clear that you are not punishing someone when you are stating consequences. As part of effective teaching you need to include all relevant information. If there is a consequence that may result from an action, then you need to ensure that your Asperger friend knows about it. Consequences help people to learn effectively and they can bring valuable meaning to a lesson.

People with Asperger Syndrome learn best when they can participate in the process. Helping them understand consequences is part of this learning process.

There are three basic rules to follow when applying consequences to the Four Pillar Teaching Technique:

- outline consequences clearly
- ensure consequences are natural and realistic
- always follow through.

7.3.1 Outline the appropriate consequences

Just as the expectation has to be stated in clear terms, so should any consequences. For example, "If after one month you are not able to increase your production speed to 16,000 entries per day, we will not be able to keep you employed." This may appear harsh; however, it is actually kind. By identifying the consequence, you are providing an opportunity for the person to rise to the demands of the job and to be successful. It would be cruel to lead people on by telling them that they are doing okay or that they need to improve without telling them the consequence if they don't. David was a twenty-four-year-old man with Asperger Syndrome who got a job in a manufacturing company. His job was to run a machine that packaged coupons. In order to meet the quota for the position, David had to be able to run the machine at full capacity. The company gave him four months to work up to this level. The job coach explained to David what was expected of him and that the consequence of him not meeting the employer's quota would be losing his job. The employer and coach worked with David to come up with the best strategy to meet the expectation. David was extremely motivated because he wanted to keep his job, but he still struggled to meet the demands. Every week he would try to out-do his best time from the week before. The employer and job coach taught him tricks and shortcuts, which helped him improve, but he was still not able to meet consistently the quota after four months. Unfortunately the company had to let him go. This may seem like a sad ending, but David came out of the experience knowing that he did his absolute best and that he tried everything possible to meet the demands of the job. He also learned that he could do this type of work as long as the focus was more on accuracy and less on quantity. Rather than feeling like a failure, David left this job feeling proud. Because of what he learned from this experience, he was confident that his next job would be a better fit for him. If David had not been told up front about the consequences of not meeting the quota, his dismissal would have come as a surprise and would have seemed very unfair. By having this information early, David was able to strive to do his best. This resulted in him learning some valuable lessons and skills that he could apply to his next job.

7.3.2 Ensure consequences are natural and realistic

Being consistent and fair in your consequences will allow an opportunity for the employee with Asperger Syndrome to be responsible for his or her actions. It is important when you are helping people with Asperger

Syndrome to learn that you ensure that any consequences you establish are equivalent to the natural consequences that would occur in a real situation. For example, if you are teaching punctuality in a job and the employee shows up to the lesson late, it would be unnatural for you to tell him to go home and come back when he can be on time. In the real world an employer would state the expectation, give a warning and tell the employee that if he is late again it will be documented and put on file. If the employee continues to be late, he will be put on probation and after three warnings, his contract terminated.

When you are helping someone learn, it is not usually realistic or desirable to terminate his employment, so you may need to modify the consequence. You can however, attune your consequences to mimic something close to natural. For example, as in the previous example you could still document behavior and put it on file, explaining that documenting behavior may lead to dismissal in a real job.

7.3.3 Always follow through

Credibility is everything when you are establishing trust. When someone trusts you, they are more likely to listen and learn from you. It is vital that you follow through with any consequences you outline in your lessons. Take the time to explain clearly the difference between consequences and punishment. Your goal is not to punish but to help with the understanding of cause and effect, of natural consequences. It is just as important to reward positive behavior and consistently follow through with the reward.

7.4 Pillar 4: Consistency

> Consistency is the glue that bonds the pillars together and makes your lessons stand the test of time.

Without consistency, you jeopardize the hard work you have put in so far. Consistency is the strength behind the other three pillars.

Steps to being consistent:

- make a teaching plan
- follow the plan
- ensure others follow the plan.

Steps in plan	Description	Example
Challenge or new skill	Identify the challenge you are targeting or the new skill you are teaching	Purge files
Description	Give brief description of the challenge or skill	Employer requires all of their files to be purged and sent to long-term storage. Anything older than two years needs to be documented and placed in a file box for pick-up by the storage company
Major objective/s	Identify the objective/s of the program/lesson	1. To teach John an efficient system to purge files 2. To work John up to a competitive level of accuracy
Procedure	Write an overview of how you plan to go about meeting the objectives	After checking with the employer, we will outline the steps involved in purging the files. John finds checklists helpful so we will create a checklist to assist him in both learning the job and ensuring accuracy. We will also write out the steps involved in the purging process and go over them with John. Then, we will show John how we want the job done and sit with him for the first few hours to make sure he has got it. We will then do regular spot checks to make sure that his accuracy remains high. After we feel secure that he is doing the job accurately, we will begin working on speed
Effective communication	List any particulars with regard to effective communication including steps, details, etc.	1. Take a box of files from the file room, starting from A and working toward Z, and take it to your desk 2. Working from the front of the box, remove the first file 3. Open the file and remove any documents with the dates 2000 and older 4. On the Purging Sheet write the name of the file and the file number 5. Do this for each file in each file box making sure to keep files in order
Expectations	Name any expectations	This project needs to be completed by September 1
Consequences	Name any consequences	If John is too slow, he may be removed from the project
Constancy plan	Identify the people who need to follow this plan and make sure they have a copy	John has two job coaches: Sandra and Amir

Figure 7.2 Sample teaching plan

7.4.1 Make a teaching plan

In this chapter you have learned how to communicate effectively, how to state clear expectations, and how to outline consequences. Whether you write it down or keep it in your head, this system is your ultimate tool for writing a good teaching plan. When you set out to teach anything significant to someone with Asperger Syndrome, it will be important to think out your teaching strategy. The Four Pillar Technique gives you the foundation for your strategy. Now you can write a solid teaching plan. Figure 7.2 is a teaching plan template you may use in your own lessons.

7.4.2 Follow the plan

Once you strike a plan that works with your own personal style and, most important, with the style of your Asperger friend, you need to follow it consistently. Your teaching style combined with the Four Pillar Technique allows you to build trust and puts you in a positive position with whomever you are helping to learn. Being consistent makes you predictable and this predictability is very reassuring and comforting to someone with Asperger Syndrome. Once you have a plan, follow it!

7.4.3 Ensure others follow the plan

You can't always expect the other people involved in the process of finding work that works to share the same style of teaching, but you can make sure that they are consistent with your lessons, methods, and messages. This is extremely important in situations where there is a team of support. If there is more than one job coach involved in the teaching process, make certain that the teaching plan is documented clearly and that everyone uses the same strategies. This ensures that every job coach is clear about how something is being taught, the exact steps involved – including the order of the steps, and that the expectations as well as the consequences are consistent. It is very frustrating and confusing to have different people teach you different ways of doing something.

7.5 Applying the Four Pillar Teaching Technique

Learning the Four Pillar Teaching Technique will be one of the most important steps you can take to help someone with Asperger Syndrome meet his or her potential both in the workplace and in life. If you can adapt your thinking and communication style to fit that of someone with Asperger

Syndrome, then you are so much closer to helping that individual achieve his or her goals. When you get stumped, think about being a stranger in a foreign country. What would help you to learn something in that situation? This can oftentimes help you look at the situation from a different angle and give you insights that you might not have otherwise.

A note on teaching style

If you were to think back to your childhood, who are the teachers you remember? More often than not, it was the teachers who had a great personality, who made you feel worthy and important, who made the lessons interesting and fun. Don't be afraid to show your personality in your teaching style. All of us have a style and when we show ourselves in our teaching, it makes our lessons more real and usually more interesting. It also helps us to build the all-important relationship that is so vital to being successful with our Asperger friends. If you are a bit quirky, be a bit quirky. I have discovered that showing my quirky side endears my clients to me. They really seem to enjoy my sometimes "off-beat" humor but I am also able to balance it with my serious and sensitive sides. Good teachers wear many hats. You will find that teaching people with Asperger Syndrome requires a trunk full of hats. If you don't have a lot of hats before you start using this teaching technique, you certainly should afterwards.

Communicating with people with Asperger Syndrome is different. It's normal to make a few mistakes and have a few misunderstandings along the way. Using this system will go a long way to helping the Asperger candidate understand what you are teaching and what is expected of him. You will find that as you get used to the system it will become natural. You may even discover that you have become a better communicator in general.

Summary

In summary, *always* ask. Don't assume anything when you are helping people with Asperger Syndrome learn. This honors intelligence and sensitivity and allows you to keep your lessons on track. Plan your lessons ahead of time and do the homework necessary to ensure that you have the steps right. It is always easier to teach something the first time than it is to re-teach it. Use directive language by avoiding hidden and implied meanings, and provide lots of detail.

It's important to state expectations clearly and outline consequences when you are helping someone with Asperger Syndrome learn. Check-in with yourself to ensure that expectations are realistic and attainable and that consequences are natural. Finally, use the Four Pillar Teaching Technique to help you write a solid teaching plan. Share the plan with all of the support people involved in the process of finding work to ensure consistency. Consistency is the glue that bonds the Four Pillars together.

8 The Employment Toolbox

The top ten tools for building successful strategies

When I was a little girl, my dad gave me a toolbox that he built himself out of wood. Inside were a hammer, saw, hand drill, some nails and screws, a multi-purpose screwdriver, a level, a tape measure, and a pencil. My dad told me that now I had the basic tools to make almost anything and the only other thing I needed was my imagination. That was probably one of the best gifts I've ever received.

Having Asperger Syndrome means seeing the world in a unique way. Processing information and relating to everyday situations therefore follows a different course. For these reasons it is important that you equip yourself with tools that the candidate with Asperger Syndrome will understand and retain. In Chapter 7 you learned the Four Pillar Teaching Technique. To develop successful strategies, you also need the right tools. This chapter contains the basic tools you need to develop strategies for working with your Asperger friend. You will still need to be creative and flexible when applying them but you will find that the tools in the chapter support effective strategies.

I have found ten tools to be most effective when developing strategies to help people with Asperger Syndrome be successful in the workplace – what I call the *Employment Toolbox*:

1. scripting

2. role play

3. video play

4. rule tool

5. formulas

6. anchoring

7. scales

8. third-party praise

9. mirroring

10. verbal reflection.

Once you learn these ten tools, and combine them with the Four Pillar Teaching Technique, you will be able to create a strategy to address almost any situation.

Remember, Asperger Syndrome affects different people in different ways and each individual is unique. What works for John, may not work for Robert or Susan. Expect some adjustment and fine-tuning to make the tool suit each individual. If something does not work right away, make a few changes to see if you are on target with that particular tool or whether you should try something different. As you gain experience, you will get to know what tools work best for different people and situations. Expect to have some trial and error in this process, and think of mistakes as opportunities to learn, gain experience, and improve.

8.1 Scripting

8.1.1 Description

Scripts are predetermined dialogues for a given situation. When someone has Asperger Syndrome, she has difficulty instinctively knowing what is appropriate in many situations. Not knowing what is expected or what to say can cause her great anxiety. When her anxiety rises, she gets more nervous and is more likely to exhibit behavior that draws negative attention. A predetermined script takes the guesswork out of a situation, lowers anxiety about what to say and sets the groundwork for appropriate interaction. This allows the person to relax, and a calm person is in a better position to succeed because she can think more clearly.

8.1.2 Instruction

Write an appropriate and common response to a specific situation on paper. You will later ask the candidate to memorize it. Keep scripts simple and get the input of the candidate you are working with so that the dialogue sounds and feels natural to her.

8.1.3 Example

Issue: Jerome interacts awkwardly, if at all, when he arrives at his job in the morning. He mumbles "hello" only if someone says it first, but usually says nothing more. A script will help him to know exactly what is appropriate to say when he arrives at work. For example: "Good morning Jack, how are you?"

8.1.4 Experience tips

- Often scripts are combined with action. In Jerome's situation, you might wish to combine the script with role play to make it effective.

- Scripting is useful for issues such as interrupting, greetings, making "small talk," and asking questions. It is also effective when teaching telephone interaction.

- Scripts are often crucial in interview preparation and help to keep the candidate calm and focused. When the candidate is prepared with set phrases to say, she can concentrate more on the questions being asked.

8.2 Role play

8.2.1 Description

Role play is the acting out of a scene or situation in order to practice for the real event. It is an opportunity to acquire skills by making mistakes in a safe environment. This is a very effective tool because it draws upon the natural ability many people with Asperger Syndrome have to act. It can also be a lot of fun.

8.2.2 Instruction

Keep your role play specific and detailed. You may choose to include other people in the role play or keep it between you and your Asperger friend. This is an interactive exercise so you want to get your friend involved by first discussing the situation. Together, answer these questions:

- Who are the players involved in the situation?

- What is the outcome that you want?

- How do you get this outcome?

Get up and move around during the role play. Use furniture and pillows as props. For example, I might use a pillow to represent a person and furniture to take the place of a photocopier.

8.2.3 Example

Issue: Frank tends to stare at people when he is in the elevator and several women have complained. This draws negative attention to him.

In this role play, Frank is instructed to take quick, hardly noticeable glances at people by using his peripheral vision. It is helpful to Frank to have the behavior modeled for him so he can see what it looks like. The glances are to be no longer than one second and are timed and practiced to give him the correct reference.

The role play begins with Frank pretending to stand in an elevator looking up at the numbers above the elevator doors. When his job coach gets on the elevator with him he practices his glance. If he stares too long, the job coach points it out and the role play is started again.

8.2.4 Experience tips

- Keep the role play specific and only work with one issue at a time.

- Do not expect to eliminate behavior but rather, try to alter or shift it to the point of being more socially acceptable, or less obvious.

- Set the role play up with you as the director and use language such as "cut," "pause," and "action." This makes it less personal and more fun, which is more conducive to learning.

8.3 Video play

8.3.1 Description

People with Asperger Syndrome have difficulty seeing themselves through the eyes of others. They are often unaware that others may perceive some of their behavior as peculiar or inappropriate. When given the opportunity to witness their behavior from an outside vantage point, they are usually more motivated to change it, particularly if they themselves can see how unusual something looks.

Video play is a means of presenting behavior in the third person. It is said that "seeing is believing" and if you videotape the behavior, your Asperger friend is able to see himself through the eyes of bystanders. The goal of using video play is to offer the candidate an outside perspective, which you hope will motivate her to alter a behavior that is inappropriate or alienating.

8.3.2 Instruction

Target a behavior that is not appropriate and then record it with your video recorder.

Once you have the target behavior on tape, watch it with your Asperger friend a few times. Have her describe what is happening on the tape play-by-play. You may find that some people view themselves in the third person, using vocabulary such as "he is" or "she is." If this happens, ask that they repeat the comment using the first person, for example, "I am…" "I" statements are important because they help the candidate to identify personally with the behavior.

Discuss how other people watching your friend act this way might perceive the behavior. Then talk about alternative behaviors or choices your Asperger friend can make to express himself more appropriately. It is important to discuss alternative methods of expression so that you don't simply identify what your friend is doing as wrong without working out a solution. This follow-through is crucial to the tool working.

8.3.3 Example

Issue: Ellen pouts when she gets upset. Her behavior is immature for an adult and draws considerable attention. Ellen is not aware of how her pouting looks or how others react to it.

When Ellen watches her behavior on video, she is very surprised. She identifies the behavior as being that of a three-year-old. She discusses how people witnessing this behavior might react to an adult who behaves like a three-year-old at work. Ellen's support worker uses an example of a bank teller pouting and making a scene because her lunch hour has been changed from 1:00 to 2:00. When the worker asks Ellen how long she thinks the teller would have her job under these circumstances, the answer is, "one day."

Ellen makes a contract with the support worker to work on being more adult in situations where she feels she is not getting what she wants. She agrees to express that she is feeling upset, frustrated or angry rather than pouting. Then they develop a strategy to work out how she can recognize and alter the behavior.

8.3.4 Experience tips

- Before you begin, tell your Asperger friend that you will be recording her. Although this may make her a bit self-conscious, she will soon get used to you following her around and you will eventually get the target behavior on tape.

- Following someone around with a camera can attract attention from bystanders. Be discreet about filming and sensitive to the feelings of your friend. If your friend objects at any time, honor her feelings and stop the taping. You are not trying to embarrass or bully anyone into doing something they do not want.

8.4 Rule tool

8.4.1 Description

The Asperger Syndrome world is one of extremes. Things are either this way or that way and the "in between" parts are difficult to live with. People who have Asperger Syndrome like things to be predictable and concrete. They find this comforting. This is the reason people with Asperger Syndrome respond well to rules and often live by them. The rule tool uses this rigid or "black-or-white" characteristic to help a candidate with Asperger Syndrome learn appropriate behavior.

8.4.2 Instruction

This is a great tool that uses the natural characteristics of Asperger Syndrome to work for the person rather than against her. People with Asperger Syndrome relate well to structure, and what is more structured than rules? If you want someone with Asperger Syndrome to learn and retain something, then make a rule to fit the situation.

8.4.3 Example

Issue: Stewart yells to people across the office when he requires assistance. This startles and distracts his coworkers.

The rule in this situation might be:

> When you require assistance, you must walk over to the appropriate person and ask for his help.

8.4.4 Experience tips

- Be specific in your rule setting. Begin with very basic, black-and-white rules and then expand them to include the necessary variations and exceptions.

- Include an *exception* rule, which allows the candidate with Asperger Syndrome to be flexible when things don't fit the regular rule. For example, the exception rule for the previous example might be, "Only when there is an emergency in the office that involves the physical safety of people, would there be a reason to yell to get someone's attention."

8.5 Formulas

8.5.1 Description

Formulas are clear, step-by-step descriptions of how to do something so that the correct result is netted. Formulas may be used to teach a task or to help make a decision or judgment.

Formulas are very logical and precise and this makes them a good tool for people who have Asperger Syndrome because they find them easy to follow. Formulas can actually help your Asperger friend to be more flexible because once learned, a formula can be applied to other situations. This gives her the tool to handle more situations, thus offering her the opportunity to be more adaptable and therefore less rigid.

8.5.2 Instruction

Outline a step-by-step system that, when applied to a situation, delivers the same outcome every time. There are numerous factors that may contribute to the complexity of the formula such as the number and detail of the steps, the people concerned and the difficulty of variables involved. You will need to factor into the formula any challenges the candidate has, such as learning and comprehension, the ability and functioning level of the candidate, and the complexity of the task or assignment.

8.5.3 Example

Issue: Marion is required in her job to answer the telephone occasionally. She has difficulty problem-solving when callers ask for something out of the ordinary. A formula is an excellent tool to help Marion address this issue.

When you are using a formula to help someone perform a job or address a specific problem, the formula should be in the form of a written step-by-step instruction as in Figure 8.1.

IF	The caller asks for someone who is not in the office	THEN	You take a message
IF	The caller wants information on a product	THEN	You take their address and tell them the information will be sent to them
IF	The caller has a complaint	THEN	You take their name and telephone number and say that you will have someone get back to them within the hour
IF	The caller asks you a question and you do not know the answer or know how to deal with the problem	THEN	Ask for the caller's name and telephone number and tell them that you will have someone get back to them

Figure 8.1 Sample formula

Sample formula: If + Problem, Then = Solution

8.5.4 Experience tips

- Always include a formula that helps the candidate when something does not fall into a category or if something out of the ordinary occurs. For example, "*If* you are unable to help the caller, *then* take their name and number and have your supervisor return the call later."

8.6 Anchoring

8.6.1 Description

Anchoring is a method that uses the power of the unconscious to get a prede-termined response. Anchoring works by making an association between a behavior and a word, touch, or action. This tool derives from Neuro-Linguistic Programming or NLP. Pavlov used a similar technique to anchoring and called it "conditioning." He used conditioning to create a connection between the hearing of a bell ring and salivation in dogs. Every time the dogs were given food a bell would ring. As a result, when the dogs heard a bell ring they thought food was coming and would therefore salivate. Once the conditioning had been established, Pavlov found that all he had to do to make the dogs salivate was to ring the bell, even when no food was given.

In NLP this type of associative conditioning has been expanded to include links between other aspects of experience than purely environment cues and behavioral responses. For example, a song might become an anchor for a particular emotion or feeling. A touch on the arm might induce a feeling of warmth and comfort. A hand signal might trigger a memory or action.

When helping people with Asperger Syndrome learn, anchoring is a useful tool because it is respectful and promotes self-responsibility since ulti-mately it is up to the individual to apply the technique. The candidate can consciously choose to establish the anchor to trigger or re-trigger a response, action or behavior in order to handle or cope with a situation more appropriately.

There are three main types of anchoring: *Verbal*, *touch*, and *silent*. They all work equally well and provide you with alternatives depending upon the person, situation, circumstance, and the required prompt level.

8.6.1.1 VERBAL AND TOUCH ANCHORS

Some people respond better to verbal prompts while others respond better to touch. Verbal and touch anchoring are used when the candidate has a behavior that requires an obvious prompt to trigger her into appropriate action. Asperger Syndrome often blocks a person from seeing subtle cues. Touch or verbal anchors are more obvious than visual anchors and are often a good introduction to the tool.

There are a number of factors that may influence the choice between using a verbal and touch anchor. These include the noise level of the environment and the proximity between you and your candidate. If it is a noisy environment, a verbal anchor may not be appropriate. If you are not within reaching distance of your friend, a touch anchor will be hard to implement. Your choice will also depend upon the preference of the person with whom you are working. Some people with Asperger Syndrome do not like to be touched, while others might find a verbal anchor embarrassing. It is important to honor the preference of the candidate. I recommend that you explain the tool to your Asperger friend and have her choose the type of anchor she feels most comfortable with, taking into account external factors such as environment and proximity.

8.6.2 Instruction

8.6.2.1 VERBAL ANCHOR

In order to establish a verbal anchor, ask your friend to assist you in choosing a phrase or word that will remind her to alter the target behavior. You might choose the word *attention*, for example, if the issue is lack of focus. Try to choose words that are somewhat related to the subject. The word is not as important as its relationship to the behavior.

Verbal anchor example:

Issue: Allan daydreams, which interferes with his productivity at work.

First, Allan and his job coach discuss why the behavior is not appropriate or why it is an obstacle and what impact it might have on Allan's job if it does not change.

> Daydreaming during work hours interferes with you being productive and getting your assignments accomplished on time. Your employer can't afford to pay you if you are not productive. If you are not able to meet your employer's expectations, you will eventually lose your job.

Now, Allan and the job coach negotiate a word or phrase to say when the behavior is taking place. "Are you distracted?" In this situation, it is most effective if you try to come up with a word or phrase that a coworker or manager might typically say.

Finally, Allan and the job coach decide what action Allan should take when hearing the word or phrase.

> When you hear me say, "Are you distracted?" this is your signal to stop daydreaming and return to work.

8.6.2.2 TOUCH ANCHOR

The touch anchor associates a behavior with a touch instead of a word. This anchor is a little subtler than a verbal anchor and can be used effectively without drawing attention to anyone.

Always ask permission to touch the candidate before showing her the touch anchor. This is a courtesy, and shows that you respect the person's boundaries. Once you have established an agreement with regard to the type of touch that will be acceptable, you do not need to ask permission every time you use the anchor.

Touch anchor example

Issue: Jennifer regularly interrupts people when they are talking.

First, Jennifer and her support worker explore why the behavior is not appropriate or why it is a challenge.

> Interrupting people when they are speaking is considered rude and can annoy the person you are interrupting.

Next, they negotiate a touch anchor that will take place when the behavior occurs. In this case, it is a touch of the hand on the shoulder.

Finally, they decide what action Jennifer will take when she feels the touch anchor.

> When you feel my hand on your shoulder, this is your reminder to say, "I'm sorry, I'm interrupting you. I'll come back when you are finished with your conversation."

In this example, Jennifer is helped to correct the interrupting behavior as it happens. Eventually, this new behavior will become habit and she will no longer need the anchor.

8.6.2.3 SILENT ANCHOR

The silent anchor is the most subtle of the anchors. It relies on a visual cue to work. The candidate will need to be taught to see the anchor but, once she gets used to it, it is a wonderful tool. The beauty of the silent anchor is that it is practically invisible to outsiders. Therefore, it is not at all intrusive or embarrassing to the candidate.

Silent anchor example

Issue: When Graham is late for work, he does not acknowledge it or apologize to his supervisor.

First, Graham and his job coach discuss why the behavior is an issue.

> Your employer expects you to be on time for work every day. When you show up late and do not acknowledge it or apologize, it looks as if you don't care that you are wasting the employer's time.

Next, they negotiate the silent anchor.

> Every time you walk in late, I will look at my wristwatch. When you see me do this, it will remind you to say: "Sorry I'm late. I will leave earlier tomorrow so I'm on time."

Experience tips for the silent anchor

- Choose silent anchors that mimic typical responses people have to the problem. If you are not there to give the anchor, then a well-chosen silent anchor will likely happen naturally because someone else will unknowingly use it.

- Ask the candidate to help choose an appropriate anchor. Be aware of other meanings that might be associated with a gesture in the workplace, depending on coworkers' cultures, beliefs, etc. You do not want to establish a silent anchor that has an insulting double meaning to others.

8.6.3 Experience tips about anchoring in general

- It is a good idea to practice anchoring before you use it in public. You want the person you are working with to be very clear about what is expected of her and confident that he or she understands what to do.

- Have your Asperger friend participate in the solution as much as possible by including her in choosing the anchor.

- You may need to verbally remind the candidate about the touch anchoring agreement until she becomes used to it. This reminder should be done in private.

- The purpose of anchoring is to bring awareness to a behavior so the candidate can correct it independently. In this way you are helping your Asperger friend to create a new habit.

8.7 Scales

8.7.1 Description

The scale tool uses numbers to help your Asperger friend measure situations. Scales may be used on issues from productivity to emotions and from behavior to anxiety or volume. This scale tool is an expansion on the tool Tony Attwood recommends using in his book *Asperger's Syndrome, A Guide for Parents and Professionals*, for measuring and identifying emotions. The scale tool is very effective and works well for two main reasons:

1. People with Asperger Syndrome comprehend specifics more easily than generalizations.

2. A scale provides a system that clearly identifies middle ground, which is typically something difficult for a person with Asperger Syndrome to grasp.

People with Asperger Syndrome live in a world of extremes. They see things in terms of black-and-white and struggle with the shades of gray. A scale identifies the extremes and then fills in the middle areas with identifiable levels. The numbers of the scale allow the gray areas to be more concrete and therefore easier to identify.

8.7.2 Instruction

Develop a scale between one and five. At either end, name the extremes and then fill in three middle levels. Identify clearly what each level looks like either by describing it or by role playing it.

After you have created the scale, identify strategies that the candidate with Asperger Syndrome can implement. You want to make sure that she can not only recognize each level, but also know what to do at each level. For example, if you are creating an anxiety scale, you might want to include breathing and relaxation exercises at level three, have the candidate take time out at level four and make certain that she leaves the environment completely before reaching level five. There is an example of an anger scale in Chapter 10 (Figure 10.1), which demonstrates how a scale may be utilized to help address behavioral and emotional challenges in the workplace. Scales are also very useful when addressing non-behavioral challenges such as volume of voice.

8.7.3 Example

Issue: Rolph has a booming voice. Everything he says is amplified, which in an office setting is disruptive.

First, Rolph is introduced to the volume scale when his job coach explains that his voice is very loud and that it distracts his coworkers. Rolph needs to become aware of the volume of his voice before he can start adjusting it for different situations. It is helpful to Rolph to have the scale demonstrated to him through role play. During the role play, each volume level is demonstrated and an example is given to indicate where that volume would be appropriately used. For example, a volume one is a whisper and might be used in a library and a volume five is a yell, which would be appropriate in a stadium when cheering at a football game. Rolph is asked by the coach to role play each volume to get a feel for the scale. He identifies that he normally speaks at a volume four and that this is a bit too loud for an office environment. He agrees that a volume three would be more appropriate for the office. His assignment is to lower his volume one notch in the office and Rolph works out a strategy with his job coach to help accomplish this.

1	2	3	4	5
Whisper	Quiet voice	Regular voice	Loud voice	Yelling
Theater	*Elevator*	*Office*	*Cafeteria*	*Football game*

Figure 8.2 Volume scale

8.7.4 Experience tips

- Try to develop prompts that do not stand out or draw attention. You do not want to be misunderstood as being condescending or embarrass the candidate in any way.

- When using scales for identifying levels of emotion such as anger, excitement or anxiety, ensure that you also assign a strategy to the higher levels to help your friend cope with the emotion as she learns to identify it. For example, at anger level three, your friend could do some deep-breathing exercises to relax.

- When you are working with emotions, it is helpful when identifying the various levels to write down what the candidate physically experiences at each level. This helps her to recognize the signals her body provides. Often our body tells us what we are feeling before our brain does.

8.8 Third-party praise

8.8.1 Description

The positive reinforcement of behavior is not a new concept. Sometimes, however, direct feedback for a behavior, even when it is positive, can cause a backlash. Third-party praise is an indirect form of positive reinforcement. If you have ever had a compliment come through a third party, you can relate to how good it makes you feel. Third-party praise is a useful tool when complimenting a positive behavior because it reinforces the behavior without drawing a lot of attention to it.

Direct positive reinforcement often draws attention to a behavior. This attention can trigger some candidates with Asperger Syndrome – or anyone else, for that matter – into doing the exact opposite of what you are complimenting them for. There are a variety of reasons for why this happens.

- Drawing positive attention to a behavior might increase the candidate's anxiety because she perceives this will now be the expectation. That can be too much stress for some people and so they may react by doing the opposite behavior to avoid the expectation.

- Some people might get embarrassed by the attention and revert to an inappropriate behavior.

- Some people may enjoy the attention negative behavior draws over the fuss or possible non-response for an appropriate behavior.

8.8.2 Instruction

The most important element of this tool is to ignore any inappropriate behavior. This of course will involve your judgment because there are some behaviors that cannot be ignored, such as aggression or actions that jeopardize safety. However, if a behavior can be ignored, you should do so.

Teach the appropriate behavior using the Four Pillar Teaching Technique. Make a point of complimenting the new behavior within earshot of your Asperger friend, but do not express it directly. Say the compliment to a coworker or some other neutral party. The effectiveness of this tool relies on your friend *overhearing* the compliment.

8.8.3 Example

Issue: Maria has a tendency to act immaturely by making funny voices, asking inappropriate questions, and fidgeting. This challenge draws negative attention to her and makes her stand out, which is an obstacle to her getting and keeping a job. When Maria is complimented on good behavior, it seems to draw too much attention to her and she reacts by reverting to the negative behavior.

First, Maria's job coach completely ignores the behavior by focusing his attention on whatever else it is that he is doing, for example reading a book, working, washing the dishes. He makes no eye contact with Maria, nor does he give any attention to her while she is exhibiting the immature behavior. This includes getting annoyed or shooting glances at her. If Maria asks questions while she is being ignored or attempts to engage him, he does not respond. By not acknowledging the inappropriate behavior he is not reinforcing it.

To reinforce her appropriate behavior, he compliments Maria within her hearing distance, by telling someone else what she did well. "Maria sat in the same seat on the bus on the way here today. She was really mature."

Remember that receiving a compliment through a third party can be more flattering and does not draw direct attention. Be specific in the compliment. Say what the candidate did well and *why* it was good.

8.8.4 Experience tips

- Don't overdo the compliment. Make it natural and genuine.

- This strategy works particularly well with people who have attention-seeking behaviors.

- In general, this is a lovely way to compliment anyone.

8.9 Mirroring

8.9.1 Description

Mirroring is a tool that the candidate with Asperger Syndrome can use to help her create rapport and build relationships more effectively through non-verbal communication. It is a process of imitating the personality of the person to whom you are speaking.

Like the anchoring tool, mirroring is derived from NLP. It is human nature to like people who resemble ourselves. This may sound a bit egotistical but, nonetheless, it is human. In other words, *anyone who is like me must be a good person*. The beautiful thing about using the mirroring tool for a person with Asperger Syndrome is that it provides an easy means of projecting positive non-verbal cues. This takes a lot of the stress out of social interaction, something that, on its own, will help the candidate to communicate better.

8.9.2 Instruction

The trick to effective mirroring is not to mimic the other person exactly. That would be too obvious and would definitely backfire! You want the candidate to mirror the other person, but to do it within her own comfort level and personality range. If your Asperger friend were a very non-emotive person with a rather flat tone of voice, for example, it would be unnatural and therefore uncomfortable for her to act overtly enthusiastic. If a very dynamic and energetic person is interviewing your friend and this does not match your friend's own personality then, rather than act unnatural, she can still be affective by widening her eyes more, leaning forward and smiling to mirror the interviewer. The objective of mirroring is not to mock the other person but to help your Asperger friend use that person as a guide to acceptable non-verbal language.

There are three aspects to effective mirroring: Voice, body, and energy.

When mirroring the voice, you want to help your friend mirror the tone, volume, and pitch of the other person. Again, you do not want this done to an extreme, to the point that your Asperger friend seems to be mocking the other person. You want to help your friend adjust her own voice to match the other person's, within your friend's own natural range.

When mirroring the body, you want the candidate to mirror the physical body movements of the other person. In other words, if the person leans forward, then a second or two later, your friend can also lean forward a bit. If the person crosses his legs or clasps his hands together, then the candidate may do one or the other or both but, again, within the candidate's own natural comfort zone.

Finally, you want to help the candidate to mirror the energy of the other person. For example, in an interview the interviewee should always try to project a positive and upbeat energy. However, this should be kept in step with the energy of the interviewer. If someone who is very low-key is interviewing the candidate, it is best that the candidate tone down her own positive energy. If the interviewer is quite hyper, then the candidate should try to bring her energy level up and act a bit more exuberant. Once again, when helping your Asperger friend learn this tool, you want to honor her own personal comfort zone and help her to mirror within that range.

8.9.3 Example

Issue: Christopher was an older man with Asperger Syndrome who always had a frown on his face, even when he was happy. People did not want to approach him because they thought he was angry, upset, or miserable all the time. In an interview, this did not help him present well. He had to practice a lot of mirroring to help him project a more positive image. This took considerable effort on his part because it did not feel natural to him. Over time, it did improve however. Although Christopher still does not exactly look happy, he does not look quite as miserable either. During interviews, he has to pay close attention to his facial expressions and make a real effort to smile occasionally, particularly during the initial greeting. The mirroring tool helps Christopher immensely in interview situations because he has learned simply to mirror the non-verbal language of the interviewer. This takes a lot of the stress out of the interview for Christopher because he is no longer concentrating on his own body language. This allows him to concentrate more on the questions he is being asked.

Mirroring can be a very fun tool to use when helping your Asperger friend learn better communication skills. Using it in a role play format provides a terrific opportunity to practice while having fun. Mirroring also allows you the opportunity to see the natural personality range of the candidate so that you can provide guidance and feedback to her if the mirroring is too strong or not enough. You may find that your Asperger friend requires a lot of practice with this technique because it is not something that she is familiar with. It is however definitely worth the effort and will serve your friend well in many situations over her lifetime.

8.9.4 Experience tips

- Teach and practice the three aspects of mirroring separately.

- Only after your friend has mastered all three aspects should you attempt to put them together.

- Arrange to have your friend practice this tool with many people to get variety.

8.10 Verbal reflection

8.10.1 Description

Verbal reflection is an effective tool that provides clear insight into the way others perceive a person's body and language behavior. This tool will help your Asperger friend understand what non-verbal cues she is projecting and differs from mirroring, which helps your friend mimic non-verbal language and build rapport. These two tools will often compliment each other.

Having Asperger Syndrome impedes a person's ability to read non-verbal language easily and accurately, including her own. This makes it extremely challenging to know what her body language is saying to others and therefore difficult to read situations accurately. Verbally reflecting your own insights to your Asperger friend helps her to have a greater awareness of what other people see. In essence, it is like holding a talking mirror up to your friend to see himself through the eyes of others. In this manner, you are becoming the talking mirror, verbally reflecting information. With this information, your friend will gain greater self-awareness and be in a position to decide if she wishes to change what she is projecting to others.

8.10.2 Instruction

It is important to introduce the verbal reflection tool to the candidate at a time when you do not have a reflection to offer. This allows your friend to understand the tool and to decide if she would like to use it. It is important to get the candidate's permission to use the tool because if she is unwilling, it is unlikely that she will listen to your reflections. Those candidates who want to grow and learn will be open to hearing the reflections. People who are reluctant may still learn from the tool but may require more support in absorbing the information or taking ownership and self-responsibility.

Once permission to use the tool has been given, you may use the verbal reflection tool when you see a behavior, action, or body language that is likely to stand out or draw negative attention to the candidate. In your head, formulate what you are seeing so that you can describe it. You also want to be able to explain how the behavior, action, or body language makes you feel so that you can offer it as insight. It is very useful to use your own first impressions and reactions as a guide. Chances are that if you have an initial reaction to something the candidate does, others will also. This is an excellent guide and will help you choose the target behaviors.

Once you are clear about how to describe the situation and how you feel about it, you can introduce it to the candidate. Make your reflection unemotional and very clear while simultaneously being sensitive. You are simply providing insight and information. You do not want to sound critical. Once you have given the reflection, discuss in general terms how people might perceive the same behavior, action or body language in other situations. Encourage the candidate to come up with insights about the situation and ask her to explain how she might react if on the receiving end. This will promote self-responsibility and ownership.

8.10.3 Example

Issue: When people speak to Robin, he constantly says "Ah ha." This disrupts the speaker, leaving him feeling as if what they are saying is not important or that he is being rushed through the conversation.

During the behavior, the support worker interrupts Robin and offers his reflection.

> Robin, I'd like to use the verbal reflection tool and reflect my insight right now. When you say "ah ha" over what I am saying, I feel like you are rushing me and that what I am saying is not important. Is this what you are thinking?

It is important to get this feedback because you want to ensure that you are on track with the tool. It is always possible that what you perceive is exactly the intent. In many situations, however, it will not be.

The support worker discusses with Robin how others might react to his behavior in various situations and encourages Robin to participate in the discussion.

> If an interviewer was feeling rushed or interrupted by the candidate, do you think that this would help or hinder that candidate's chances of being offered the job?

> How do think that people would respond to you rushing them in this manner in a social situation? Do you think that this would encourage or discourage them from wanting to continue the conversation?

By posing these types of questions, the support worker is helping the candidate with Asperger Syndrome come up with her own insights. Notice that the questions are not open ended; that each offers choices. This often makes it easier for the candidate to participate in the discussion and see that her action or behavior will ultimately have a consequence. Empowered with this knowledge, the candidate is in a position to decide if she wishes to alter the behavior. When this occurs, a strategy can be developed to address the challenge.

8.10.4 Experience tips

- Use the verbal reflection tool in private. Bringing up your reflections in front of others could embarrass the candidate and therefore it is important to be sensitive to timing.

- Always get permission ahead of time to use this tool as not everyone wants to, or is ready to, hear the reflections.

- Be sensitive when offering the reflections. You do not want to be misunderstood as being critical.

Summary

Now you have a toolbox filled with the basic tools you need to help you develop effective strategies. It's very different than the one my dad gave me but the same advice applies.

- Use your imagination when building your strategies and lessons.

- Customize tools to match the personality, needs, and learning style of the candidate.

- Don't get discouraged if things don't go exactly as you imagined.

- Use your errors to create more lessons, if not for the person with whom you are working, then for yourself.

- Remember that you are human and showing your own mistakes to others can be a lesson for them in how to deal with disappointment and change.

You may discover more tools to add to your toolbox as you gain experience. Unlike the wooden toolbox my father gave me, your toolbox is always with you and you can use the tools at any time and in any way. When you combine these tools with the Four Pillar Teaching Technique and some experience, you can do a lot of good in the world.

9 The Big Picture
Assessing employment skills

Assessing someone with Asperger Syndrome is like putting together a jigsaw puzzle. When you start with the edges and work inward, you see the picture come together.

Your friend with Asperger Syndrome might be the next Albert Einstein or Glenn Gould but it is unlikely that he will reach full potential in today's world without a little help. Even geniuses need support at times. Employers want to hire people with excellent social and communication skills. In fact, these are among the top skills that employers look for in a candidate. It is extremely difficult for a person with a social/communication disorder like Asperger Syndrome to compete in today's job market without first clearly identifying his challenges and then putting strategies in place to address them. There is no cure for Asperger Syndrome but there are some very effective ways to help people with this disorder develop compensating skills to move forward.

Given the social demands of today's workplace, it is more important than ever for people with Asperger Syndrome to develop a foundation of skills that will enable them to succeed. This process begins with clearly defining the areas where they are lacking skill and helping them learn exactly what they need to improve. The Big Picture Assessment is a system I developed for assessing the work skills of people with Asperger Syndrome. It will allow you to define and prioritize the areas where they require the most support in a job. Chapter 10, The Strategy Guide, will help you learn how to develop strategies to address the challenges you identify in this chapter.

The best place in which to assess the work skills of a candidate with Asperger Syndrome is in a competitive work environment. Since people with Asperger Syndrome have difficulty expressing what they are feeling and thinking, this allows you to observe first-hand where exactly their challenges lie. Relying on second-hand information from family or other supports, although useful and insightful, does not offer the same perspective as seeing the challenges through your own eyes. By observing behavior and skills yourself, you are able to measure the candidate's skills from a dual perspective, that of an employer and that of a support worker. These two perspectives are critical to seeing the "Big Picture."

From the perspective of the employer, you will be able to determine what is acceptable and what needs to improve before an employer would consider hiring the candidate. From the eyes of the support worker, you are able to introduce strategies to address the issues and challenges that you observe. The two perspectives work beautifully together and, by using this dual perspective method to get the Big Picture, you will quickly and easily be able to define your strategy to build a skills foundation.

To demonstrate the value of getting the Big Picture before jumping into a job search, I'd like to tell you about my experience with Tory. At the time I met him, Tory was in his early forties. He was a tall, sinewy man who rode his bicycle everywhere he went. When you spoke to Tory, you would likely be struck by his advanced vocabulary and academic air, although he only had a grade eleven education. It was clear upon meeting Tory that he was a very bright man. He loved to analyze life and would often hang around the local university passing as an eccentric grad student. Although Tory had never actually attended university, I'm sure he could win a debate with anyone on campus.

When I first met Tory, like most others who knew him I believed that he was capable of far greater feats than loitering around a university campus. At his request, I took him on as a client and we began the process of assessing skills to get the Big Picture of Tory.

Despite his intelligence, Tory had difficulty with basic tasks such as folding letters, operating office machines, and sweeping. He had very limited skills: His computer skills were practically non-existent and, because of poor hand–eye coordination, he had difficulty learning and operating the computer keyboard. Tory had very poor time management skills and often struggled to get to appointments on time and finish assignments. Through a family connection Tory had managed to get a job at a small shop doing yard maintenance, shoveling snow, sweeping, and raking leaves. The shopkeeper would give him work, but Tory really had no work ethic and it was frustrating for the employer. There were times when the shopkeeper would tell him to come in on Tuesday to help unload a delivery truck and Tory would show up late, sometimes even a week late, and would be dressed looking as if he had spent the night on the street.

Tory was very set in his ways, which is a common characteristic of Asperger Syndrome, and had become more so as he got older. He had firm beliefs that would not be shaken regardless of the logic presented. Tory was also very good at debating and shifting responsibility. When I began assessing him, I was amazed at the dichotomy between his intellectual ability and his ability to perform basic tasks. Here was a very bright man who could converse with scholars, but would not be able to keep a job clearing tables at McDonald's.

It was not until I began the Big Picture process with Tory that I discovered this extreme gap between his intelligence and his functioning level. Tory was amazing to debate with but it was unlikely that an employer would hire him for that skill. In fact, he could be quite disagreeable at times, which made matters even more challenging.

Before I did the Big Picture Assessment on Tory, I would have been fooled into believing that he could do things with which, in fact, he ended up struggling. Once I got the Big Picture and had a clear idea of who Tory was, I was in a position to introduce strategies to address some of his challenges. I was able to develop realistic employment goals with him and outline the necessary steps to reach those goals. To Tory's credit, he worked very hard on himself and, although he had many setbacks, he kept at it. It took Tory four years, but today he is a tour guide at a museum and is a sharp dresser as well!

9.1 The Big Picture Assessment

The Big Picture Assessment examines the most important elements that employers want to see in an employee but which are typically challenging for people with Asperger Syndrome. It is divided into seven categories, each sub-divided into skills that are important to building a foundation for successful employment. In each sub-category, you will rate the Asperger candidate on a competitive employment scale between 1 and 4, as in Figure 9.1.

1 Unsatisfactory	Requires considerable attention. Must be addressed in order to move forward
2 Requires attention	Needs to be addressed to be at a competitive level
3 Adequate	Borderline – needs improvement but will not prevent employment
4 Competitive	Employer would consider the skill comparable or superior to general population

Figure 9.1 Competitive employment scale

Remember that you are rating the candidate's skills using the dual perspective method. In other words, you must look at him through the eyes of the employer and the support worker.

9.1.1 Setting up the assessment venue

The most effective way to assess people with Asperger Syndrome is to observe them in a competitive work environment. In most cases, you will need to create that environment. There are various ways you can go about this. If the Asperger candidate is in school and has a cooperative education placement, you can discuss the possibility of your conducting the Big Picture Assessment during the coop. It may also be done at a summer job if the employer agrees. If there are no employment experiences currently set up for the candidate then you can set one up through a volunteer organization. Many cities have volunteer agencies listed in the local telephone directory or community center. A volunteer agency will help place the Asperger candidate in an unpaid job. You will want to be upfront about your role during the job and make sure that the employer is in agreement. Alternatively, you may choose to approach employers on your own whom you think will be sympathetic. The benefit for the employer is that he will have a supervised volunteer for a few weeks.

I recommend that the Big Picture Assessment take place over a minimum of two weeks. The hours should ideally be part-time; either half-days or three days per week depending upon the schedules of the employer, you, and the candidate with Asperger Syndrome. Set up the schedule and write it down. Make sure that the candidate is clear about what he should wear to the assessment and what jobs he can expect to be doing. You also want to ensure that the candidate understands that this is not a paid placement, nor is there an expectation of paid employment from the employer at the end of the assessment, (unless, of course, there is!).

9.1.2 Insurance and liability

The employer may ask you about liability or insurance coverage. Here you are on your own. My agency has by law to carry liability insurance and any of our programs that are paid for by the government are covered under government insurance. As an individual, you may need to do some research. In most cases, when you are using an employer who might otherwise have volunteers, he will likely have his own insurance. If not, you may have to consider a liability waiver to appease the employer.

The assessment

The Big Picture Assessment has seven categories, each sub-divided into specific skills that are important to building a foundation for successful employment. Read through the description of each category and then each specific skill within the category, before using the rating system provided. When you have completed making ratings in each category, calculate the average rating by adding together all the ratings and dividing the total of the ratings by the number of sub-categories. There is space for you to make comments to help you remember any relevant details that you might need later when developing strategies.

9.2 Personal presentation

People make judgments and form opinions within the first few seconds of meeting others. The attitude formed in these few minutes often affects the way in which an individual is accepted. In today's society, where image is of utmost importance, it is important that all employees portray an appropriately professional and friendly manner.

Employers are often willing to make accommodations for people with disabilities but they are rarely willing to make accommodations in the area of personal presentation. Employees represent the company image. There are no exceptions for individuals with Asperger Syndrome.

Take a close look at the candidate when he shows up for the assessment. Remember that you will have informed him beforehand exactly how he should present himself in the work setting. Make note of anything that makes him stand out, both good and bad. If he looks exceptionally well groomed, then make note of this. If he wears running shoes when you specified dress shoes, make note of that. Look for details such as dirt under the fingernails and clean, brushed teeth. This may seem very picky but I can tell you from experience that, while people may not notice good grooming, they are sure to notice if it's bad!

There are eight sub-categories of personal presentation (see Figure 9.2). Read the description of each carefully to know exactly what you are looking for before rating them.

Ratings:

1 – Unsatisfactory 2 – Requires attention 3 – Adequate 4 – Competitive

	Personal presentation	Rating	Comments
1	Appropriate clothing		
2	Footwear		
3	General cleanliness/hygiene		
4	Hair		
5	Teeth		
6	Fingernails		
7	Greetings		
8	Handshake		
	Average rating		

Figure 9.2 Personal presentation assessment

9.2.1 Appropriate clothing

The candidate is expected to wear clean clothes that are appropriate for the work setting in which you are doing the assessment. If it is an office environment, then the clothes should be pressed and tucked in. Pants should be held up with a belt and clothes should not have stains or odors. If the work environment is other than professional, rate the clothing on suitability for that environment.

9.2.2 Footwear

Footwear should be in good condition and suitable for the work environment; for example, dress shoes for a professional environment and work boots for a warehouse.

9.2.3 General cleanliness/hygiene

There should be no discernable body odor and it should be apparent that grooming has taken place. Men should arrive at the assessment clean-shaven or with beard trimmed. This can be a challenge for many young men. I suggest they make it a rule to either shave daily or come to the assessment with a full beard grown in. "In-between" facial hair looks messy and unkempt.

9.2.4 Hair

Hair needs to be clean, combed, and reasonably styled.

9.2.5 Teeth

Teeth need to be reasonably clean and breath should be fresh.

9.2.6 Fingernails

Fingernails should be clipped and clean.

9.2.7 Greetings

Look for basic greetings such as "good morning," "hello," or "how are you?" Note whether the candidate initiates a greeting, just responds to the greetings of others, or does nothing at all.

9.2.8 Handshake

The handshake is important in business so you want to greet the candidate with a handshake on the first day. You are looking to receive a firm and confident handshake.

9.3 Social skills and behavior

Social skills and behavior issues are primary challenges for people with Asperger Syndrome in the workplace. Since the challenges of people with Asperger Syndrome are so individual, it is impossible to encompass here all the challenges different people with Asperger Syndrome might experience in a job. Therefore, this category identifies some of the key areas that prove problematic for employers with Asperger Syndrome employees.

People with Asperger Syndrome find learning social skills and appropriate behavior by observing others challenging. They have to make a very conscious effort to pick these up. This category rates the candidate's skills so that you can clearly identify what areas you and the candidate will need to focus on to help him be competitively employable.

You will need to pay close attention to how the candidate interacts with coworkers and supervisors. You view yourself as the equivalent of a supervisor or manager because how candidate relates to you will be similar to how he will relate to a boss in the future. Make full use of the dual perspective method in this category.

There are ten sub-categories in the social skills and behavior section (Figure 9.3). Read the description of each sub-category so that you know exactly what you are looking for before rating them.

Ratings:
1 – Unsatisfactory 2 – Requires attention 3 – Adequate 4 – Competitive

	Social Skills/Behavior	Rating	Comments
1	General manners		
2	Table manners		
3	Awareness of personal space		
4	Obsessive-compulsive/ perfectionism		
5	General comfort level with others		
6	Unusual sounds		
7	Unusual behaviors		
8	Appropriate touching of others		
9	Aggressive behavior		
10	Racial/sexual prejudice		
	Average rating		

Figure 9.3 Social skills/behavior assessment

9.3.1 General manners

People can be embarrassed, even appalled by poor manners. Having good manners is an important element of being successful both personally and professionally. Without good manners, the Asperger candidate will stand out and risk alienation.

I have seen clients bulldoze their way through a room practically knocking everyone in their path onto the ground. Some might sit in a chair with their legs stretched halfway across the room and do not think of moving or excusing themselves when someone practically trips over them. Because having Asperger Syndrome can make people awkward and unaware of how they should be conducting themselves in public, they may need to look at some of the basics, such as how to walk and sit appropriately in a work setting.

The influence that manners have cannot be stressed enough. People have been refused work because of poor manners. Poor manners may not be typical grounds for dismissal but it can motivate people to look for other reasons. You do not want the candidate to draw this type of negative attention to himself.

Having appropriate manners makes life a little easier in the workplace for someone with Asperger Syndrome. You will find that people will be more willing to assist and accept someone who is polite and pleasant than someone who is not.

9.3.2 Table manners

Table manners are an important part of social etiquette at work. It is common for people in the workplace to take breaks together and to go out for a social lunch or dinner upon occasion. If someone eats with food all over his face or talks with his mouth full, this can be quite off-putting for the people around them. Table manners may not directly impact employment, but they may turn off coworkers and employers and add to isolation or alienation.

9.3.3 Awareness of others' personal space

Personal space is the comfort level people have around their body. It is uncomfortable for most people to have someone stand in their personal space; in other words, to stand too close for their comfort. An invasion of this sort can have a number of negative effects on the person whose space is being invaded and subsequently on the Asperger employee who is unaware he is doing this. Invading personal space can be interpreted as intimidation, bullying, or as a sexual advance; or it may be just plain annoying to the other person. People tend to avoid people who make them feel uncomfortable. Although poor awareness of personal space may not lead to dismissal often, it can make coworkers uncomfortable, which may lead to other problems.

9.3.4 Obsessive-compulsive behavior/perfectionism

Obsessive-compulsive disorder (OCD) usually involves having both obsessions and compulsions, though a person with OCD may sometimes have only one or the other. Obsessions are thoughts, images, or impulses that occur over and over again and feel out of one's control. Compulsions are the actions that one takes to fix the obsessions. For example, a person with an obsession about contamination may wash constantly to the point that his hands become raw and inflamed. Perfectionism is part of OCD. A diagnosis of OCD or traits of OCD is common amongst people who have Asperger Syndrome. This often manifests in behavior such as habitually checking work assignments to make sure there are no errors, keeping things in a specific order or place, and doing something repeatedly until it is perfect.

People with Asperger Syndrome who have a tendency to be obsessive and compulsive find that it interferes with their work performance and level of acceptance on the job. If the behavior is odd, it can draw negative attention to them in the workplace. If an employee is obsessed with getting something perfect, it will slow his productivity.

While employers require that a job be done well, they also need employees to meet deadlines. If the employee is a perfectionist or has other challenges related to OCD, this may have a significant impact on his ability to be competitive in the workplace.

9.3.5 General comfort level with others

Since individuals with Asperger Syndrome don't understand many of the rules around socializing, they may develop high levels of anxiety in social situations. This can cause them to act oddly or say unusual things. How this manifests may make them stand out or look peculiar to others.

When anxiety levels increase, they may:

- become more rigid, more insistent on routine, or defensive

- retreat to talking about a special interest

- become more argumentative

- begin to show physical signs of discomfort such as scratching or picking.

9.3.6 Unusual sounds

People with Asperger Syndrome can utter uncontrollable or unpredictable sounds. These may include repeated throat-clearing, grunting, snorting, giggling, animal noises such as barking, and other unusual sounds, including repeating their own or someone else's words under their breath.

Although unusual sounds may not impede employment, they can draw negative attention to the person, which may contribute to him being alienated in his work environment. Because people with Asperger Syndrome often tend to isolate themselves, you want to help them avoid any behaviors that contribute to that isolation or alienation whenever possible.

9.3.7 Unusual behaviors

As with unusual sounds, any behavior that draws negative attention to a client is something that you should note. A candidate with Asperger Syndrome may display unusual behavior; for example, staring, walking into people, rocking or swaying, talking to himself, or making odd gestures. Some of these behaviors might be related to an obsessive-compulsive disorder, while others might simply be due to a lack of social awareness.

Once again, it will be part of the assessment for the job coach to identify any unusual behaviors that might attract negative attention to the candidate. If the behaviors are obvious or might impede getting or keeping a job, then it is the role of the coach to develop a strategy to address them.

9.3.8 Appropriate touching of others

In a work environment, there are strict rules around touching others. Generally, it is acceptable to touch another person on the shoulder or shake his hand. Any contact beyond that type of touching is risky in terms of how others might interpret it. Having Asperger Syndrome makes it difficult to judge what is and is not appropriate. In a world that is sensitive to sexual harassment, teaching what touching is appropriate and not appropriate in a work setting is crucial for both the comfort of coworkers and, in some unfortunate cases, the safety of the candidate himself.

Upon occasion, you may have to deal with the candidate's sexuality. This can be difficult as it presents a number of issues. Depending upon the situation, you will have to make a judgment call as to whether or not you are the appropriate person to be dealing with the subject. During the Big Picture Assessment, it is not considered your place to teach the facts of life, only the rules. The facts regarding sexuality or sex should be left for the family or a chosen professional to discuss. The candidate can also take a sexuality workshop if he requires more information. If the challenge is around the rules of touching, then you should proceed to deal with the issue.

9.3.9 Aggressive behavior

People with Asperger Syndrome can get deeply frustrated and disappointed with themselves and their situations. It can be difficult for many who lack the ability to identify and talk about their feelings to find emotional outlets. Anger is common amongst people with Asperger Syndrome because they often do not know how to express it appropriately, and may explode. Those explosions usually draw a negative response from the people witnessing the behavior, so many people with Asperger Syndrome learn to suppress their angry feelings. I have had clients who look as if they are always on the edge of blowing up. They appear to carry anger in every inch of their bodies. It is very difficult to work around a person who is on the edge, angry or bitter, or worse, if the anger seeps out in destructive behavior. Employers do not have time to deal with, nor should they have to deal with, aggressive behavior. They are usually understanding of the occasional upset. Yet, when the anger turns into a behavior and is seen as aggression or violence, it is considered unacceptable in the workplace. The repercussions of aggression or violence in a job setting are usually very serious and the consequences are often severe. They can range from a warning to dismissal or even criminal charges. All of these consequences are serious and are documented in the employee's file.

If the candidate has challenges with anger or aggression, then the job coach needs to deal with this as a priority. He should think very carefully about working with a candidate who has displayed aggressive behavior recently. Not only may it present liability issues for him, but someone may get hurt. It is important to investigate details and extenuating circumstances before making a decision to assess anyone who has a history of aggression. This helps protect the safety of staff, the candidate, the job coach, and the employer.

9.3.10 Racial or sexual prejudice

In the workplace, there is zero tolerance for any form of discrimination. I have heard candidates with Asperger Syndrome make what might be interpreted as derogatory or discriminatory comments out of innocent curiosity. Couple this with a loud voice and you could have a difficult situation on your hands in some environments. It is important to help the candidate understand what comments are inappropriate.

Upon occasion you might experience genuine prejudice or sexism. This, too, must be documented and addressed as it could lead to serious consequences including dismissal from a job.

To rate candidates on their social skills and behavior, observe them over a two- to four-week period on the job, making notes in each category as you go along. You should minimize any interventions to change the behavior during this period. At the end, rate the candidate on his overall behavior. As you become more skilled at assessing skills and behavior, you will begin to overlap the assessment and teaching stages so that you can address issues as they arise.

9.4 Communication skills

People with Asperger Syndrome understand things in terms of black or white. They tend to like things to be concrete and predicable and they have great difficulty understanding gray areas. Their often extensive vocabulary can hide poor comprehension skills, particularly of more abstract language. Language is often stiff and pedantic and quite logical. When people with Asperger Syndrome are conversing with others it is often more in terms of talking *at* the person rather than *with* them. They will frequently focus on a topic of their own interest or fascination without considering the interest level of the other person and then miss cues that the person is bored or not interested. This is exacerbated by their difficulty in reading non-verbal cues, such as facial expression and tone of voice. It is this lack of reciprocity and understanding in conversation that may make it hard for a person with Asperger Syndrome to initiate and/or maintain a conversation.

People with Asperger Syndrome tend to either show little facial expression or inaccurate facial expression. This makes it difficult for others to read what they are feeling or thinking. Their expressions may be inconsistent with their words or feelings. For example, a candidate who appears to be angry all the time because of his body language, when asked if he is feeling angry, might respond that he is actually feeling fine and not at all angry or upset. This lack of continuity between what the candidate is feeling and what he is projecting makes reciprocal communication even more challenging.

Many people with Asperger Syndrome also tend to speak in a monotone voice. Their restricted range of intonation may result in a flat tone of voice that seems inconsistent or unrelated to the content and discussion. They may speak in an unusually loud or quiet voice, frequently with precise diction. They do not always realize that the tone and emphasis of a sentence can change its meaning.

People with Asperger Syndrome generally do not go through the process of censoring their thoughts. They will often say whatever comes into their minds without considering first whether it is appropriate to the situation. They may need support around determining what topics and language are appropriate for various situations and environments.

There are ten sub-categories of communication skills (see Figure 9.4). Read the description of each sub-category to know exactly what you are looking for before rating them.

Ratings:
1 – Unsatisfactory 2 – Requires attention 3 – Adequate 4 – Competitive

	Communication skills	Rating	Comments
1	Ease of conversation skills		
2	Appropriate choice of conversation topics		
3	Interrupting		
4	Ability to read non-verbal cues		
5	Level of unprompted interaction with others		
6	Listening skills		
7	Ability to understand humor		
8	Level of response to others		
9	Eye contact during regular interaction		
10	Volume of voice		
	Average rating		

Figure 9.4 Communication assessment

9.4.1 Ease of conversation

Each person with Asperger Syndrome is unique and his or her comfort level when conversing with others will vary. There are some people with Asperger Syndrome who are quite comfortable making conversation with people, and many more who struggle to engage. In the Big Picture Assessment, you need to evaluate how easily the candidate engages in conversation and whether he or she needs to improve in this area. Although this skill is something that an employer will likely be understanding about and make some accommodation around, it still plays an important role in how someone fits into the environment and builds a social network.

9.4.2 Appropriate choice of conversation topics

One of the most characteristic traits of Asperger Syndrome, and perhaps one of the most compelling and interesting to those who do not have this syndrome, is the special interests. People with Asperger Syndrome can get engrossed in a specific topic easily if it is within their area of interest. This does not mean that they are not capable of discussing other topics, just that they are drawn to the topics of their interest. They will often manipulate a conversation to bring it into or back to, the area of their interest and, once on the topic, will dominate the conversation. These topics can range from common interests such as sports, politics, or cars, to obscure or bizarre interests such as mosquitoes, hearses, or washing machines. Whatever the interest, you can be sure that they know a great deal about it. The special interest may be something that lasts for years or for weeks and then changes. Regardless, if the topic is inappropriate for the workplace or even if it is appropriate but dominates conversations regularly, it is likely to interfere with employment.

Aside from special interests, the candidate may make irrelevant or inappropriate comments or statements or ask questions that are not linked to the conversation. Because he or she may not grasp many of the rules around appropriate conversations, topic choices or comments can be misinterpreted or considered rude. For example, some of my clients have made comments about the way someone dresses or the weight or age of a coworker, or have been very opinionated about religion or politics. In a social setting, such comments or opinions might be acceptable or at least open for debate. But in the workplace, judgment is required to determine what is and is not appropriate. Such judgments can be very challenging for a person with Asperger Syndrome to make.

9.4.3 Interrupting

People with Asperger Syndrome generally lack awareness of their environments, which can contribute to a problem of interrupting others. Being rather self-focused, when an employee with Asperger Syndrome approaches another person to discuss something or to ask a question, he or she can be oblivious to the fact that the person is occupied or speaking with someone else. The employee can blurt something out regardless of whether the person is ready to hear it.

This is problematic in a work environment because it is considered rude and disruptive. Everyone must learn to wait his or her turn. Interrupting or talking over someone is quite a common challenge for many Asperger employees.

9.4.4 Ability to read non-verbal cues

Communications theorists estimate that 55 per cent of communication is non-verbal, for example, body language, gestures, and facial expression; 38 per cent is tone of voice; and 7 per cent is words alone. This places candidates with Asperger Syndrome at a serious disadvantage since so many are unable to read non-verbal cues. They don't realize that people's expressions can be a source of information about how someone is feeling. In fact, for some people with Asperger Syndrome, looking at a person's face may be distracting or cause confusion.

In a work environment, a great deal of communication is conveyed non-verbally. When assessing the candidate, you must determine how much information he or she is actually receiving, including that conveyed non-verbally, to know how competitive the candidate will be and what support he or she will need to be independent in the workplace.

9.4.5 Level of unprompted interaction with others

Initiating and participating in conversation is also difficult for many people with Asperger Syndrome. You need to determine how much of a challenge this is for the candidate. Some candidates need prompting to answer a direct question, either because they don't know what to say or because they are unaware that a person is speaking to them. Unprompted interaction includes asking and answering questions and independently starting and participating in conversations or discussions.

Even patient, understanding employers cannot wait very long for an answer to a question. It is not up to the employer to draw information out of staff. The employer needs employees to respond one way or another within a reasonable amount of time. If the candidate has difficulty interacting with coworkers or supervisors without a lot of prompting, you need to note this and develop a strategy to address it.

9.4.6 Listening skills

It is common for people with Asperger Syndrome to take longer to process information and to respond. This is different than the person not listening. Employers need to feel confident that their employees are listening and absorbing what they are being told.

If your candidate appears not to be listening, you may want to look deeper into why. Poor listening skills may be a result of poor hearing, poor attention or focus, distraction or even disinterest. In the employee with Asperger Syndrome, it may also be due to too much information being provided, anxiety, confusion, or high expectations, which may cause the employee to "shut down."

Regardless, you need to make note of the candidate's listening skills and, if they are poor, you should investigate why.

9.4.7 Ability to understand humor

It is a misconception that people with Asperger Syndrome are humorless. It may just take some time to determine exactly what it is that each candidate finds funny. Some candidates will possess a strong wit, while many are drawn to slapstick or physical humor, which can prove awkward at times. I recall a client who rarely laughed at anything. One day his employer slipped on a wet floor and my client doubled over in laughter. Perhaps because the employer was so shocked to hear him laugh, he didn't get perturbed by this reaction or that the client showed little concern for the employer's well-being.

People with Asperger Syndrome will generally find double meanings challenging or will take idioms or metaphors very literally. This makes it difficult for them to relate to types of humor such as sarcasm, joking or teasing. Since in most work environments, joking and teasing are a common way of connecting with people and making them feel comfortable, this often hampers the employee with Asperger Syndrome's ability to fit into a work team.

It is quite possible that the Asperger employee will simply not find many forms of humor funny. This is fine. However it is helpful if you can convey this to an employer in the future so that the employer and staff understand that this may be part of that employee's personality and are not insulted by a lack of reaction.

9.4.8 Level of response to others

Since most individuals with Asperger Syndrome have difficulty reading others' emotions and expressions, they may respond inappropriately during interactions or not at all. You may have to coach a candidate to respond to a greeting or a question, as he or she may be unaware that a person has spoken to them.

In a work environment, it is reasonable for an employer to expect a response to a question or greeting. You want to assess the level of response the candidate exhibits to determine his or her level of awareness and how much support you need to offer to help the candidate become competitive in this area.

9.4.9 Eye contact during regular interaction

Eye contact can be a challenge for people with Asperger Syndrome. They may find it difficult to maintain eye contact or they may find it interferes with their ability to absorb information. At the other extreme, others with Asperger Syndrome will stare; which can make the people around them uncomfortable.

9.4.10 Volume of voice

The volume level of speech is important. If people speak too quietly, it is difficult to hear them. This can impede their employment because the employer is always straining to hear them or may not hear something correctly. Many people with Asperger Syndrome speak too loudly, which can be distracting to others in the work environment. If the candidate is also prone to making inappropriate comments, then making them in a loud voice increases the challenge.

9.5 Mindful skills

Mindful skills refer to one's ability to be aware in and of the situation at hand. This category will help determine the candidate's ability to process information as it relates to the workplace. The sub-categories represent areas that are generally challenging for people with Asperger Syndrome. Depending upon the job you are targeting for the candidate, he or she needs to have a basic level of competency in most, if not all, of these sub-categories for an employer to consider hiring him or her.

In this section in particular, it will be helpful if you look at your Asperger friend through the eyes of the employer. Keeping in mind that there will be some amount of accommodation, ask yourself the question, "Would my investment of time and money result in a profit if I were to hire this candidate?" The answer to that question will help you rate the candidate realistically for the competitive job market.

There are thirteen sub-categories of mindful skills (see Figure 9.5). Read the description of each sub-category to know exactly what you are looking for before rating your candidate.

9.5.1 Problem-solving

People with Asperger Syndrome have difficulty problem-solving since they have a challenge applying common sense. They often don't know what to do when a problem arises or how to go about solving it. Something that might appear simple to address may cause the candidate with Asperger Syndrome a great deal of frustration. They often don't realize that some solutions or strategies can be applied to more than one scenario or situation. Therefore, every situation is new and just as difficult to solve.

People with Asperger Syndrome require support to absorb and apply lessons and strategies to different situations. They might believe that a solution can be applied only to a specific situation and do not realize that a problem may have more than one solution or that one solution may solve many problems. This incapacity to generalize makes it really hard for the candidate to compete in this area.

Problem-solving skills are highly rated by employers. They want employees who can think independently and handle problems as they arise. When assessing a candidate's problem-solving ability, look closely at his or her limitations and how well the candidate can apply one solution or lesson to other situations.

Ratings:

1 – Unsatisfactory 2 – Requires attention 3 – Adequate 4 – Competitive

	Mindful skills	Rating	Comments
1	Problem-solving skills		
2	Comprehension of verbal instruction		
3	Comprehension of written instruction		
4	Comprehension of hands-on instruction		
5	Judgment skills		
6	Flexibility		
7	Focus		
8	Memory retention		
9	Ability to follow steps		
10	Ability to take initiative		
11	Ability to multi-task		
12	Overall speed/productivity		
13	Ability to organize work		
14	Fine motor skills		
15	Gross motor skills		
	Average rating		

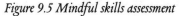

Figure 9.5 Mindful skills assessment

It is possible to put strategies in place to improve the candidate's problem-solving skills but you need to know up front how much support he or she will require, particularly later when you will be helping the candidate choose an appropriate career path. If the candidate has great difficulty with problem-solving, you will need to ensure that the jobs you target in the job search do not rely heavily on this skill.

9.5.2 Comprehension of verbal, written, and hands-on instructions

There are three styles of learning: Auditory, visual, and kinesthetic.

- *Auditory – learning through listening (verbal instruction).* Auditory learners learn best by listening. They like verbal instruction, discussions, talking things through and listening to what others have to say and often benefit from reading text aloud and using a tape recorder.

- *Visual – learning through seeing (written instruction).* Visual learners tend to think in pictures and learn best from visual displays including diagrams, illustrated books, videos, and checklists.

- *Kinesthetic – learning through touching, moving, and doing (hands-on instruction).* These people learn best through a hands-on approach, actively exploring things around them. They may find it hard to sit still for long periods and may become distracted by their need for activity and exploration.

How a person learns impacts how they comprehend instruction. The way the candidate processes information will help you determine how best to explain a job or task. With many people with Asperger Syndrome, the way they are taught something the first time is how they will continue to do it. In a job, an employer will expect employees to follow instruction. Knowing how the candidate learns not only helps you to teach effectively but also helps you to choose effective strategies that job coaches and employers can continue to use to support the candidate in being productive in his or her job.

9.5.3 Judgment

People with Asperger Syndrome typically lack the intuitive "common sense" that is learned by observing others and watching how they respond in different situations. They tend not to apply information and lessons they have learned to different scenarios or situations. This drastically restricts their ability to make sound judgments. Although there are some things that you can do to help the candidate diminish this challenge, it will not be totally eliminated. However, lack of judgment and common sense need not be a barrier to employment. With effective strategies in place to address challenges with judgment and a well-chosen career path, the candidate will be successful.

9.5.4 Flexibility

People with Asperger Syndrome will frequently depend on structure and routine to make their lives more predictable, provide order and consistency, and reduce the level of anxiety they feel. Consequently, they tend to be very rigid when asked to make changes. Any change in routine can cause some candidates to experience anxiety.

Employees need to be flexible. They need to be able to switch tasks depending upon priority and change with the demands of the job. Employers value this skill and look for it when they are hiring.

You want to determine how flexible or rigid the candidate is in the workplace in order to identify what jobs the candidate should target or avoid.

9.5.5 Focus

Busy environments can easily distract some people with Asperger Syndrome. They may not be able to focus on one task for too long. It is important to determine how long the candidate can focus since this may affect the type of employment pursued.

9.5.6 Memory retention

Long-term memory is a truly impressive attribute shared by many people with Asperger Syndrome. Some have the capacity to memorize large amounts of data, such as telephone numbers, addresses, dates, license plates, directions, and any other number of facts that fascinate them. Even those who appear not to have some of these more exceptional memories will often remember intricate details of the past quite vividly.

The amazing capacity of people with Asperger Syndrome to store detailed information is a godsend for helping them learn. Their rote memory may be incredible, but they don't necessarily understand the meaning of what they memorize. It is the job coach's job to use the candidate's ability to memorize as a tool to help him or her remember how to perform certain tasks and social skills at work.

9.5.7 Following steps

For the most part, once tasks or instructions are broken down into distinct steps, candidates with Asperger Syndrome can follow them quite well. If they have difficulty, it may indicate that there are other issues involved, such as Attention Deficit Disorder (ADD) or an intellectual disability. If this is the case, this will make your job more challenging because it takes longer for people with ADD and intellectual disabilities to learn steps and to retain information.

9.5.8 Initiative

People with Asperger Syndrome frequently get "stuck" when they are left without direction. They perform best when there is some amount of routine and structure. If they do not know what to do, they may sit around waiting for someone to notice that they have nothing to do or they might guess and, because of their impaired judgment skills, do something the employer would not want done. You will find that many people with Asperger Syndrome do not take a lot of initiative without having strategies in place to support this.

9.5.9 Multi-tasking

Asperger Syndrome frequently impedes one's ability to do more than one job at a time or "multi-task." The candidate with Asperger Syndrome may get confused and anxious when multi-tasking is required. As a general rule, it is advisable not to place clients in jobs that require them to multi-task. The job coach should assess how many tasks the candidate can handle simultaneously and make note. Begin by having him or her perform one job and add a second and third. This gives you a clear indication as to the level of multi-tasking the candidate can handle and gives an indication as to how to structure job responsibilities in the future.

9.5.10 Overall speed and productivity

Many people with Asperger Syndrome are detail-oriented, which is an attribute to an employer. However, if speed and productivity are not at a competitive level, then it is difficult for an employer to justify keeping an employee, regardless of how well he or she may perform the job. The challenge for many people with Asperger Syndrome is to maintain their level of detail and quality while sustaining a competitive level of speed and productivity.

9.5.11 Organizing work

Some people with Asperger Syndrome are excellent at organizing them-selves and their work assignments. Others do not have good organizational skills and require support. If the candidate has difficulty in this area, it is likely to affect his or her performance on the job and he or she will need to learn how to improve in this area.

9.5.12 Fine and gross motor skills

Research suggests that between 50 and 90 per cent of people with Asperger Syndrome have poor motor coordination. This can make some candidates slow and laborious workers. The simple task of bending down to file can be extremely demanding. Some candidates may appear clumsy and walk with an unusual or odd gait. Some have very lax joints, which causes them to hold objects such as utensils or pens awkwardly. Difficulty with eye–hand coordi-nation makes some tasks such as throwing, catching, kicking, and moving objects more challenging. Balance may be affected as well as manual dexter-ity, which makes handwriting more difficult. You may find that the candidate has difficulty using scissors or putting labels on folders, folding letters or putting them into envelopes. All of these factors can influence his or her per-formance on the job.

The lack of motor development and coordination is a conspicuous feature that affects many people with Asperger Syndrome in the workplace. The severity of poor motor coordination can affect the type of employment the candidate can pursue. If a candidate has severe motor difficulties, he or she should be referred to an occupational therapist or physiotherapist for professional support.

9.6 Personal characteristics

It would be difficult for anyone to succeed in a job without a good score in the personal characteristics category. Employers value employees with a good work ethic, yet today this is increasingly difficult to find. It is good news that many candidates with Asperger Syndrome do well in this area. Their honest, straightforward personalities combined with their innate sense of honesty and integrity are wonderful selling points to employers.

If the candidate rates poorly in this area, it may be an overwhelming impediment to employment unless you can establish what the problem is and change it. If the candidate does not want to change or does not really care if he or she moves forward, it is likely that the candidate will always have trouble in a job. With support and encouragement, the employee can turn this around, sometimes by having just one positive experience. Interestingly, the one positive experience is often this assessment.

There are four sub-categories of personal characteristics (see Figure 9.6). Read each description carefully to know exactly what you are looking for before rating them.

Ratings:

1 – Unsatisfactory 2 – Requires attention 3 – Adequate 4 – Competitive

Personal characteristics		Rating	Comments
1	Attitude		
2	Motivation		
3	Independence		
4	Punctuality		
	Average rating		

Figure 9.6 Personal characteristics assessment

9.6.1 Attitude

People with Asperger Syndrome may be more susceptible to low self-esteem, lack of confidence and depression. Throughout their lives, they have heard phrases such as, "You're bright but lazy" and "How can you be so clueless?" They are easy targets for bullying and often have negative experiences in the school system. They generally do not know the difference between friendly teasing and malicious teasing and can overreact or be overly sensitive as adults. Many people with Asperger Syndrome do not have friends and suffer from loneliness. A lifetime of such experiences will make anyone belligerent, angry, and frustrated. Combine this with the fact that people with Asperger Syndrome typically do not adapt well to change and you can begin to understand why some candidates suffer from a negative attitude and display harsh, uncooperative, belligerent, and even aggressive mind-sets.

The workplace does not tolerate poor attitudes. Employers do not want employees who talk back, become aggressive, argue, or act belligerent. If the candidate displays any of these traits, then the issue will need to be addressed before placing him or her in a job.

9.6.2 Motivation

Few people are motivated to complete a job that is unimportant to them. Although it is important to find work that is interesting and motivating, even the most exciting jobs have some aspect that is boring or tedious. This is important for the candidate with Asperger Syndrome to understand. It is also important that the candidate demonstrate that he or she is motivated to work, even in areas that are not of interest to him or her. Employers need all aspects of a job done well and cannot afford to retain employees who lack motivation and require constant incentives to produce basic results.

When you are assessing the motivation level of a candidate, the most important element is that he or she demonstrate a desire to work and a willingness to do what it takes to reach his or her potential.

9.6.3 Independence

There are many factors that may impede the candidate's level of independence on the job. These include functioning level, ability to take initiative, confidence, and self-esteem. All of these factors play a part in the ability of the candidate to be independent on the job.

If the candidate is not able to function independently in a job within a reasonable time frame, it will be more difficult for him or her to be competitively employed. In this situation, it is important to investigate the reasons behind the candidate's lack of independence and then develop a strategy to work toward building greater independence. The sooner you assess the needs of the candidate in this area, the sooner strategies may be set in place to develop the necessary skills.

9.6.4 Punctuality

Punctuality can be a problem for some people – with or without Asperger Syndrome. If the candidate is consistently late, strategies must be implemented to address the issue before it puts his or her job at risk. An employer will only put up with so much tardiness before reprimanding the employee.

9.7 Education/skill

There is a category of employment called "unskilled" jobs that generally do not require a high level of education or specialized training. These may include cashier, gas bar attendant, retail clerk, and assembly worker. Although these are considered unskilled jobs, they still have basic educational requirements such as the ability to read, write, and perform basic math. As people move up the ladder into more skilled and more professional positions, the educational and skill requirement levels will be higher. You need to document what level of education and skill the candidate has to assist you in his or her job search in the future.

In the Figure 9.7, comment on the candidate's education and skill level. Make sure you inquire about any informal training, which includes on-the-job training. If the candidate has any special licenses, such as a driver's license or credentials or certificates such as CPR or first aid, make note of that, too.

	Educational skill	Comments
1	Highest academic level completed	
2	Strongest subjects	
3	Weakest subjects	
4	Learning challenges	
5	Specialized training or courses, licenses and/or credentials	

Figure 9.7 Education assessment

9.8 Environment

Before beginning a job search for a candidate, you need to determine what type of environment will best suit him or her. Because many people with Asperger Syndrome have poor motor coordination, they may have difficulty lifting and standing or sitting for long periods. They may also have sensitivity to temperature and thus be unsuited for working in high temperatures, such as in a bakery, or low temperatures, such as in a meatpacking plant.

Environment	Well Suited	Not well suited	Occasionally
Physical conditions			
Cold weather			
Hot weather			
Indoor			
Outdoor			
Noise level			
Quiet			
Outdoor noise level, for example street traffic			
Loud noise level, for example construction site			
People tolerance			
Work alone			
Small number of people (under 10)			
Medium number of people (11–25)			
Large number of people (26–50)			
Working with the public			
Children			
Seniors			
Shifts			
Full-time hours			
Days			
Afternoons			
Evenings			
Nights			
Weekends			
Rotating shifts			
Physical tolerance			
Lifting light weight (up to 10 pounds)			
Lifting heavy weight (11 to 30 pounds)			
Bending			
Standing			
Sitting			

Figure 9.8 Environment assessment

Some will be capable of working full-time hours while others will not. Some will perform better in the afternoon or evening than in the morning.

Use the checklist in Figure 9.8 to determine what environmental conditions best suit the candidate.

Summary

- Observe the candidate's work skills in a competitive work environment so that you can see for yourself what his strengths and challenges are.

- Assess the candidate both through the eyes of the employer and as a support worker. This gives you a realistic perspective.

- Keep an open line of communication with the candidate as you assess his skills. This helps the candidate trust you and the process.

10 The Strategy Guide

Building a foundation of skill

Only by choice can anyone truly embark on change.

Everyone has challenges in life, those things that hold us back from getting where we want to go. It is not so important what challenges you face in life but rather what you choose to do about them. If you are reading this book, then you have made the decision to support people in their choice to grow and change so that they can reach their potential. But understand that you cannot do it for them. You cannot *make* someone change. Your decision to support your Asperger friend in her endeavor to improve will only be successful if it is something that your friend wants. You can support and guide the candidate, but you cannot make change happen on her behalf.

My father used to tell me to choose my battles in life. Basically he meant that I needed to decide what was most important to me and what was worth my effort. It is time for you and your Asperger friend to choose your battles. In Chapter 9, you worked with the candidate to identify the areas in which she needs to improve in order to be competitive in the workplace. Together you will now prioritize those challenges and develop strategies to address them.

This chapter contains the Strategy Guide, which outlines effective strategies for each item in the Big Picture Assessment. Use this guide to help you and the candidate decide on which strategies are most appropriate for each situation.

10.1 Prioritizing challenges

Prioritizing challenges can be a bit of a balancing act. It is not uncommon to feel overwhelmed after doing the Big Picture Assessment. It may seem as if there are a lot of challenges to address. Do not get discouraged. Each challenge will get addressed in due course. They say that Rome was not built in a day and there is no expectation that significant life changes should take place immediately. This is a life process. Begin by developing one strategy at a time and build from there. Change does not happen quickly, especially when the changes involve shifting behavior. As long as the candidate is committed to improving, it will all come together, if not today, then a month or a year from now. If everyone remains focused, it will happen. People can turn their lives around through sheer determination and will. The power is in the will to succeed!

When prioritizing challenges there are three factors to consider:

- what challenges are the greatest impediments to employment
- what aptitudes/skills do employers value most
- what is the candidate most capable of altering.

Based upon the information you gathered in the Big Picture Assessment, consider any items that rated below a three. Highlight no more than ten items that you believe are the candidate's biggest challenges to gaining or maintaining employment. It is likely that the most significant challenges will jump out at you quickly. If they are not obvious to you, then perhaps your Asperger friend is well on her way to competitive employment. If there are many significant challenges, then you will know that you need to develop a longer-term strategy. Either way, this is good information.

Now let's consider what the employer values most. Every employer will have his own idea of what skills or attributes are most important. Generally speaking, however, employers want the same thing. They want an employee who comes in on time, is personable and does her job well.

If your Asperger friend rated poorly in the personal characteristic section of the Big Picture Assessment, this will be the place for you to begin building strategies. Bad attitude and lack of motivation are killers in the workplace. Employers won't put up with it and really, why should they when there are many other people they can hire who will be positive and want the job?

Beyond this, you will need to use your own judgment in deciding what is most important to address. Having some idea about where the candidate wants to work will be helpful. For example if she wants to work in construction or on a farm, then personal presentation will not rate as highly as if the choice is to work in an office or retail environment. Your objective is to target those challenges that will most likely impede the candidate's chances of getting and keeping a job based upon the person as an individual. It is this individualized approach that helps you to develop effective, targeted strategies.

In Chapter 2, the ten most desired skills employers look for in new hires today was outlined. Consider this list when you are prioritizing the challenges you will be addressing with your Asperger friend:

- communication (oral and written)
- honesty/integrity
- teamwork (works with others)
- interpersonal skills (relates well to others)
- motivation/initiative
- strong work ethic
- analytical skills
- flexibility/adaptability
- computer skills
- time management/organizational skills.

Finally, factor the candidate's ability to alter each challenge. You do not want your friend to get discouraged or overwhelmed. You may want to put a few easier challenges on the priority list, such as improving greetings and handshakes or modifying wardrobe. When working with candidates, it is typical to target between three and ten challenges over a four-week period. By staggering the strategies the candidate is less likely to get inundated.

The strategy guide

Building a foundation of skill takes time and energy on your part and on the part of your Asperger friend.

Now that you have identified and prioritized the challenges you will be working on with the candidate, you need to develop strategies to address them. To make your job easier, here is a guide to assist you in choosing effective strategies. I have developed many tools and methods over the years and have compiled them into this easy-to-use reference guide. When you are using this guide, it will be helpful for you to refer back to Chapters 7 and 8, "The Four Pillar Teaching Technique" and "The Employment Toolbox." These chapters lay the groundwork for the strategies in the guide. When you are implementing any strategy, be sure to apply the Four Pillar Teaching Technique. This will ensure that your message is getting through clearly to your Asperger friend.

I have also made a number of references in the Strategy Guide to the tools in Chapter 8. These tools are fundamental to many of the strategies in the guide. If you have not already read Chapter 8, then I strongly recommend that you do so before implementing any of the strategies in this guide.

For the sake of ease, the guide has been organized to follow the same sections and sub-sections of the Big Picture Assessment in Chapter 9. This will allow you to reference one to the other and develop your strategies quickly and effectively.

10.2 Personal presentation

10.2.1 Appropriate clothing

Dressing appropriately for the workplace is an important element of finding and keeping work that works.

Strategies

Candidates working in an office environment should purchase three pair of pants/skirts, one navy, one black and one tan or kaki. They should purchase five shirts/blouses, one for each day of the week. Most colors go with navy, black and tan so there should be few mismatched combinations if any. For men, socks should be dark in color, black is always safe. For women who wish to wear skirts or dresses, natural nylons/stockings are appropriate. They should have two pairs of casual/dress shoes, black and brown. Match belts with shoes.

If the candidate cannot afford to purchase this clothing then he should build up to it. Here is an example of a starter package for a man:

1 pair navy pants

1 pair tan pants

3 business casual shirts in different colors

1 pair black dress shoes

1 black belt

3 pair black socks

It will also be important to tell the candidate not to wear the same shirt two days in a row. Discuss when and how to launder and iron the clothes to maintain a neat and clean appearance.

10.2.2 General cleanliness/hygiene

Proper hygiene is important to being successful in a job. Employers should not be telling an employee to shave, wash or get a hair cut, brush their teeth, bathe, or enact any other form of personal hygiene. This may seem trivial; however, if you have ever had to work with a person who had body odor, you will relate to this point. If the candidate has issues with hygiene, they should be addressed promptly.

Strategies

The job coach should make a schedule and outline in detail what is expected of the candidate with regard to cleanliness and hygiene. A parent or a support person involved on the home front can help the candidate ensure that the schedule and routine gets established and is adhered to. A checklist is also a helpful tool to make sure that everything gets done.

A common problem often faced with male candidates is that they won't shave on a regular basis. The result is that they look scruffy. When this happens they should be given two choices: Either grow a beard or shave every day. It needs to be explained to them that if they grow a beard they may still have to shave a little bit. Most candidates are not pleased with this rule but they all abide by it and usually choose to shave. Accept no middle ground and send them home if they show up unshaven.

> Helpful tools from the Employment Toolbox (Chapter 8) to build strategies for this challenge are: Rule tool, mirroring, formulas, third-party praise, verbal reflection

10.2.3 Greetings and handshake

Every day that an employee goes into work, she should greet people. A simple "hello" or "good morning" will suffice. Although handshaking is not necessary every time you meet someone, it is a common part of the greeting process when being introduced to someone new. Refer to Chapter 12 for a detailed outline of the greeting and handshake process.

Strategies

- Outline clearly what is expected of the candidate when greeting someone.

- Break the greeting and handshake down into steps that are easy to learn and follow. This will reduce the stress level when meeting a new person.

- Help the candidate to set goals, first to greet one, then two, then three people each day at work.

> Helpful tools from the Employment Toolbox (Chapter 8) to build strategies for this challenge are: Scripting, role play, mirroring, formulas, anchoring, third-party praise

10.3 Social skills and behavior

10.3.1 General manners

Manners are very important in the workplace. If your Asperger friend's manners are a weak point, then this is an area that should be addressed. Make a list of the basic manners that the general public expects. Go over each one with your friend then point out the ones which are already being done well, then discuss the ones which are not being done adequately.

Strategies

The best way to teach manners is to first help the candidate become aware of what is expected, spelling out very clearly when and how to use manners. Start with the main ones such as saying "please," "thank you" and "excuse me," then move to the more subtle manners such as not staring, opening doors for others, and reducing body sounds.

Some candidates have gotten into trouble because they stare at people, more specifically people of the opposite sex. Although *you* may know that the candidate means no harm, you cannot expect that others will have the same knowledge. In fact this can present real problems in the workplace for an employee if his or her actions are misunderstood. This is particularly a problem with males staring at females. I recall hearing about a man with Asperger Syndrome who was fired because he had stared at women in his office building. Someone had filed a complaint about him and he was dismissed. This demonstrates how easily innocent actions might be misunderstood and, when this occurs, the serious consequences that may result.

When addressing the topic of staring and approaching people of the opposite sex, set out clear guidelines. Here are a few examples.

- Do not stare at people for more than two seconds. (Practice the time limit.)

- If you are a man, do not approach women whom you do not know and engage them in conversation unless it is work-related.

- Again, if you are a man, do not follow women.

- Make guidelines specific to the issues your client is facing.

> Helpful tools from the Employment Toolbox (Chapter 8) to build strategies for this challenge are: Scripting, role play, video play, rule tool, formulas, anchoring

10.3.2 Table manners

Although table manners may not have a direct impact on finding or keeping a job, they are important because if they are unusual, they draw negative attention.

Strategies

The "Rule" or "Formula" tool described in Chapter 8 works well for learning good table manners, depending upon what the candidate responds to best. Here are few of the basic rules of table manners:

- chew with your mouth closed
- wait until your mouth is empty to before speaking
- wipe your mouth regularly to remove any food from your face
- ask for things to be passed rather than reach across the table for them.

You may want to customize your list or add rules.

Formulas work well when the candidate has never really learned a skill such as eating neatly.

Here is an example of an eating formula:

1. Take a small/medium sized bite of food.

2. Chew with your mouth closed.

3. Swallow.

4. Wipe your mouth.

5. Speak.

You may also want to include a non-verbal anchor (see Chapter 8) such as the coach putting his hand to his own mouth to help as a prompt.

> Helpful tools from the Employment Toolbox (Chapter 8) to build strategies for this challenge are: Rule tool, formulas, anchoring, third-party praise

10.3.3 Awareness of personal space

Have you ever been at a party where some stranger came over to you and leaned so close to your face that you felt like if they got any closer you'd have to marry them? That's an invasion of personal space.

In a work setting and, for that matter, any setting, no one likes his personal space invaded. If your Asperger friend inadvertently makes an invasion of this sort, it can have a number of negative effects on people and, subsequently, your Asperger friend. Without knowing it, his or her behavior could be interpreted as intimidating, bullying, or just plain annoying. This can lead to a serious problem and even dismissal.

Strategies

There is an effective strategy for teaching the candidate personal space. I call it the "Arm's Length Rule." Have the candidate stand in front of you and put her arm straight out in front. The outstretched arm should have enough room so that it is about one inch away from touching you. If the candidate can't extend her arm fully, then she is too close. The rule is, simply, "If you are less than an arm's length away from someone, you are too close. Take one step back."

Note: There may be some cultural exceptions to this distance rule relative to personal space.

> Helpful tools from the Employment Toolbox (Chapter 8) to build strategies for this challenge are: Role play, rule tool, formulas, anchoring

10.3.4 Obsessive-compulsive/perfectionism

Obsessive-compulsive disorder (OCD) is an anxiety not a thought disorder. Many people with Asperger Syndrome also have OCD or high anxiety. If the candidate's OCD or anxiety challenges are serious, she should refer to a specialist. If the challenge mildly interferes with work, here are a few strategies you can try.

Strategies

- Create an "anxiety scale" so that you and your Asperger friend can rate the level of anxiety and make note of the things that cause it. By also identifying the physical sensations or symptoms associated with each level, your friend will be able to recognize the anxiety coming on and take action to calm himself.

- Let your Asperger friend learn a task really well to prove to himself that the job can be done. Then support the candidate in trusting that she will do it well. Limit the number of times the work can be checked or re-checked.

- Set speed or productivity goals and explain that perfectionism or OCD is interfering with meeting the goals. See if this limits the number of times needed to repeat a behavior.

- Use rules to outline what is appropriate if the obsession is dominant in the workplace.

- Set clear boundaries as to what is off-limits relative to topics and behavior at work.

> Helpful tools from the Employment Toolbox (Chapter 8) to build strategies for this challenge are: Role play, video play, rule tool, anchoring, scales

10.3.5 General comfort level with others

People with Asperger Syndrome tend to take longer to feel comfortable around people. If they are very shy or timid, this makes it difficult for them to fit in to the workplace.

Strategies

Getting comfortable with people takes time, particularly for people with Asperger Syndrome. You can support your Asperger friend in this challenge by encouraging contact with a few people. Select one or two coworkers and introduce the candidate to them so she knows their names. Then script greetings and have the candidate greet these coworkers each day. All of the social skills and communication assignments, which are given to the candidate, can then be practiced on these one or two coworkers. Usually within a few weeks, the candidate is comfortable with the coworkers and might even be socializing with them independently.

It is a good idea to speak with the coworkers beforehand to make sure that they are open to helping the candidate out. By creating a social and safe environment for the candidate, you set her up for success.

> Helpful tools from the Employment Toolbox (Chapter 8) to build strategies for this challenge are: Scripting, role play, anchoring

10.3.6 Unusual sounds and behaviors

Any unusual sounds or behaviors that draw attention to your Asperger friend impact how coworkers will perceive her. Your objective is to help the candidate blend into the worksite. If she is going to stand out for anything, you want it to be for something positive, not unusual or negative.

Strategies

The first step in addressing unusual sounds and behaviors is to bring it to the attention of the candidate. She may or may not be aware of the behavior that draws this attention. You want the candidate to start becoming aware of others' perceptions.

One excellent tool that addresses this challenge is the "Video Play" (Chapter 8). Should the candidate be unaware of the behavior or require proof of it, playing back a video recording of the behavior is an excellent way of bringing it to her attention. Often seeing the behavior from an outsider's perspective is enough to motivate the candidate to make changes.

Many unusual behaviors are habitual and therefore take a concerted effort to alter. The candidate must want to change the behavior. Most candidates will not want to draw negative attention to themselves. When they have an opportunity to see what is alienating them or drawing negative attention to themselves, they are frequently motivated to change it. This effort combined with a strategy such as "Verbal Reflection" that helps the candidate be self-aware, will frequently get a positive result.

> Helpful tools from the Employment Toolbox (Chapter 8) to build strategies for this challenge are: Role play, video play, anchoring, third-party praise, verbal reflection

10.3.7 Appropriate touching of others

People with Asperger Syndrome can lack boundaries. Today's workplace is very sensitive to issues around sexual harassment. If your Asperger friend touches someone inappropriately, however innocently, there is a risk of job loss.

Strategies

If the candidate has difficulty in this area, you should develop a strategy that clearly outlines what is and is not considered appropriate touching.

Depending upon the needs of the candidate, the outline may need to be very detailed. If he or she has extremely poor boundaries, simply put a rule in place that there is zero touching (other than the handshake). This is the safest thing to do if the candidate cannot learn boundaries. I suggest that the only body parts safe for touching in a professional environment are the hands and the shoulder. Everything else is off-limits.

Here is a list of some general rules pertaining to sexuality/touching and the workplace. You may need to make more specific rules for your Asperger friend based upon the situation. Go over these rules with your friend. If you feel a little uncomfortable doing this just remember that you will both feel even more uncomfortable if you have to deal with an employer about these rules at a later date.

- Do not touch your fellow workers.

- Do not bring up, discuss or make reference to anything sexual. This includes media stories, TV programs and movies.

- Do not talk about what you do sexually in your private life.

- Do not talk about what your friends or family do sexually in their private lives.

- Do not make sexual comments about anyone, particularly anyone who has anything to do with your work.

- Do not touch your genitals at work unless using the washroom.

If these rules seem cut and dried it is because they are. Do not expect the candidate to be able to generalize because this is one of the more difficult things for someone with Asperger Syndrome to do. He or she will have more success and less trouble if there are steadfast rules to follow.

Helpful tools from the Employment Toolbox (Chapter 8) to build strategies for this challenge are: Role play, rule tool, mirroring, formulas, third-party praise

---

10.3.8 Aggressive behavior

There is no place for aggression or outrageous behavior in the workplace. It is critical to take a zero tolerance stand on this issue. Not addressing aggression will result in a negative experience for all involved should an incident occur. If a candidate displays aggressive or violent behavior at the worksite, then remove him or her. The bottom line is if your Asperger friend displays any aggressive behavior, he or she is not ready for the workplace.

Strategies

Anger and aggression are difficult issues to work with. They can be very deep rooted and complex. Use your judgment when working with this issue. There are situations where you can help the candidate manage his or her anger and aggression and then there are situations that require professional guidance and expertise. The candidate should be referred to a professional for support if the issue is serious and people or property are at risk of being harmed.

It is important that you explain clearly to the candidate why aggression is not acceptable and why it needs to be addressed before continuing in a work environment.

The scale tool (Chapter 8) is an effective tool to help the candidate recognize and manage aggression issues. An anger scale helps the person with Asperger Syndrome become aware of the signs he or she experiences leading up to the aggressive behavior. As the candidate becomes better at identifying the signs, he or she is in a better position to recognize behavior before it happens and then take action to either calm it or remove himself from the situation.

- Develop an anger scale between 1 and 5.

- Help the candidate identify the level of anger by identifying the symptoms of each level. For example, at level 1 there might be a feeling of calm, at level 2 stomach muscles get tight, at level 3 the shoulders and back get tense, at level 4 the face gets really hot, the stomach feels upset and the candidate starts talking under her breath, and at level 5 swearing and yelling begins.

- Role play each level of anger so that both of you get familiar with what each level looks/feels like.

- Identify a strategy for every level; for example, level 1 = take a deep breath, level 2 = practice some relaxation techniques, level 3 = go out for a drink of water, or write in a journal, level 4 = leave the office and go for a short walk, level 5 = too late, one should never get to level 5! Before an explosion (level 5), the candidate should have removed himself from the situation to avoid negative consequences.

- Get the candidate to begin identifying the levels on his own. "What number are you at now Paul?"

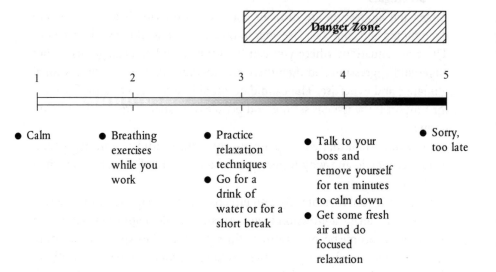

Figure 10.1 Anger scale

> Helpful tools from the Employment Toolbox (Chapter 8) to build strategies for this challenge are: Role play, video play, rule tool, formulas, anchoring, scales, third-party praise, verbal reflection

10.3.9 Racial/sexual prejudice

Today's workplace does not tolerate racial or sexual prejudice. Candidates can unwittingly make comments or observations that could easily be misinterpreted as prejudice. More often than not, the candidate makes these comments or observations naively with no bad intent. However innocent, if said to or overheard by the "wrong" person, such remarks could have serious ramifications.

Strategies

Asperger Syndrome affects judgment skills. People with Asperger Syndrome do not automatically know what is acceptable and what is not acceptable in the workplace. Therefore they need it to be spelled out. People with Asperger Syndrome may forever struggle with judgment skills; however, when they are aware of and avoid inappropriate topics, they greatly lessen the impact of poor judgment.

Anything about sex:

- sexual body parts
- jokes
- sexual orientation
- anything personal (sexual about self).

Racism/sexism/prejudice:

- stereotypes
- gender roles
- religion
- jokes
- sweeping judgments (generalizations).

Personal questions regarding:

- salary
- sexual orientation
- political views
- age
- religion.

Figure 10.2 Unsafe topics

Helpful tools from the Employment Toolbox (Chapter 8) to build strategies for this challenge are: Role play, rule tool, mirroring, formulas, anchoring, verbal reflection

An effective strategy to address this challenge is the use of the "unsafe topics" list (see Figure 10.2). This list outlines in detail what topics are generally not acceptable for discussing in a work environment. Conversely you may also compile a list of "safe topics" (see Figure 10.3).

10.4 Communication skills

10.4.1 Conversation skills

Balanced conversation does not come easily to people with Asperger Syndrome. Candidates do not have to be great conversationalists to be employable but they should be able to converse at a basic level. This will help them fit into their work environment and is considered "normal" behavior in the workplace.

Strategies

One of the best ways to support your Asperger friend in developing conversation skills is a game I call "the reporter." This is a role playing game that gets your friend to interview someone, perhaps yourself the first time, and get information.

The reporter role playing involves introducing "open-ended questions" to your friend. This consists of who, what, where, when, why, and how. Set the scene by establishing what the interview is about. For example, you may play a zookeeper at the local zoo and the candidate has to interview you for the local paper. She needs to find out what you do, why you do it, where you do it, with whom you do it, etc. This strategy works best if there is a third party present. This allows someone free to direct (the "director"), or help out during the scene.

The objective for the candidate is to begin a two-way conversation where she is asking the questions and the other person is answering. The answers should lead the candidate to the next question. This takes some coaching and practice for the candidate because she will not always see what the next question might be. To assist in this, write who, what, where, when, why and how on a piece of paper and let the candidate hold it as a visual prompt. The director can help the candidate determine what is appropriate to ask next based upon what was said in the answer.

The logical next step in teaching conversation is to introduce three-way conversations. This may be done in much the same way as the "reporter" two-way conversation role play. A topic is introduced and then the rules are outlined for a three-way conversation as follows:

- The first player asks a question on the topic that has been predetermined.

- The second player answers the question. Then asks one.

- The third player answers that question and then asks one.

The role play continues for several minutes. As the candidate becomes more comfortable, you may wish to increase the level of difficulty by "forcing" the

Helpful tools from the Employment Toolbox (Chapter 8) to build strategies for this challenge are: Scripting, role play, rule tool, mirroring, formulas, anchoring

candidate to follow the flow of conversation in a more complex format. For example, the questioner may ask two or three questions before accepting a response. Another example would be to change the order of the questioners, i.e. move from the 1, 2, 3, order.

This strategy takes a long time to perfect but it works extremely well.

10.4.2 Appropriate choice of topics

Choosing what is appropriate to discuss in the workplace can be a real challenge for people with Asperger Syndrome. They tend to blurt out whatever is on their minds. This is a challenge in the workplace if what they are thinking is not appropriate to be said aloud.

Strategies

People with Asperger Syndrome respond well to guidelines. They are almost relieved that they do not have to guess. A wonderful strategy to help them with appropriate topics is to make a list of what are considered "safe topics" in the workplace. These are topics that are generally inoffensive to people. Of course there will always be exceptions. You and your Asperger friend will want to customize your list. If for example there are topics on the list that the candidate obsesses about or dominates a conversation about, they might well need to be removed. Figure 10.3 gives a sample of safe topics.

The weather	Weekend plans	Famous people
Sports	Vacation plans	Awards shows
Movies	Past vacations	Olympics
Television shows	Museum exhibits	Cars
Books	Art galleries	Hobbies/leisure activities
Musicals/theater	Technology	Architecture
Restaurants	Domesticated animals	Horticulture

Figure 10.3 Safe topics

Helpful Tools from the Employment Toolbox (Chapter 8) to build strategies for this challenge are: Scripting, role play, rule tool, mirroring, formulas, anchoring

10.4.3 Interrupting

Interrupting is one of the most common problems encountered among employees with Asperger Syndrome in the workplace. If it is not addressed early in pre-vocational work, it can have a crippling effect on the success of the candidate's career. One of the missions for the support person is to help the Asperger employee become independent and competitive in the job. One should never rely on the patience or generosity of an employer because even the best employers may lose these qualities when they are pushed.

A step-by-step strategy to address problems with interrupting follows.

Strategies

1. Clearly describe the social rules around interrupting.

    Example: "Do not interrupt people when they are speaking or when they are on the telephone." Do not assume that a person with Asperger Syndrome will know that speaking also includes phone conversations.

2. Clearly outline how to handle the situation.

Example:

(a) If someone is on the phone:

○ Wait until the person has hung up.

○ It is polite to leave the room when someone is having a telephone conversation. Do not stand at his desk and wait for more than five seconds.

○ Come back in ten minutes to see if the person is off the phone.

○ Do not interrupt a phone call unless there is an emergency [you may need to discuss in detail what an emergency consists of].

(b) If someone is already speaking to another person and you need to speak to him:

○ Come back in ten minutes.

○ If the person is still busy and your question is important to finishing your assignment you should do the following: Interrupt by saying, "Excuse me, sorry to interrupt your conversation but I have a question to ask you. When would be a good time to speak to you?"

○ When the person has named a time, leave and come back at the scheduled time.

(c) If the person is working:

○ Say, "Excuse me for interrupting, may I ask you a question about my assignment?"

○ Wait until the person looks up.

○ Make direct eye contact.

○ Ask your question.

○ Continue with your assignment.

Helpful tools from the Employment Toolbox (Chapter 8) to build strategies for this challenge are: Scripting, role play, rule tool, mirroring, formulas, anchoring

10.4.4 Ability to read non-verbal cues

Only 7 per cent of communication is relayed by the spoken word. The rest relies on non-verbal cues including tone of voice, facial expression, and body language. People with Asperger Syndrome have great difficulty picking up non-verbal cues. This is a real set-back in the workplace because they may miss important information that they are expected to know. Although candidates may not be able to change this about themselves 100 per cent, they can increase the number of non-verbal messages they are able to read.

Strategies

To help your Asperger friends increase their ability to read non-verbal cues, you need to expose them to the cues and explain what they are. During regular interaction, when you notice yourself giving a non-verbal cue, ask how they are interpreting the cue.

You can also set up an exercise that does this through role play. Use your imagination. One of my favorite exercises is to sit across from one another and make faces. The candidate has to guess what I am silently saying to them and *vice versa*. It is very enlightening because I also get the opportunity to see how the candidate expresses himself non-verbally. This gives me insight into how well the candidate might be communicating to others with non-verbal messages.

Improvisational theater classes are an excellent way for people with Asperger Syndrome to gain better non-verbal skills. Check to see what is available in your community.

> Helpful tools from the Employment Toolbox (Chapter 8) to build strategies for this challenge are: Role play, video play, anchoring, verbal reflection

10.4.5 Level of unprompted interaction with others

Some people with Asperger Syndrome are very timid and will not initiate conversation. It is not vital that they initiate conversation if this is really uncomfortable for them; however, employers will expect employees to answer questions without a lot of prompting.

Strategies

Explain to the candidate why it is important to respond to people. Clearly outline the expectation of the need to respond to direct questions. The natural consequence of not responding may include job loss.

Here are some strategies to support candidates in responding to direct questions:

- Determine if they understand the question and, if they do not, script a response such as "I don't understand your question" or "Could you please rephrase your question?"

- If they do understand but don't know how to answer, script a response for that as well. An example might be, "I'm not sure. Can you go over my options?"

- If they need more time to respond, script something like, "Can I get back to you?" or "I need to think about the answer. Can I get back to you in a few minutes?"

You will need to script whatever is appropriate for the situation or challenge candidates have. The objective is to help your Asperger friends convey that they are not ignoring people, but that they are having some difficulty answering them.

> Helpful tools from the Employment Toolbox (Chapter 8) to build strategies for this challenge are: Scripting, role play, video play, formulas, anchoring, verbal reflection

10.4.6 Listening skills

Asperger Syndrome is not a hearing impairment. However, it is wise for your friend to check for any medical reason if she is having problems listening before addressing the issue as behavioral. Once this possibility has been eliminated, you should develop a strategy to help her listen and then retain information.

Strategies

It is important to have a person's attention before speaking to him. This optimizes the chances of him listening. One strategy is to say the candidate's name and then pause until you know she has focused on you. You may want to set this up with the candidate beforehand so that she recognizes this as a prompt. Begin speaking to your Asperger friend in very clear direct phrases. Make your point brief. Ask the candidate to repeat what you have said. Once you are confident that your instruction has been heard and understood, ask that the instruction be acted upon. If truly understood, it will be indicated if the appropriate action follows.

Another strategy is to also write the instruction down. Sometimes this dual method of communicating is helpful. What the candidate does not pick up through oral instruction, can be seen in writing.

> Helpful tools from the Employment Toolbox (Chapter 8) to build strategies for this challenge are: Role play, anchoring

10.4.7 Ability to understand humor

Humor is helpful when fitting into a work environment. Some people with Asperger Syndrome have an excellent sense of humor while others struggle with this. People with Asperger Syndrome may miss some of the more subtle forms of humor that involve play on words, double meanings and sarcasm because they take things very literally.

Strategies

- Try to discover what the candidate finds humorous. Use this sense of humor to draw her out and create a comfort level.

- Joke with the candidate and then ask if she thinks you are joking or being serious. This offers you some idea of the candidate's perspective.

- Explain some of the non-verbal cues that go along with joking. For example, a wink of the eye usually means that someone is teasing.

> Helpful tools from the Employment Toolbox (Chapter 8) to build strategies for this challenge are: Role play, anchoring, verbal reflection

10.4.8 Level of response to others

Because Asperger Syndrome is a communication disorder, you may find that candidates have difficulty responding to others. The following strategies are two examples of solutions for this issue.

Strategies

- Teach the candidate to look at a person and to give a brief verbal acknowledgment when spoken to. This may simply be a matter of saying "yes," "no" or "okay."

- Set the expectation that the candidate make an effort to greet people in the morning. This can be built up over a period of time. For example, begin with insisting on a greeting to one pre-established person. You may add more as the candidate becomes more comfortable.

> Helpful tools from the Employment Toolbox (Chapter 8) to build strategies for this challenge are: Scripting, role play, video play, formulas, anchoring

10.4.9 Eye contact

Eye contact is an important part of communication and social interaction. The better your Asperger friend is at eye contact, the easier she will find it to blend in at work.

Strategies

- If it is really uncomfortable for the candidate to maintain eye contact, have her look at your forehead. This sometimes makes it easier and it looks as if eye contact is being made.

- Have the candidate make eye contact at the beginning of each sentence she speaks.

- Have the candidate make initial eye contact for the first three seconds when someone speaks. Build the contact up from several seconds to minutes.

Helpful tools from the Employment Toolbox (Chapter 8) to build strategies for this challenge are: Role play, video play, anchoring, verbal reflection

10.4.10 Volume of voice

It is common for people with Asperger Syndrome to speak either too quietly or too loudly. They have difficulty gauging what volume is appropriate for different situations.

Strategies

- Develop a volume scale to help the candidate determine what volume she normally speaks at. The scale can be from one to five with one being the equivalent of a whisper and five the equivalent of yelling across a ball field.

- Demonstrate each level on the volume scale and have the candidate repeat after you to get a feel for each volume.

- Give an example of where the candidate should use each volume. For example, a volume three is appropriate in the office, a volume one in the elevator and a volume five when trying to get someone's attention across the street.

- Clearly outline the volume level expected in the work environment.

- Set up a verbal anchor to help prompt the candidate when her volume is not appropriate for the environment.

- Eventually you will find that the candidate will require fewer prompts and will begin independently adjusting her own volume.

Helpful tools from the Employment Toolbox (Chapter 8) to build strategies for this challenge are: Role play, anchoring, scales, verbal reflection

10.5 Mindful skills

10.5.1 Problem-solving skills

Problem-solving skills are what one uses every time one is faced with a new problem. These are valuable skills, which many employers are looking for in prospective employees. Technical problem-solving is often a *forte* of people with Asperger Syndrome because of the systematic approach it requires. Problem-solving that involves a great deal of common sense or people skills is usually very challenging, however. Most major problem-solving in a business is left up to the managers; however, employees at any level need to have some skill in this area in order to excel in a job.

Strategies

- Work alongside the employee to teach the steps involved in basic problem-solving. Example:
    1. Define the nature of the problem by breaking it down.
    2. Identify possible causes of the problem.
    3. List a number of possible solutions for each cause.
    4. Select the best solution by making a list of pros and cons and then talking about what is most important.

- Come up with formulas for common problems. For example, if the boss is away and an answer is required to a question, always ask a coworker. You can develop a multi-tiered formula if it is appropriate, which is basically a list of things which your Asperger friend tries in turn in order to solve the problem. Your objective is to limit the judgment involved in the problem-solving process since this, too, is an area of challenge for people with Asperger Syndrome.

Helpful tools from the Employment Toolbox (Chapter 8) to build strategies for this challenge are: Role play, formulas

10.5.2 Learning style

Everyone learns a bit differently (section 9.5.2 outlines the various learning styles). Defining the candidate's learning style is important as it allows you to teach more effectively. If your Asperger friend is not absorbing information, here are some strategies to try.

Strategies

- Combine different teaching techniques to improve information absorption and comprehension. For example, combine a checklist with a demonstration.

- Break the task down into smaller steps.

- Demonstrate the instruction three times and then have the candidate do the task. If an error occurs, try to get the candidate to figure out what went wrong rather than providing her with the answer. This develops problem-solving skills while at the same time helping to determine the logic behind the steps. Once the logic is determined, the candidate is more likely to perform the task better.

> Helpful tools from the Employment Toolbox (Chapter 8) to build strategies for this challenge are: Role play, mirroring, formulas, anchoring, verbal reflection

10.5.3 Judgment skills

All jobs require at least minor judgment skills. This is typically an area of challenge for people with Asperger Syndrome. If your Asperger friend is having difficulty with judgment, try the following strategies.

Strategies

Confine the use of judgment skills by limiting the projects or assignments that require a lot of judgment. When judgment is required, develop a formula that will help the candidate make the correct judgment. For example, write out a formula such as this:

- If the document is missing a signature, then put it in this tray.

- If the document is missing a file number, then set it aside to give to the supervisor at the end of the day.

This type of formula removes the guesswork from the assignment and gives the employer and the employee greater confidence that the job will be done well.

> Helpful tools from the Employment Toolbox (Chapter 8) to build strategies for this challenge are: Role play, video play, rule tool, formulas, anchoring

10.5.4 Flexibility

Asperger Syndrome can make people quite rigid and therefore they might struggle to shift from one assignment to another. Employers, however, often need employees to be flexible.

Strategies

One of the most effective ways to help candidates who have difficulty switching from one task to another is to use a verbal anchor word. A good anchor word to use is "priority." I explain to my clients that when they hear me say a job is a "priority," they are to take two minutes to come to a reasonable place to stop their current work. Then they are in a position to begin the next assignment. This allows them a little time to make the adjustment, which seems to help them with the transition to the next task. With this allowance and preparation time, they seem much more able to be flexible.

> Helpful tools from the Employment Toolbox (Chapter 8) to build strategies for this challenge are: Role play, video play, anchoring

10.5.5 Focus

Employers want employees to be able to focus for a minimum of one hour at a time and preferably two hours. If the candidate has difficulty meeting this expectation, you need to address it or it will become an issue in the workplace.

Strategies

If your Asperger friend has difficulty focusing, it is important to investigate why. Once you have determined why she is lacking focus it will be easier to develop a strategy to address the issue.

- *Is she tired?* Examine sleep habits and make suggestions to improve sleep patterns. Observe if there are any changes in the level of focus over the next few weeks.

- *Is she bored?* Set goals or targets to make the job more challenging or more interesting or choose different types of jobs to offer variety. Observe if this makes a difference in the level of focus.

- *Is she easily distracted?* Earplugs can be helpful in reducing noisy distractions. Have the candidate work in an area where there is less stimulation to see if this helps.

- *Does she have Attention Deficit Disorder (ADD)?* Suggest a medication review with the family doctor and break the assignment down into small steps with a written checklist as an aid.

> Helpful tools from the Employment Toolbox (Chapter 8) to build strategies for this challenge are: Role play, video play, anchoring

10.5.6 Memory retention

Generally speaking, people with Asperger Syndrome have good long-term memory retention. If they are at all challenged with memory skills it will likely be in short-term memory retention.

Strategies

Upon occasion one might meet someone with Asperger Syndrome who has poor short-term memory retention. For example, you might see the candidate forgetting the steps to an assignment readily done the day before. If this occurs regularly or consistently, it will need to be addressed.

- Write the steps down so that the candidate can refer to them independently.

- If the difficulty persists then you may need to group the steps or reorganize the steps in a way that will make better sense to the candidate. This might take some trial and error.

- If the candidate continues to have difficulty, break the job down into components. For example, if the candidate was performing a mailing task, you might begin with folding all the letters, then inserting all the folded letters into the envelopes, then putting the labels on all the envelopes...etc. rather than completing all of the steps for one letter then moving on to the second letter.

Helpful tools from the Employment Toolbox (Chapter 8) to build strategies for this challenge are: Role play, formulas, anchoring

10.5.7 Ability to follow steps

When you are working with someone who has difficulty remembering or following steps, it is important to determine where the difficulty is. It is possible that there may be other issues complicating matters, such as Attention Deficit Disorder (ADD) or a learning disability.

Strategies

If you suspect that the candidate has ADD, there are several steps that you may take to help improve performance.

- Work with your Asperger friend to set up a structured routine. Including the candidate in establishing the routine will result in greater motivation to follow it.

- Provide lots of positive reinforcement. People with Asperger Syndrome can be extremely sensitive to feedback and they need to hear positive reinforcement. This will help them feel motivated.

- Work on improving concentration by using gentle "quizzes" which sets the candidate up for success. For example, "What is the next step after you fold the letters?" This will help build confidence and memory in completing assignments.

Helpful tools from the Employment Toolbox (Chapter 8) to build strategies for this challenge are: Role play, rule tool, formulas, anchoring

10.5.8 Ability to take initiative

Initiative skills are frequently a challenge for people with Asperger Syndrome. It either does not occur to them to take initiative or, if it does, they often do not know what to do and may make errors.

Strategies

- Work with the employer to develop a list of tasks, assignments and jobs that would be considered valuable but are not necessarily part of the job description. Call this list "initiative jobs."

- Teach the candidate how to perform these jobs.

- When the candidate runs out of work, instruct her to refer to the list of "initiative jobs" and begin performing them until asked to do something else.

- Make sure that the candidate is aware that the jobs on the "initiative jobs" list are not priority jobs. Once asked to work on something else, the candidate should oblige.

Initiative is one of those things that will impress an employer but that many people, regardless of ability, fail to do. If you succeed in teaching the candidate to take initiative, you greatly increase her potential for successfully maintaining a job.

> Helpful tools from the Employment Toolbox (Chapter 8) to build strategies for this challenge are: Role play, rule tool, formulas, mirroring, anchoring

10.5.9 Ability to multi-task

Multi-tasking is a challenge for many people with Asperger Syndrome. Most jobs will require *some* amount of multi-tasking and, frequently, candidates are capable of handling this when it is set up for them appropriately.

Strategies

- Begin building skill by assigning one task and adding a second and possibly a third.

- Limit the multi-tasking to no more than three tasks at one time (two is generally preferable).

- Establish a routine to multi-tasking whenever possible.

> Helpful tools from the Employment Toolbox (Chapter 8) to build strategies for this challenge are: Rule tool, formulas, anchoring

10.5.10 Overall speed/productivity

The inability to be productive and quick in a job can be influenced by a number of factors, such as lack of focus, perfectionism, lack of motivation. Determining the cause behind a problem with speed or productivity will point you toward a solution.

Strategies

- Clearly outline what the employer's speed and productivity expectation is for a task. Then set realistic and attainable goals with your Asperger friend that work up to the competitive level. Make a chart together and document the level of productivity each day. This visual will let the candidate see progress and help with motivation.

- Once the candidate is improving, set the goals to meet the competitive level. For example, if the expectation of the employer is to have five boxes packed in an hour, setting the goal of packing three boxes an hour in the first week, four in the second and five in the third will help the candidate meet the goal within a reasonable time frame. You must set time frames based upon what is realistic for your Asperger friend and balance these with what the employer will accept as a reasonable learning curve. Set the stage for success.

- Develop a speed scale between one and five and then an accuracy scale between one and five. Use the scales together to help the candidate gage expectations for each assignment. For example, a mailing job might require a speed four and an accuracy rating of five. Shredding documents might be a speed five and an accuracy rating of one.

- Set targets and goals to help the candidate increase speed and productivity. Setting attainable goals builds confidence.

> Helpful tools from the Employment Toolbox (Chapter 8) to build strategies for this challenge are: Scales, mirroring, formulas, anchoring, third-party praise

10.5.11 Ability to organize work

Not everyone with Asperger Syndrome is able to organize work effectively and some people may require support.

Strategies

Ten ways to improve organizational skills:

1. Establish a routine.

2. Use checklists.

3. Prepare in advance.

4. Create "to-do" lists.

5. Keep things in the same place.

6. Label, date or color code things.

7. Establish reasonable (competitive) time frames to complete jobs and stick to them.

8. Break assignments down into manageable pieces.

9. Maintain an orderly workspace.

10. Establish a list of priorities (or have someone help with this).

> Helpful tools from the Employment Toolbox (Chapter 8) to build strategies for this challenge are: Role play, rule tool, mirroring, formulas, anchoring

10.5.12 Motor skills

People with Asperger Syndrome can have difficulty with motor coordination. They may be clumsy, bump into things or struggle with writing or other fine motor tasks.

Strategies

- Limit the jobs that require fine motor skills if this is a problem.

- Help the candidate be more aware of the environment by having her look ahead rather than at the ground, watch for people or objects that might be in her path, learn what areas of the environment have more traffic or require greater attention to maneuver around.

- Encourage the candidate to slow down.

> Helpful tools from the Employment Toolbox (Chapter 8) to build strategies for this challenge are: Rule tool, formulas, anchoring, verbal reflection

10.6 Personal characteristics

10.6.1 Attitude

It is very difficult to change anyone's attitude. Really, only the candidate can change her attitude if it is problematic; however, it is possible to put some things in place that set the stage for positive growth.

Strategies

- Give candidates positive feedback whenever possible.

- Encourage them to feel good about themselves.

- Build confidence by giving assignments that they will do well at.

- Be gentle and sensitive when giving constructive feedback.

- Point out when you are offering a compliment because the candidate may not always hear or absorb it.

- Help your Asperger friend be aware of a negative attitude by talking about how it will impact success in the workplace.

> Helpful tools from the Employment Toolbox (Chapter 8) to build strategies for this challenge are: Role play, anchoring, third-party praise, verbal reflection

10.6.2 Motivation

As with attitude, it is very difficult to motivate someone who does not want to be motivated. Only the person himself can decide to be motivated. This being said, it is important to determine the reason behind any lack of motivation in order to see if there is anything you may offer to help.

Lack of motivation *can* look like laziness. People with Asperger Syndrome often get accused of being lazy, but this is usually not the reason behind issues with motivation. Here are a few things to investigate further if you observe a lack in motivation from your Asperger friend:

- poor self-confidence and self-esteem
- depression
- lack of interest in the assignment/boredom
- fear of success or fear of failure; fear of having greater expectations being placed on her.

Once you have determined the underlying cause of the lack of motivation, you can begin to build a strategy to address it.

Strategies

- Set candidates up for success. Choose jobs and assignments that they can do well. A positive experience goes a long way to building self-esteem. People who have successful experiences are more likely to be motivated to keep working at something.

- Vary the assignments to avoid boredom. People with Asperger Syndrome are frequently only motivated to do things they are interested in. If they are bored, they tend to stop working. Keep things interesting and this will help to motivate them.

- Give honest and positive feedback. Remember that candidates might be very sensitive to criticism. Reinforce what they are doing well and guide them to improve in the other areas. If they feel you are pleased with their performance, they are more likely to be motivated.

Helpful tools from the Employment Toolbox (Chapter 8) to build strategies for this challenge are: Role play, third-party praise, verbal reflection

---

10.6.3 Independence

Candidates need to be independent in a job before an employer will be confident in keeping them on. This may take time to achieve but, eventually, it needs to happen in order for employees to be considered competitive.

Strategies

After going through an assignment together, stay with the employee until she is clear about the steps. Slowly remove yourself by spending time away from the employee. Depending upon the candidate, this could happen between five and thirty minutes. Come back to check on the candidate and ensure that she is working and doing the job properly. You want to increase the span of time to two hours of independent work.

As additional strategies, you will want to encourage candidates to ask questions when they have difficulty. If they sit idle, waiting for someone to notice that they are not working, this will impede their productivity and progress. They need to be confident that they can ask for help.

Helpful tools from the Employment Toolbox (Chapter 8) to build strategies for this challenge are: Rule tool, mirroring, formulas, third-party praise, verbal reflection

---

10.6.4 Punctuality

Punctuality can be a problem for some people with Asperger Syndrome, and it will definitely be a problem for an employer. An employer will only put up with so much tardiness before getting annoyed, and when an employer gets annoyed, the placement can be at risk.

Strategies

- Set clear schedules with your Asperger friend. Allow for travel time, traffic, setting up once at work, and so on.

- Establish why the employee is coming to work late and problem-solve ways to correct this. This could mean setting the alarm earlier, leaving home sooner, or going to bed earlier, etc.

- Create a morning checklist together as a tool to help the candidate adhere to the schedule or routine.

- Be clear about expectations regarding punctuality and the consequences if they are not met. Be consistent in following through on the consequences. If you are clear, fair, and consistent, the candidate can turn this challenge around.

> Helpful tools from the Employment Toolbox (Chapter 8) to build strategies for this challenge are: Rule tool, mirroring, formulas, third-party praise

Summary

- Consider what challenges are most problematic, what employers will value most and what your Asperger friend is capable of altering as a guide to prioritizing challenges.

- Use the Strategy Guide to help you develop strategies but always individualize the strategies to meet the learning style and personality of the candidate.

- Always combine strategies with the Four Pillar Teaching Technique (Chapter 7).

- Use the Employment Toolbox to help you vary and customize strategies (Chapter 8).

Part 3
The dream

11 The Career Direction Formula

Everyone has the capacity to make a contribution when they are brought up knowing they can.

What would your life be without electricity, the telephone, the computer, or eyeglasses? Many inventions were inspired by fascinations. Fascinations have led to many wonderful contributions to our society like the ones just mentioned. It is possible to convert an obsession or fascination into a career if you take the time to explore its potential.

People with Asperger Syndrome have the ingredients to make a contribution to their communities. The fact that many people with Asperger Syndrome have unusual interests, fascinations, obsessions, and even fixations, may be the very thing that will assist them in finding their niche in the workplace. Although not all fascinations or fixations will hold the key to a career, it is surprising how often they point one in the right direction. It is important that you and your Asperger friend do not discount an obsession or fascination before fully exploring its potential in the market. The story of Tony demonstrates this point very well.

Tony loved to fish. In fact, Tony was an expert fisherman and, not surprisingly because of his Asperger Syndrome, he was driven to know everything there was to know about fish. At the age of seventeen, Tony began tying his own flies to catch fish. At first, he copied the fly designs that he saw in the local fishing stores. After some time, he decided that with his extensive knowledge of local fish he could design better, more effective flies than those available in the local tackle shops. He began experimenting and came up with his own fly designs that would lure local trout. He would go down to the stream with his special flies and out-catch the local fishermen. This of course drew some attention and the fishermen were curious. They wanted to know his secret. Tony would whip out his selection of home-tied flies to show the fishermen. Right there on the stream, he would make a sale.

Before long, Tony had built quite a reputation for himself in the local industry. He was asked to put on workshops to help others learn how to tie their own flies, he got coverage in trade magazines and the local tackle shops began carrying his fly designs. Last season Tony made $12,000 tying flies. This did not include what he made through his workshops, and his business was just starting out. Who would have thought that an interest in fishing would make Tony a living? Even though he was at first skeptical that he could make an income this way, Tony had taken what he loved and turned it into money. Today, when Tony is not tying flies, he is fishing.

Not every person with Asperger Syndrome will have a marketable interest, fascination, or obsession. Some may not even have a unique or special interest or they may lack the skill necessary to develop an interest or fascination into a career. This does not mean that they cannot still be successful in the workplace. Determining career direction for people with Asperger Syndrome requires strategy, imagination, and research. It is also possible to determine what someone's potential will be if he were to obtain further skills training before entering the job market.

I have developed a formula that encompasses all of the steps necessary to determine realistic, viable job matches for your Asperger friend. If you follow this formula, you will come up with a targeted list of jobs that the candidate will be good at and enjoy. You will also determine in what specific areas the candidate will require work accommodation for a particular job. This will be valuable to you later when you are conducting the job search. Potential employers need to know up front what is involved when they are considering hiring an employee with Asperger Syndrome. You too need to be prepared with the appropriate strategies and supports to offer the employer.

> Taking the time to determine the best job matches for the candidate with Asperger Syndrome is crucial to long-term, meaningful employment.

11.1 Three-step formula to career direction

Making a good job match for a person with Asperger Syndrome can be easy when you follow this three-step Career Direction Formula. The formula will rely on the information you gathered in the Big Picture Assessment in Chapter 9. If you have not done the Big Picture Assessment, you may jeopardize the accuracy of the career direction process. It is important that you do not guess at the skills the candidate has, as this can have a damaging impact on his success. After all, this is about a person's future and is not something to play with or base on a hunch. If you are a parent and believe that you know your child well enough, you may decide to continue with the Career Direction Formula without conducting the Big Picture Assessment (Chapter 9). One word of caution, however: The observations from the Big Picture Assessment, which have been made in a competitive work environment, usually differ from those observed at home. If you choose to rely on information you have gathered as a parent and not on observations seen through the eyes of an employer as the Big Picture Assessment offers, you may find the results of the Career Direction Formula inaccurate.

Although the Career Direction Formula cannot guarantee a perfect match 100 per cent of the time, it will dramatically increase the chances of making a viable and realistic job fit. Having a formula for career or job matching systematically generates ideas and then eliminates those that are not feasible, leaving you with a list of viable jobs that, based upon the information you have gathered, your Asperger friend or relative will be good at and enjoy.

Finding work that works for people with Asperger Syndrome is a process that requires considerable effort. Although it may be tempting, short cuts do not reap the same successful end results. Take the time accurately to assess and build a foundation of skill. This will set the candidate up for success in the workplace. By doing this, you will be far more pleased with the outcome and your Asperger friend will benefit immensely because the learning will be continuous and one of growth.

The three steps involved in the Career Direction Formula are:

- examining special interests, fixations, and fascinations
- putting fascinations to work
- the job viability checklist.

11.2 Step 1: Examining special interests, fixations, and fascinations

Dr. Temple Grandin is a designer of livestock-handling facilities and an associate professor of animal science at Colorado State University. She has designed facilities for livestock around the world. Almost half of the cattle in North America are handled in the center track restrainer system that she designed for meat plants. Her writings on the principles of grazing animal behavior have helped to reduce stress on livestock. She also developed an objective scoring system for assessing the handling of cattle and pigs at meat plants. Many large corporations are using her scoring system to improve animal welfare.

Dr. Grandin has high-functioning autism and, at the age of five, she would daydream of a mechanical device that would apply comforting pressure. When she was eighteen, she built the device and called it the squeezing machine. This machine applied gentle pressure on large parts of her body, relaxing her and alleviating anxiety. Her high school science teacher used her fixation on cattle chutes to motivate her to study psychology and science and encouraged her to research why the machine had a relaxing effect. As it turned out, the machine also had a relaxing effect on livestock. Dr. Grandin used her fixation on cattle chutes to create a career.

> The world is a better place due to Dr. Grandin's unique contribution. Not to mention that being a cow is much more pleasant!

Special interests, fascinations, and fixations are often part of Asperger Syndrome. They need to be recognized for their potential and encouraged and broadened. They may lead indirectly or even directly to a career if they are used to motivate the candidate to expand his knowledge base and to grow.

11.2.1 When fixations are too much

There will be cases where a fixation, fascination, or obsession is extreme and will actually interfere with work. This is worth noting because it will be counter-productive for everyone involved when this is the situation. This point is demonstrated by Nancy, a young lady who was obsessed with shoes. Naturally, you might think that was a good thing and that working in a shoe store might be one obvious job match. Wrong! Nancy was so obsessed with shoes that she would stare at them, ask questions about them and want to try them on, *all* the time. She would ask strangers where they bought their shoes and what size the shoes were. Of course there were more challenges here to address than the obsession with shoes, but you get the point. Nancy was so distracted by her obsession that there was no way a job coach would consider placing her within ten miles of a shoe store. In these situations, you need to exercise your judgment. If you can come up with something related to the obsession that will not impede work performance, then go for it. You want the person to be motivated and interested, but they must be able to perform the job.

The first step in the Career Direction Formula is to examine interests, fixations, and fascinations. You do this by working with the candidate to create a detailed list of every interest, fixation, fascination, and/or obsession he has. Don't leave anything out. In this process everything counts because you never know what it might lead to. Include small things and big things; include ridiculous and outrageous things. Get everything down on the list that you can come up with. You will have an opportunity to edit your list later in the process.

11.2.2 Sample interest list

Jeremy is a twenty-four-year-old man with Asperger Syndrome. His functioning level is moderate on the Asperger spectrum. He has a grade twelve high school diploma and he completed eight months of college in travel and tourism but dropped out because he found the coursework too challenging. He has provided a list of his interests (Figure 11.1).

Trains	Airports	Maps	Movies
Trucks	Airplanes	Geography	Computer games
Subways	Cars	Travel	Video games
Streetcars	Motorcycles	Buses	Sitcoms

Figure 11.1 Interest list

Your Asperger friend's list may be short or it may be very long. Try to go into as much detail as you can. For example, if the candidate is interested in transportation, as in the sample above, list all the modes of transportation that are of interest.

11.2.3 What if there are no apparent interests, fascinations, or fixations?

Some people with Asperger Syndrome do not have any apparent interests, fascinations, or fixations. If this is the case, then all you can do is come up with a list of jobs that seem reasonable based upon the person's strengths in the Big Picture Assessment (Chapter 9). The beauty of having interests, fascinations, and fixations to work with is that these are likely to be motivating for the candidate. When there are no apparent interests, you are left with only your and your candidate's observations; however, the formula can still work.

11.3 Step 2: Putting fascinations to work

The second step in the Career Direction Formula is to extrapolate ideas from the interest list that you have just created. The idea behind extrapolating from the interest list is to help you and your friend or relative find work that will be within his interest range and to expand the options. For example, if the person is obsessed with baseball, it may not be viable to become a baseball player but working in a stadium might be appropriate. Later in the process you will determine whether the candidate has the skills or potential to do the job. For now the focus is on expanding choice.

You begin the process of extrapolation through an exercise that I call "Brain stretching," which is the term I use to describe brainstorming. It is a *stretching* rather than *storming* process because you are actually stretching your imagination and exercising your creativity. Take each item on the list of interests you both created above and begin listing every job that is remotely

Trains	Airports	Maps	Movies
Public transit: subway driver bus driver information attendant ticket seller	*Travel agency:* travel agent office support on-line ticket agent	*Place where they make globes:* assembly worker machine operator	Ticket seller
Truck driver (delivers shipments to trains)	Ticket seller	Printer	Guy who counts the money
Conductor	Flight attendant	City planner	Concession stand attendant
Engineer	Air traffic controller	Tour guide	Usher
Porter	Ground traffic controller	Public transit (list under trains)	*Video store:* manager shelf stocker cashier shipper/receiver
Luggage handler	Security officer	Graphic designer	Cleaner
Lost and found attendant	Shuttle driver		Movie critic for local newspaper
Ticket booth operator	Information booth attendant		
Information booth attendant	Luggage		
Maintenance person	Cleaner		
Cleaner	Maintenance person		
Train terminal: cleaner security officer	Courier		

Figure 11.2 Brain stretching exercise

related to the fascination, fixation or special interest (see Figure 11.2). Go wild and give yourselves permission to write down anything. Nothing is too crazy or ridiculous. You may find that you go off on tangents. This is fine. For example, in brain stretching the word "trains," one might think of "public transit," which might inspire a whole list of jobs. Remember the abilities of your Asperger friend: If he is highly skilled or qualified, you should be brain stretching jobs at the appropriate level, although it is recommended that you do not limit yourselves to only those jobs.

Inviting other people to get involved in brain stretching helps to generate ideas. Have fun with it! I have had many team meetings at the office where I get my staff involved in brain stretching. It makes for a fun time and the results are always more varied and plentiful. You may find that there are repeated jobs or ideas in different lists. This overlap is good because it means that themes are forming. Keep at it. Brain stretch every item on your interest list. If you don't know the name of a job, make it up. For example "guy who hands out flyers" or "person who builds web sites." The idea is to expand the possibilities beyond the obvious. Later in the process, you will fine-tune the list.

Once you have brain stretched every item on your interest list (as in Figure 11.2), you want to eliminate any job that would realistically be out of reach for the candidate. For example, if the candidate has not completed high school and is thirty years old, he is unlikely to become an astronaut, regardless of how great the desire to be one.

Returning to the example case of Jeremy, he has a grade twelve education and has no interest in going back to college. Therefore, for him we would eliminate the jobs that require considerable education but keep jobs on the list that might have on-the-job training or apprenticeships because Jeremy has expressed an interest in this type of learning (see Figure 11.3).

11.3.1 Check-in

Now check in again with your Asperger friend. Is there anything on the list that he finds unappealing or is opposed to? If there is, this is a good time to take it off the list. Keep the original list however, in case you want to re-visit it at a later date.

In Jeremy's example, he is not at all interested in being a cleaner nor is he interested in working in a factory. He does not have his driver's license but the idea of being a bus, train, or subway driver appeals to him. He says that he is not interested in fixing things and would like the maintenance jobs

Trains	Airports	Maps	Movies
Public transit: subway driver bus driver information attendant ticket seller	*Travel agency:* ~~travel agent~~ office support ~~on-line ticket agent~~	*Place where they make globes:* ~~assembly worker~~ ~~machine operator~~	Ticket seller
~~Truck driver~~ (delivers shipments to trains)	~~Ticket seller~~	Printer	Guy who counts the money
~~Conductor~~	~~Flight attendant~~	~~City planner~~	~~Concession stand attendant~~
~~Engineer~~	~~Air traffic controller~~	Tour guide	Usher
~~Porter~~	~~Ground traffic controller~~	Public transit (list under trains)	*Video store:* ~~manager~~ shelf stocker cashier shipper/receiver
~~Luggage handler~~	Security officer	~~Graphic designer~~	~~Cleaner~~
Lost and found attendant	Shuttle driver		~~Movie critic for local newspaper~~
~~Ticket booth operator~~	~~Information booth attendant~~		
~~Information booth attendant~~	~~Luggage handler~~		
~~Maintenance person~~	~~Cleaner~~		
~~Cleaner~~	~~Maintenance person~~		
Train terminal: ~~cleaner~~ security officer	~~Courier~~		

Figure 11.3 Job elimination

removed. Jeremy also explains that he does not want to work with food or money, so any jobs that are related to this are removed. When Jeremy took travel and tourism at college, he decided that he didn't want to work in that industry so he wants the travel agency jobs removed as well.

It is vital that the candidate's wishes are honored. It is the individual's life and choice although it is okay to offer your advice and opinion. Understand that this may or may not alter the candidate's wishes, however.

11.3.2 Further reduction

There is one more area that you want to explore that may reduce the jobs on your list. Environmental conditions will have an impact on whether or not a job will be suitable for the candidate. Refer to the "environment" category in the Big Picture Assessment from Chapter 9. This will tell you exactly what your candidate can tolerate. Adjust your list accordingly.

In Jeremy's case, he can't tolerate large crowds although he likes to talk to people. He does not mind working outside every once in a while but does not want an "outdoor" job. Jeremy can handle moderate noise and has no apparent phobias or fears. Jeremy does not like to lift heavy things but is capable of doing it if absolutely necessary. He wants to avoid jobs that involve a lot of heavy lifting. Therefore it is time to eliminate the jobs that take place predominately outdoors and the ones that involve being around large crowds of people and have on-going heavy lifting.

After removing the jobs that were either of no interest or did not meet environmental conditions, this is what Jeremy's list looks like.

- Security officer at a train/bus station or airport.
- Information booth attendant/ticket seller at a train/bus station or airport.
- Driver, truck/bus/shuttle/train/subway.
- Printer.
- Shelf stocker/shipper/receiver at a video store.
- Usher/cashier/ticket sellet at movie theatre.

11.3.3 Research

There is one final, yet extremely important component of Step 2. There may be some jobs on your list that you are either unfamiliar with or need to learn more about. You and your Asperger friend need to educate yourselves. One of the most convenient and effective ways to do this is to look up job descriptions on the Internet. If this does not work or you don't have Internet access, you can usually find job information in trade magazines, the library, or by calling a company and asking the operations manager or someone in human resources to give you an overview of what is involved in a particular job. As you gather more information, you may find that some of the jobs on the list become less interesting to your friend or relative with Asperger Syndrome. In this case, you can take them off the list. You only want jobs on the list that are of interest to him. Whether or not they are viable choices will be determined in the third and final step of the Career Direction Formula.

11.4 Step 3: The job viability chart

The final step in the Career Direction Formula is the job viability chart (see Figures 11.4 and 11.5). This chart will determine if your Asperger friend has the skills necessary to be competitive in a particular job. By completing this chart, you will easily determine:

- job or career choices that are immediately viable

- the support areas required to be fully competitive

- the choices that will require further skills training prior to seeking the job

- the choices that are not viable.

Skill level is assessed on a scale from 1 to 4 as follows:

      1 = None (requires or has no skill)

      2 = Minimal (requires or has minimal skill)

      3 = Moderate (requires or has moderate skill)

      4 = Strong (requires or has a strong skill base)

      T = Further testing required**

** *There will always be some skills that you will need to test further or were not able to observe in your assessment. In this situation, make note of them with the letter "T."*

Skills list	Job #1 Security officer	Candidate	With training and support
	Minimum requirements	Jeremy's current skill	With support, Jeremy is at or can get to:
Education	2	3	3
Special training	3	T	3
Experience	2	1	2
Knowledge	2	1	2
Computer skills	2	3	3
Safety Awareness	4	2	4
Speed	3	3	3
Accuracy	4	4	4
Gross motor	4	4	4
Fine motor	3	3	3
Social interaction	3	3	3
Written communication	3	3	3
Oral communication	3	3	3
Organizational skills	3	4	4
Time management	4	2	2.5
Multi-tasking	2	2	2
Judgment	3	2	3
Decision making	3	2	3
Initiative	3	2	3
Focus	3	3	3
Independence	4	4	4
Flexibility	3	3	3
Analytical skills	3	4	4
Interaction with people	3	3	3
Total:	72	64	74.5
Match	YES		

Skill level

1 = None   2 = Minimal   3 = Moderate   4 = Strong   T = Further testing required

Figure 11.4 Job viability chart 1

Skills list	Job #2 *Truck driver*	Candidate	With training and support
	Minimum requirements	*Jeremy's current skill*	*With support, Jeremy is at or can get to:*
Education	3	3	3
Special training	4	T	T
Experience	3	1	2
Knowledge	3	T	T
Computer skills	1	3	3
Safety Awareness	4	2	4
Speed	3	3	3
Accuracy	4	4	4
Gross motor	4	4	4
Fine motor	3	3	3
Social interaction	2	3	3
Written communication	3	3	3
Oral communication	3	3	3
Organizational skills	3	4	4
Time management	4	2	3.5
Multi-tasking	4	2	3
Judgment	4	2	3
Decision making	4	2	3.5
Initiative	3	2	3
Focus	4	3	4
Independence	4	4	4
Flexibility	3	3	3
Analytical skills	2	4	4
Interaction with people	2	3	3
Total:	77	63	73
Match	**With Training and Support**		

Skill level

1 = None   2 = Minimal   3 = Moderate   4 = Strong   T = Further testing required

Figure 11.5 Job viability chart 2

To use the chart, write one job choice under "job" at the top of the table. Using the skills list to the left of the job column, rate the skill level required for a person to be competitive in this job. If you have not already done so, you may have to do some research to educate yourself about the requirements of the job. For example, a bookkeeper is required to have strong computer skills while a file clerk is required only to have moderate computer skills. When you are unsure of the skill level, either conduct further research or, if you are comfortable, use your best judgment. You can often find job descriptions on the Internet. These are very helpful when rating the skills required for any particular job.

At the top of the table under "candidate," write in the name of your Asperger friend or relative. Again, using the skills list at the far left of the table, rate the candidate's current skill level. Because you have already conducted the Big Picture Assessment in Chapter 9, you will have gathered this information.

At the top of the table under "with training and support," write in the name of your Asperger friend again. You will now rate your Asperger friend's skill level as to what you predict he could *realistically* attain if given appropriate support, such as job coaching or on-the-job training. Support may take place over several days or up to several months depending upon the requirements of the job, the employer and the needs of the candidate. Although you are using your judgment to rate what skills your Asperger friend will achieve with support, you are basing your judgment on what you assessed during the Big Picture Assessment. The experience from the assessment puts you in a position to be able to determine how much progress your Asperger friend will be able to make in a given category of skill.

Finally, total each column and put the number at the bottom. The total needs to be within 10 points of the job column for it to be considered a viable job match. For example, in Figure 11.4 the total of the first candidate column is 64. The total of the security officer job column is 72. The candidate column total is less than 10 points below the job column total, so this means that the job is a viable match.

Based on this formula, Jeremy's skills are not within 10 points of the truck driver job, so this is not a viable match; however, with training and support, he scores within 10 points. This means that if Jeremy wants to pursue this option and is willing to get the training, it is likely to be a viable job match for him.

11.5 Getting the final approval

Once you have created your list of viable job matches, it is time to consult your Asperger friend, if he has not already been actively involved in the process. Go over the list together and talk about each job, where it will take place, what will be involved (the job descriptions are useful here) and why you have determined that the job is a viable/good match. Your Asperger friend has the last say. If a job is not acceptable, then take it off the list. You can offer your advice and opinion but ultimately it is his choice. When you feel strongly that a job should be on the list, respect the decision of the candidate and simply set the job aside. You can always re-visit job lists at a later time if necessary.

11.5.1 The shortlist

Finally, you want to prioritize the list. Work with the candidate to decide in what order to put the jobs. In other words, which job is most desirable and which job is least desirable to the candidate. You can advise your Asperger friend regarding what jobs might have the best potential for success based upon your local employment market research; however, ultimately the choice is the candidate's. If you have a lot of jobs on your list, pick the top three to five choices. More than five will broaden your search too much. You want to focus your job search on the top job and move down the list when it becomes apparent that for one reason or another, the job search is not showing results.

11.6 Occupations suitable for people with Asperger Syndrome

People with Asperger Syndrome are better suited to some types of jobs than others simply because of the nature of the disorder. Jobs that involve a lot of judgment, fast decision-making, multi-tasking, strong interpersonal and social skills and pressure do not bode well for people with Asperger Syndrome. Unfortunately, this will eliminate a number of occupations. Management positions, for example, are very challenging for people with Asperger Syndrome because they require people skills, decision-making and judgment skills and usually have a higher level of pressure. As well, most managers have to be very good multi-taskers. Human resource positions are generally not suitable for people with Asperger Syndrome nor are many health occupations, unless they are behind-the-scenes technician jobs. Some people with Asperger Syndrome relate extremely well to children and are also excellent teachers. As a general rule, however, teaching jobs are not the best for people with Asperger Syndrome because of the high demand for social interaction, judgment, organization, and multi-tasking. It might be a more appropriate alternative for these individuals to select a career in instructional design, developing curricula, and courses.

Occupations that people with Asperger Syndrome tend to excel in are ones that draw upon their strengths. Jobs that require a logical or analytical approach, such as accounting or bookkeeping, engineering, statistics, and research, are good examples. Industries that value employees who are detail-oriented and technical are also excellent – computer programming, software design, and testing. Jobs that have a highly repetitive or structured component can be suitable for some people with Asperger Syndrome. These are jobs such as shipping and receiving, packaging, assembly line, mailroom, and file clerks. There are some people with Asperger Syndrome who are very creative and do well in occupations such as graphic and web design, music, architecture, and computer animation.

Figure 11.6 is a sample list of occupations that are suitable for people with Asperger Syndrome and may help you to brain stretch. Of course, what jobs are appropriate for a candidate with Asperger Syndrome will depend upon his level of skill, education, and interests and, of course, these must be balanced with personal challenges and environmental preferences. The labor market is always changing. It is heavily influenced by the economy, inflation, demographics (the study of the human population for purposes of identifying consumer markets), and consumer supply and demand. Factors influencing the labor market will be discussed in greater detail in Chapter 13. For now, I have marked the occupations that are likely to show significant growth over the next decade.

Accountant

Actuary

Audiologist* – research

Automotive service technician and mechanic*

Baggage handler

Cartoonist

Computer and information scientist, research**

Computer animator

Computer software engineer/applications/systems software*

Computer support specialist*

Computer systems analyst*

Copy editor

Data entry operator*

Database administrator*

Desktop publisher

Dog groomer or assistant

Dog trainer

Drafting**

Economist

Electrician*

Engineer**

Gaming dealer*

Graphic designer

Health information technician*

Information clerk*

Insurance underwriter

Inventory clerk

Janitor/cleaner*

Journalist

Laboratory technician*

Landscaping/grounds keeping worker*

Library technician

Machinist*

Maintenance and repair worker, general*

Maintenance, building or factory

Mapping drafter

Market research analyst*

Mechanic

Mechanical designer*

Medical records technician*

Medical scientist*

Musician

Office clerk, general*

Packer and packager – by hand*

Painter (house)

Pharmacist*

Photographer or assistant

Piano tuner

Researcher

Security guard

Shelf stocker

Statistician

Taxi driver*

Technical support specialist**

Technical writer

Technician and technologist**

Telecommunications line installer and repairer*

Tool and die maker*

Truck driver*

Veterinary assistant and laboratory animal caretaker*

Veterinary technician*

Web site designer

Figure 11.6 Occupations list

* Occupations that expect above average growth through 2010
** Occupations that cover a wide variety of specializations suitable to people with Asperger Syndrome

YOUR JOB/CAREER TARGET LIST

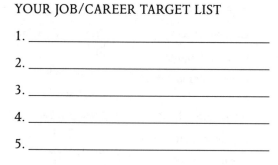

1. _____

2. _____

3. _____

4. _____

5. _____

Summary

- Don't cut corners. Do your homework before doing the Career Direction Formula.

- Every interest, fixation and fascination holds the potential for a marketable skill and career direction. Regardless of how obscure or unusual the fascination, do not discount it. It may turn into something that no one else would have thought of.

- Whenever possible, put fascinations to work.

- Use the Internet as a research tool to find job descriptions.

- Be realistic in your rating and evaluations, look at the candidate through the eyes of the employer.

- The candidate always has the final say in the decision of career direction.

12 Interviews, cover letters, and resumés

How many interviews does it take to get a job? As many as it takes!

There is no set formula for how many interviews it takes to get a job. Some people get the job on the first interview while for others it may take twenty interviews or more. Unfortunately, you cannot control the outcome of an interview. Every employer has the right to choose who he feels will be the best person for the job. The only thing you can do is to help the candidate to be as prepared as possible, encourage her to learn from experiences and provide support through the interview process.

Preparing someone with Asperger Syndrome for an interview takes a concentrated effort. You can't just throw out a few sample questions and wish her luck. To be effective with the candidate, you need to adopt a systematic approach to virtually everything you teach. This chapter will provide you with a five-step process to help the candidate prepare for an interview.

How you sell a candidate on paper is almost as important as how the candidate sells himself in the interview. Many people with Asperger Syndrome have had erratic work histories or limited work experience, which creates challenges when writing a resumé. This chapter will address the common issues that arise when formulating an effective resumé and cover letter.

12.1 Interview preparation

Part of becoming work-ready is preparing for an interview. This is not a skill that comes naturally to many people with Asperger Syndrome. To help your friend or relative, you need to understand the typical challenges faced in an interview and how to help the individual overcome these challenges. Once you have an understanding of the challenges the candidate might face, you can follow my five-step process to help the candidate have a successful interview.

There are eight main challenges that people with Asperger Syndrome face in an interview:

- personal presentation
- greetings
- anxiety
- answering questions
- selling themselves
- attitude
- body language
- ending the interview.

12.1.1 Personal presentation

First impressions count. It is said that people form a judgment within the first thirty seconds of meeting a person. That is why personal presentation is so important. For the candidates with Asperger Syndrome, it could be even more important because they have to overcome people's misconceptions and concerns about their disability. Presenting professionally is setting oneself up for success. If a person shows up tattered and disheveled, there is a risk of a bad first impression even before the interview process has begun.

Many candidates with Asperger Syndrome have needed support around how to present themselves in an interview. The following presentation guidelines will help you and them ensure that they show up for the interview dressed appropriately and looking good. I encourage you to go over this with your friend or relative.

12.1.1.1 PRESENTATION GUIDELINES

Choosing what to wear

Before practicing for an interview, work with the candidate to decide what is appropriate to wear to the interview. Here are some pointers:

Men – business casual:

- Dress pants.

- Dress shirt with a collar or a nice sweater if it's cold outside.

- The belt must be the same color as the shoes, e.g. brown shoes + brown belt, black shoes + black belt.

- Always wear dark color socks.

- Dress shoes – no running shoes or boots.

- Wear a regular outdoor jacket but make sure that it is in good condition and clean.

Men – business formal:

- Dark blue or black suit.

- Nice clean tie that is pressed and in tame colors – not too flashy.

- The belt must be the same color as the shoes, e.g., brown shoes + brown belt, black shoes + black belt.

- Always wear dark color socks, black or navy are best.

- Dress shoes – no running shoes or boots.

- Wear a dress coat or trench coat in good condition.

Women – business casual and formal:

- Dress pants or skirt (or suit if formal).

- Nice top.

- The belt must be the same color as the shoes, e.g., brown shoes + brown belt, black shoes + black belt.

- Match socks with pants, or wear natural nylons with a skirt.

- Dress shoes – no running shoes or boots.

- A regular outdoor jacket that is in good condition and clean. For a formal interview, a dress coat or trench coat is most appropriate.

Hygiene:

- Make sure that hair is clean and neat.

- Ensure teeth are brushed and free of any debris.

- Fingernails should be trimmed and clean.

- Breath should be fresh – brushing teeth usually does this but it's also a good idea to gargle with mouthwash.

- Shoes should be clean.

- Clothes should be pressed or ironed – no wrinkles.

- Clothes should be clean – no stains or odors.

12.1.2 Greetings

Greetings can be a challenge for some people with Asperger Syndrome because they don't know what to say and may feel awkward. It can make them feel anxious or nervous because they don't know what is expected of them. If they have never been taught how to greet someone in a professional manner, then you can't expect them to know it.

There are four steps to a professional greeting, outlined below, with exercises to help the candidate improve their greetings:

- eye contact

- the handshake

- what you say

- putting the greeting together.

12.1.2.1 EYE CONTACT

Eye contact is important in Western culture because it implies to an interviewer that a person is honest, trustworthy, and confident. Many people with Asperger Syndrome have difficulty making and/or maintaining eye contact. Candidates often say that it feels too personal or uncomfortable for them. Nonetheless, eye contact is something that an interviewer will look for and expect.

If a candidate is uncomfortable with eye contact, you first need to clearly explain why eye contact is important to an interviewer. The messages conveyed by eye contact, or the lack of eye contact, will affect the impression with which the interviewer is left.

One way to get around the poor eye contact dilemma is to have the candidate look at the interviewer's forehead. That may sound a little strange but if you have someone look at your forehead, you will notice that you can't really tell that she is not looking into your eyes. This is perfect for the person with Asperger Syndrome who finds this a challenge. Practice is needed, however, because it will still require an effort to remember to look at a forehead.

12.1.2.2 THE HANDSHAKE

The handshake has a long history. In the 16th and 17th centuries and the beginning of the 18th century, the handshake was used to show that a hand was free of a weapon and to seal the peace between two parties or as a contract for closing business deals. Even husbands and wives would shake hands after a domestic quarrel! It is believed that the Quakers made the handshake popular. They opted for the handshake over more grandiose gestures such as bowing, hand-kissing, and hat-tipping.

Today, the handshake is commonplace in both business and social greetings. Studies have shown that a handshake plays a role in how a person is perceived. For a handshake to be most effective, it should be firm, confident, and friendly. About 90 per cent of my clients do not know how to shake hands properly or with confidence.

To teach someone with Asperger Syndrome how to make a confident, firm handshake, you must first explain why a handshake is required:

> Your handshake is an important part of making a first impression to the interviewer. If your handshake is too soft, they will think you are not confident and may have trouble doing the job. If it is too hard, you will hurt the interviewer.

Then you need to guide the candidate step by step in how to shake hands properly:

- In most of the developed world, the handshake is done with the right hand.

- The skin between your thumb and first finger must touch the same place on the hand you are shaking.

- Clasp your fingers around the other hand firmly, yet gently.

- Shake the hand up and down three times. If you have trouble with this, let the other person do the shaking – that's okay, too.

Next, you need to help the candidate develop the appropriate words to say when greeting. Those include an introduction as to who you are and, an acknowledgement of who you are greeting. In most interview situations, a greeting is done in the standing position.

Depending on how comfortable the candidate is, I will script the greeting. If she is very comfortable, I will make the greeting a bit more involved. For example:

- Simple greeting: "Hello, nice to meet you."

- Basic greeting: "Hello, my name is Jason. Nice to meet you."

- Involved greeting: "Hello, you must be Miss Austin. My name is Jason, nice to meet you."

Finally, practice the entire process with the candidate several times to ensure that there is a good comfort level in putting all the elements of the greeting together:

1. Make eye contact with the interviewer when you first meet.

2. Stand up for the greeting.

3. Hold the eye contact until the end of the entire greeting.

4. Outstretch your hand to shake the hand of the interviewer.

5. When you are shaking hands, say "Hello, nice to meet you."

12.1.3 Anxiety

During an interview, it is natural for anyone to be nervous or anxious. The anxiety level of the candidate might be very high. This is okay because the interviewer will expect a certain amount of nerves. However, you will still want to address the issue of anxiety and nervousness with the candidate before the interview and offer some strategies to help your Asperger friend remain calm. For example:

- If the candidate displays really nervous or anxious behavior, it is a good idea to persuade her to tell the interviewer about the nervousness. This will bring out the compassion and understanding of the interviewer, as most people can relate to the situation.

- Teach the candidate to breathe properly. That means deep breaths in through the nose, hold for three seconds and then exhale through the mouth. Breathing gets oxygen to the brain, which helps a person to relax and get thoughts clearer.

- If the candidate does not understand a question or doesn't hear all of it, teach her to ask the interviewer to repeat the question or to ask it differently.

12.1.4 Answering questions

Some candidates with Asperger Syndrome interview exceptionally well. They answer questions and are charming and charismatic. But this is not the rule. Frequently, people with Asperger Syndrome struggle to scrape by in an interview. Preparation and practice are needed.

The premise of an interview is for the interviewer to ask questions and the interviewee to answer them in a way that demonstrates ability and potential. If the interviewee cannot answer the questions, it makes it difficult for the interviewer to learn what the candidate knows, or is capable of doing.

People with Asperger Syndrome generally have difficulty answering questions in an interview. They can get confused easily or don't understand the question. If the questions are compound – that is, a series of questions – it is even more difficult for the person with Asperger Syndrome to answer. In this case, the candidate doesn't know which question to answer first or can't remember what any of the questions were in the first place. Some interview questions may not make any sense to a person with Asperger Syndrome because they are abstract or poorly worded. That makes it very challenging for the candidate to respond.

There are basically five types of questions that an interviewer most commonly asks in an interview: Questions about credentials, experience and opinions, silly questions and behavior questions. Knowing the types of questions that may be posed will help the candidate prepare to answer them.

12.1.4.1 CREDENTIAL QUESTIONS

"What were your grades in school?" and "How long were you at Company ABC?" The purpose of these questions is to measure the background of the candidate.

12.1.4.2 EXPERIENCE QUESTIONS

"What were your responsibilities in that position?" and "What did you learn in that course?" These questions aim to get the candidate to expand beyond their resumé to demonstrate whether her experience is relevant.

12.1.4.3 OPINION QUESTIONS

"What are your strengths and weaknesses?" and "What would you do in this situation?" Such questions explore how the candidate would respond in different situations.

12.1.4.4 SILLY QUESTIONS

"What is your favorite color and why?" and "How many people can fit into a telephone booth?" These kinds of "silly" questions try to get the candidate past pre-programmed answers to show how she thinks spontaneously. Such questions make no sense to people with Asperger Syndrome, they find them frustrating and purposeless.

12.1.4.5 BEHAVIORAL QUESTIONS

"Can you give me a specific example of how you dealt with conflict?" or "What were the steps you followed to accomplish that job?" Perhaps the most challenging type of question for people with Asperger Syndrome, this aims to anticipate future responses based upon past behaviors.

Most interviewers rely on the first four types of questions during an interview. However, the higher the level of job, the more complex the interview questions are likely to be. Candidates interviewing for professional positions, for example, will likely encounter some behavioral questions, as this type of interviewing is gaining greater acceptance and is the most reliable indicator for determining future results.

Below are some sample questions frequently asked during interviews. Practice them with your Asperger friend or relative. To get to know the candidate, the interviewer may first pose some general questions, such as:

- If you could have your choice of any job, what would it be and why?

- What are some of your hobbies?

- What are some of your weaknesses?

- Tell me about the best and worst jobs you've ever had.

- How do you take constructive criticism?

The interviewer will also want to learn about the candidate's experience and reasons for seeking a new position and may ask the following questions:

- How long have you been out of work?

- What have you been doing since you left your last job?

- What did you like most and least about your last job?

- At your last job, how much of the work did you perform independently?

- At your last job, how much was performed by a team?

- Do you prefer working independently or as part of a team?

- What were some of the problems you encountered in your past jobs?

- How did you solve the problems?

To learn about plans for the future and the candidate's motivation for applying for the job, the interviewer may ask the following questions:

- Why do you want to work here?

- If you feel you have any weaknesses with regard to this job, what would they be?

- How do you feel about evening work? Weekend work? Shift work?

Sometimes the interviewer will ask open-ended or vague questions. If unexpected, these may be difficult for someone with Asperger Syndrome to answer. Prepare the candidate to answer questions such as:

- Tell me about yourself.

- Since you are overqualified for this position, what do you hope to gain from it?

Although this may not come up during a first interview, eventually money will be discussed. Among the questions that may arise pertaining to compensation are the following:

- What are your financial needs?

- What is the minimum salary you will accept?

- What are your salary expectations?

12.1.4.6 GIVING EXAMPLES

While interviewers for most entry-level jobs will ask few behavioral questions, they will ask questions that require examples. One of the most difficult things for people with Asperger Syndrome to do in an interview is to give examples. Candidates have a hard time filtering through past experiences and coming up with appropriate examples that demonstrate a point. Providing examples is part of the interview process and will be expected. The interviewer will want to hear how the candidate reacted to or handled a past situation to help them judge how well-equipped that person is to handle the current position.

Since this is a challenge for many people with Asperger Syndrome, you will need to help them prepare examples beforehand. Sit down with the candidate and discuss past work experiences in detail. You may use the following questions as a guide. Choose the questions you feel are appropriate for the candidate.

"Give me an example of when you..."

- had to adapt to a difficult situation

- had to be tolerant of an opinion that was different from your own

- needed to complete a project on a tight deadline

- dealt with an angry customer or coworker

- took constructive criticism from a coworker

- handled a difficult situation with a coworker

- had to make an important decision

- persuaded team members to do things your way

- prioritized the elements of an assignment

- solved a difficult problem

- had to work under a lot of pressure

- had to be flexible with your schedule.

12.1.5 Selling themselves

One of the objectives of an interview is to sell oneself. If you are supporting the candidate by conducting the job search, you will likely have done a lot of the selling for her before reaching the interview stage. But when the candidate is in the interview it will be up to that individual to sell himself. After all, the employer is thinking about hiring the candidate, not you. It will be the candidate who clinches the deal.

Here are some tips to help the candidate sell himself in an interview:

- Make a list of strengths; support may be needed for this.

- Memorize the list and make sure that each one of those strengths are mentioned in the interview at some point.

- Smile in the interview.

- Make eye contact with the interviewer.

- Lean slightly forward when answering questions.

- People with Asperger Syndrome are often very good at acting. The candidate could choose a role model who would interview well and imitate her (within reason) during the interview.

12.1.6 Attitude

In an interview, the interviewer is looking for a person who has a positive attitude. People with Asperger Syndrome can at times appear arrogant or dismissive. This can be a problem during an interview. If you have not already addressed this issue with the candidate, you will need to work hard now to make sure that a poor attitude is not projected.

A great tool for working on this challenge is to set up a series of mock interviews. Do the first one straight through without interruption and give your feedback at the end. In subsequent interviews stop when the candidate does something that portrays arrogance, dismissiveness, or reflecting an attitudinal problem. Role play back to the candidate what you saw so that she in turn can see it. Discuss how you felt when the candidate acted that way and then role play alternative ways of the candidate expressing himself.

Keep practicing this. Nothing turns an interviewer off more than someone who seems to show a bad attitude.

12.1.7 Body language

People with Asperger Syndrome not only have a difficult time reading non-verbal cues such as body language in others, but they also have great difficulty accurately modeling it as well. What they are expressing through their non-verbal language is not necessarily what they are feeling. This is problematic in an interview because they may give the interviewer wrong messages.

The mirroring tool (Chapter 8) is very useful in helping people with Asperger Syndrome project positive body language during an interview. It is an excellent tool for anyone to use, especially people who have difficulty building rapport and relationships.

12.1.8 Ending the interview

Ending an interview can be an awkward moment for anyone, and for a person with a social disorder, it can cause extreme anxiety. One's best defense is to teach the candidate what to expect at the end of the interview and to make a list of points for her to cover, such as:

- Expressing interest in the position and thanking the interviewer for the interview.

- Asking for a business card or otherwise ensuring that the candidate has the interviewer's name, title, and address so that a thank-you letter can be sent. Make sure the letter arrives within 24 hours of the interview.

- Asking the interviewer when to expect a decision or when a follow-up inquiry would be acceptable.

12.1.9 Five steps to a successful interview

To make it easier for the candidate to prepare for an interview, I have broken these skills down into five manageable steps and developed exercises for the candidate to personalize each step.

The five steps to a successful interview are:

1. Know yourself.

2. Know the company.

3. Smile and show a positive attitude.

4. Build rapport.

5. Sell your strengths.

12.1.9.1 STEP 1: KNOW YOURSELF

- Make a list of your skills and strengths.

- Beside each point on your list, think of one example where you used that skill or strength and tell how it changed the situation for the better.

- Memorize what you have on your resumé.

12.1.9.2 STEP 2: KNOW THE COMPANY

- You *must* be familiar with the *position* and the *organization* so that you can demonstrate how and why you will be an effective worker. Read any literature they publish and look at the company's web site.

- Obtain information, if you can, on who you will be meeting with and the schedule for the interview period. If you can, find out about your interviewer in advance – for example, his name, title and role – so you can use this information during the interview.

12.1.9.3 STEP 3: SMILE AND SHOW A POSITIVE ATTITUDE

- First impressions really matter and you only have about thirty seconds to make a positive one.

- Dress appropriately and be well groomed for the interview – take care of details such as trimming and cleaning under your fingernails and brushing your teeth.

- Your attitude can actually mean as much or more to an employer than your skills. A highly skilled person with a bad attitude might get passed up for a lesser skilled person with a great attitude and the motivation to learn and work hard.

12.1.9.4 STEP 4: BUILD RAPPORT

"Rapport" means making a connection with a person. In an interview, this has to happen quickly.

- Use the mirroring tool to help you connect with the interviewer.

- Practice your interview skills with a variety of people to get comfortable with different personality types.

12.1.9.5 STEP 5: SELL YOUR STRENGTHS

In the first step, you made a list of your strengths. Now you want to put them to use.

- Make it a goal of the interview to mention each of your strengths at least once.

- Provide the example you came up with in Step 1 to demonstrate how you used your strengths in past jobs. The only way the interviewers will know about your strengths is if you tell them, so make sure that you do!

12.1.10 The candidate's rights in the interview

There are certain things that by law cannot be asked in an interview. Every country has its own laws regarding human rights. It is wise to check the laws in your own country and advise the candidate accordingly.

The following are some areas that may be restricted information in an interview:

- birthplace, ancestry, ethnic origin, place of origin

- sex, sexual orientation, marital status, family status

- age

- race, color

- religion, creed

- record of offenses

- disability.

12.1.11 Interview tips

- Pick out your interview clothes ahead of time, press them and hang them in their closet so that they are always ready on short notice.

- There are only two acceptable ways for men or women to sit during an interview: With both feet flat on the floor or with one leg crossed over the other at the knee. Make sure that you sit with your back straight and do not slouch in the chair. This posture will tell the interviewer that you are alert and listening as well as interested in what is being asked and said.

- Keep your resumé in a briefcase or an envelope until you are seated in the interview room. Once everyone sits down, the resumé, if this has not already been done prior to the interview, can be taken out and handed to the interviewer.

12.2 Disclosure

What to say about a person's disability and when to say it are important questions to address. By law, no one is obligated to disclose that they have a disability; however, it can be a great advantage to do so. This is an individual decision that the candidate will need to make. When I talk to my clients about disclosure, I make sure that they are clear about the advantages and disadvantages of disclosing their disability. It is also important to discuss their strategy of disclosure, which includes when to disclose and what to disclose.

I feel strongly that a person should disclose a disability early in the job-search process. Some candidates have a hard time with this. They are afraid that if they disclose their disability, they will not get offered the job. I counter this with, "If the employer will not hire you because you have a disability, is this an employer you should be working for? How understanding and accommodating will they be when you tell them you have a disability at the time of a problem?" The point is, when an employer decides to hire a person with full knowledge of a disability, then they are making a statement that they are willing to support the process. This sets the stage for long-term success.

Some candidates insist on not disclosing their disability. This is their decision to make. Sooner or later, however, they call to say that their job is on the line and that they want someone to step in to see if the situation can be rescued. The employer often feels betrayed at this point. It is very difficult to salvage a job after that has happened. The employer often expresses in these situations that if he had known earlier about the disability, the company probably would have still hired the person and things would have been handled differently.

If the candidate insists on not disclosing her disability then that limits the support you can offer in the job-search process. After all, what are you supposed to tell a potential employer about why you are calling on behalf of another adult? It will be perceived as odd without a reasonable explanation. The employer will not understand why the individual is not making the call himself. In this case, you can only support the candidate in doing her own job search.

12.2.1 Options for disclosure

Figure 12.1 outlines the pros, cons and possible problems that may arise when disclosing a disability at various stages in the job-search process.

Stage of disclosure	Pros	Cons	Possible problems
1. Job application – resumé or form	Honesty provides peace of mind. Easy/allows employer to decide if disability is a concern.	Might disqualify you with no chance to present yourself and your qualifications and no recourse.	If you disclose at this early stage you may have a harder time finding work but usually have no disability-related problems when you do.
2. At the interview	Honesty provides peace of mind. Opportunity to respond briefly and positively, face-to-face, to specific disability questions. Face-to-face discrimination less likely.	Forces you to handle disability issues in a clear, non-threatening way. Too much emphasis indicates possible problem, you are not being evaluated on your abilities.	How comfortable do you feel discussing your disability? These are very difficult questions, but ones that you can prepare in advance.
3. After the interview (when a job is offered but before you begin work)	Honesty provides peace of mind. If the disability information changes the hiring decision, and you are sure that your disability will not interfere with your ability to perform job, there is legal recourse.	Employer might feel you should have told him or her before you were hired. Personnel department might distrust you.	Honestly evaluate condition of disability in light of specific demands of job. Explain how disability will not interfere with ability to perform job, including job safety.

4. Once you begin work	Opportunity to prove yourself on job before disclosure. Allows you to respond to disability questions with peers at work. If disclosure affects employment status and the condition doesn't affect ability to perform job or job safety, you may be protected by law.	Nervousness at work. Employer may accuse you of falsifying your application. Could affect interaction with peers.	The longer you wait to disclose, the harder it may become. It may be difficult to identify whom to tell.
5. Following a problem at work.	Opportunity to prove yourself at work before disclosure.	Possible employer accusation of falsifying your application. Can perpetuate disability myths and misunderstandings.	Coworkers may feel hurt if they think you have been untruthful with them. It may be difficult to re-establish trust.
6. Never	Employer can't respond to your disability unless he or she is aware you have a problem.	If disability is discovered, you risk being fired, e.g. for safety reasons. Can lead to disability myths and misunderstandings.	If you are certain there will not be an issue with job performance, the issue of disclosure becomes less critical.

Figure 12.1 Options for disclosure

Adapted from Aase and Smith (1989) University of Minnesota Disability Services – Career Development Course Sequence

12.2.2 Disclosure script

I believe that people with Asperger Syndrome should understand what their disability is and how it affects their life. They should also be able to explain Asperger Syndrome to the average person who frequently has never heard of it. If they are able to talk about themselves in an intelligent and open manner, it will calm people's fears and clear up misconceptions.

Talking about Asperger Syndrome requires some effort. If they don't already know what it is, candidates will need to learn about it. They may need support to do this. The Internet is an excellent resource for this. Once they get a basic idea of what Asperger Syndrome is, they need to determine how it affects them personally. Finally, they need to be able to identify what support they need to be productive in a job and be able to ask for it. This information will give them everything they need to write a disclosure script that is informative and personalized.

Figure 12.2 is an example of a disclosure script that one candidate wrote.

General description of Asperger Syndrome

Asperger Syndrome is a disorder that is caused by an imbalance in the brain. It does not affect intelliegence or language skills but it does make it more difficult to interact in general conversation because we don't always get the "gist" of what is being said. People with Asperger Syndrome have difficulty reading non-verbal communication such as body language and facial expressions. We tend to think in logical terms and often interpret things literally.

How AS affects me

Asperger Syndrome contributes to my strengths as an employee in that I am very good at applying logic. This has contributed to my gift for learning languages and technical code. I am an excellent analytical thinker because of my Asperger Syndrome and my ability to hyperfocus on topics makes me a superb researcher when the requirement is for very detailed information. It is also an inherent trait of Asperger Syndrome to be honest and moral. These are qualities I am proud of.

Things that help me to be productive

I have difficulty organizing projects and I need assistance in setting up realistic time lines, even breaking down the priorities of an assignment. I need people to be very clear with me about exactly how they want a project done, when they want it completed by, and what is and is not important or relevant in the project. I can sometimes spend too much time on an area that is not crucial to a project if I have misinterpreted the instruction, so I need a main contact person to "bounce" things off to make sure I am on track. Regular on-going feedback helps me to stay focused and gives me an opportunity to improve in areas that may be lacking.

Figure 12.2 Disclosure script

12.3 Preparing a resumé and cover letter

Among the challenges that candidates with Asperger Syndrome encounter when preparing their resumé are how to address gaps in employment history, how to expand the resumé when lacking work experience, and how to deal with disclosure. These and more will be outlined in this section. First, the basics of resumé writing.

The reason a candidate should have a resumé is because it is a primary tool in the job-search process. A resumé is a marketing or promotional document that outlines the work experience and strengths of the candidate. A good resumé should not just be about work history. It needs to reflect the energy of the person behind it. It should tell a story about that person's accomplishments, how he performed in the past, what he was responsible for; and it should assist the reader in predicting how the candidate can contribute to the company.

The first step in writing a resumé is to decide on a job target. You did this in the Career Direction Formula in Chapter 11. Having a clearly stated goal or objective doesn't have to confine you if it's stated well. You want to describe the job objective in five or six words. For example, "Position as a data entry operator." Beyond that, the objective becomes muddy and indicates a lack of direction. If the candidate has several job targets, then write a separate resumé for each. This will make each resumé clear, targeted and easy for the employer to understand.

12.3.1 Resumé styles

There are two main types of resumés, chronological and functional.

A *chronological* resumé lists work experience and history in order from newest to oldest. It is preferred by employers because it is easy to follow and works well for those people who are moving within the same job industry.

A *functional* resumé rearranges employment history into sections that highlight areas of skill and accomplishment. This works well for those who are switching industries or have gaps in employment history.

A combination of the two types is useful because often candidates with Asperger Syndrome have a limited or sporadic work history and a lack of experience. The combination resumé (see Figure 12.3) is primarily a functional resumé with a short chronological employment history. Relevant skills and accomplishments are provided first, followed by the employment history. This format has been gaining in popularity and is one that works well for many candidates with Asperger Syndrome.

12.3.2 Cover letters

Every resumé that is sent out should be accompanied by a cover letter. The cover letter is another chance to sell the candidate. When finding work that works, the cover letter should be in the candidate's own words. It needs to be personal. If a relative or job coach is submitting a resumé on behalf of the candidate, he will likely have already spoken to the potential employer. Any employer will be far more impressed to receive a cover letter from the candidate explaining why she will be a good candidate for the job than if this letter is written by a relative or job coach. Here are some tips to help the candidate write a good cover letter:

- Always check for grammar and spelling mistakes.
- Make it personal by addressing it to the person who will do the hiring. Be formal and use prefixes such as Mr., Mrs., Ms., Miss, Dr., etc.
- Try to write the letter in your natural, conversational style to reflect your personality.
- Research the company and in the letter show that you know something about them. You want the employer to know that you chose their company for specific reasons and not just at random.

A sample cover letter (Figure 12.4) is provided to give the candidate an idea of how he can represent himself.

Rhonda Good

#505-778 Greenlawn Ave.

Rochester, NY 12345

(555) 777–1234

OBJECTIVE

Full-time administrative support position

Certificate in Microsoft Office and Desktop Publishing

CPU Computer College   *Aug. '02 – Jan. '03*

Courses include:

Microsoft Word Level II, Microsoft Access Levels I and II, Microsoft Excel Level II, Microsoft PowerPoint Levels I and II, Outlook, Accounting Overview, Office Procedures, Photoshop, Illustrator, and Quark XPress

Banking and Financial Services Diploma

Rochester School of Business   *Feb.'01 – Aug.'01*

Courses include:

Customer Service Representative Function, Foreign Exchange and Audits, Investments Consumer and Mortgage Credit

B.A. Sociology

University of Rochester   *Sept.'96 – May '00*

Majors: Statistics, Health Psychology, and English Literature

Completed second year Bachelor of Commerce program in the Faculty of Commerce

Electives: Marketing, Financial and Managerial Accounting, Excel, Business Communication

Achievement: First class standing in Business Communication

Completed second year Bachelor of Commerce program in the Faculty of Commerce

Figure 12.3 Combination resumé, continued on next page

WORK EXPERIENCE

Bookeeper (Self-employed)

Jan. '03 – Present

Market Research Representative (Part-time evening)

Access Research – Rochester   *June '02 – Aug. '02*

Customer Service Representative (Contract)

Bank of America – Rochester   *Oct. '01 – Feb. '02*

Telemarketing Representative

Club Intrasonic – Rochester   *Jan.'00 – Jun.'00*

VOLUNTEER EXPERIENCE

Income Tax Return Prep

Central Region Community Center   *March '01 – April '01*

General Laborer

Kibbutz Ein Hahoresh   *Aug. '01 – Sept. '00*

Figure 12.3 Combination resumé, continued

Joseph Jacobs
123 Rhodes Ave.
Winchester, NC 12345
123-555-1234

Mrs. Martha Genovese
Cover to Cover Book Sellers
123 Commissioners Rd.
Winchester, NC 12345

April 2, 2003

Dear Mrs. Genovese,

I am really excited about sending you my resumé because I think that I am a good match for the position you spoke about with Miss Aberdeen on Tuesday.

You want an experienced picker/packer for your warehouse and I have experience working as a picker/packer at a publishing company for over a year. I am always on time and take my work seriously. I was honored at the company's staff Christmas party last year as best new employee because of my attention to detail and dedication to the job. Unfortunately the company was sold this summer and I was laid off, along with several other staff.

I understand how important it is to an employer to find good employees who have a solid work ethic. I was well liked by my coworkers and my supervisor has offered to give me a reference. I think you will find that I am an excellent worker and have what it takes to be a real asset to your business.

Miss Aberdeen will be calling you early next week to follow up on this letter. I look forward to meeting you in person in the near future.

Sincerely,

Joseph Jacobs
Enclosure: resumé

Figure 12.4 Cover letter

12.4 Frequently asked questions about resumés

What if the candidate does not have experience in the type of work she wants to target?

Employers want to see that the candidate has experience. If the candidate has limited or no experience in the job target choice, then she needs to get some. This can be done through unpaid work experience. You can help the candidate arrange to work for an employer on a part-time or temporary basis to learn the job and gain more experience. It is not necessary to work in the position for a long time to put it on the resumé. A couple of days/shifts per week for four weeks is adequate.

What if the candidate has a lot of gaps in her work history or a string of short-term jobs?

It is important on a resumé not to leave gaps but at the same time you should not fabricate experience. Try to fill in the gaps with truths that reflect experience. For example, if the candidate was cutting lawns and raking leaves for the neighbors:

- 1998–2001 Grounds keeping

If the candidate was at home but learning new skills, possibly related to their special interest:

- 1996–1997 Private study – computer programming, networks, operating systems

A lot of short-term jobs do not look good on a resumé to an employer because it reflects instability. A great way to get around this is to group the short-term jobs into categories. For example:

- 1998–2000 Shipper Receiver, Karem Packaging, Gigi Wholesalers, The Open Book Publishers, R4U Packaging

- 2001–2003 Office Assistant, Johnson's Computer Systems, ABB Management, and Crossfire Welders

You can also drop some of the very brief and less important jobs as long as they were not jobs in which the candidate learned important skills.

How far back in a work history should the candidate go?

You want to make the resumé look fresh. Ten years of history is probably enough if the candidate's work goes back that far. Only put *earlier* jobs on a resumé if they offer relevant experience.

Is it a good idea to list hobbies and interests?

You only want to include hobbies and interests that are somewhat related to the job target or reflect characteristics that the employer will find relevant. For example, computer gaming would be relevant to working in the computer industry and graphic/game design industry, but it would not be relevant for an office job.

What should the resumé look like?

Resumés should always be printed in black ink on plain white paper unless you are a graphic designer or some other profession where graphic presentation is important. (Even then, you take a risk.) Whenever possible, the resumé should be printed on a laser printer or a good inkjet printer. Do not include a picture of the candidate on it. It is best to make the first impression in person. A picture is worth a thousand words but, in this case, you want to choose the words, not have the employer fabricate them in his head.

Try not to fold the resumé. Keep it in a large envelope and either hand it to the employer or mail it.

How does the candidate present cooperative and volunteer work experience on a resumé?

Any work experience is valuable and, if related, should be on the resumé. Simply putting a heading on the resumé – for instance "Volunteer and coop work experience" or "Unpaid Training," whatever reflects the situation – will work. Then write the span of time, for example 2000–2003, and list the experiences.

Does the candidate disclose a disability on the resumé?

The short answer is no. This is not recommended for the same reason that you should not put a picture on the resumé. It risks pre-interview conclusions. You want the opportunity to explain the situation to the employer. This is better done in person or beforehand on the telephone. This will be discussed in more detail as part of the job-search process in Chapter 13.

Summary

- The candidate has only one opportunity in an interview to make a good impression. Take the time to develop effective interview skills with her and give the candidate ample opportunity to practice in mock interviews.

- Help the candidate create a list of strengths that she can memorize, as well as the content of the resumé.

- It is helpful to set up mock interviews with a variety of people to offer the candidate variety in personality and interview styles.

- A well-rehearsed greeting and handshake go a long way to making a positive first impression.

- Decide on a disclosure strategy before beginning the job-search process.

- Develop a disclosure script with the candidate so that she can speak in an informed and intelligent manner about strengths and challenges. This will diminish fears and clear up misconceptions.

- A resumé and cover letter is a primary tool in the job-search process. Take the time to create good ones that reflect the personality of the candidate.

13 The job search

Sometimes you have to cut a hole in the wall to create a window of opportunity.

When I first started finding employment for my clients I was so afraid of making cold calls that I would get myself worked up and totally stress out. I was self-conscious and afraid of how my calls would be received. I remember setting my hand on the telephone receiver for ten minutes, staring at the phone, waiting for my other hand to get up the courage to dial the number. When I finally started to dial the phone number, my hand would refuse to dial the last digit. It was as if my hands had a mind of their own and were not connected to my brain.

I started thinking a lot about how to make these calls easier on myself. It occurred to me that I should talk to the experts to get some advice. So I started asking friends and colleagues who they knew who could teach me how to do cold calls. It wasn't long before I was introduced to a number of people who worked in recruiting. They were happy to sit down with me and offer advice. What I learned from them, and then put into practice with my own spin, will also help you to become very good at finding work that works. Don't let this part of the process intimidate you. All of my secrets and tricks of the trade are found in this chapter. Just follow each step of my job-finding process and watch as everything starts to come together. It's not magic, but it works! But first, I think it is important to put things in perspective.

13.1 The labor market and employment trends

Dramatic changes have occurred in Western economies over the last few decades that have affected the labor market. Changes and advancements in technology, consumer demands and new workplace policies, processes and expectations have shifted what employers need from their employees. This has created a shift in attitude about work. It is now commonplace for people to have many jobs over a lifetime. However, an increasingly new concept is that people will have many career changes as well. The current generation can expect between five and seven career shifts over the span of their life. Many candidates and their families struggle with this notion. It is exceedingly unlikely today that the first job someone gets will be the job from which they will retire in fifty years. It is as useful for our Asperger friends to know this as anyone else.

It is important to understand that employment opportunities are driven by demand. What the public wants and needs determines the trends in the labor market. To produce the goods and services that the public demands, employers need to hire people who have specific skills, knowledge, and abilities, and it is up to the people looking for work to acquire what employers demand. Over the past two decades there has been a shift from goods-producing to service-producing employment and this is expected to continue. The services industry is the largest and fastest-growing major industry group in the Western world and is expected to add millions of new jobs by 2010. To give you an idea of the scope, the service-producing industry will account for three out of every five new jobs created in the United States economy. Service-producing industries include finance, insurance, real estate, government, transportation, communications, utilities, and the wholesale and retail trades. This is important to realize because it is necessary to look for jobs in the areas where jobs do or will exist. It can be hard enough for our Asperger friends to find jobs without their looking in the wrong place.

Another very important factor that impacts the labor market is changing demographics. Demographic trends became very important, particularly after the Second World War. Factors such as birth rate, fertility rate, and life expectancy have had the greatest impact on the labor market. For example, baby boomers (the population surge in some countries after the Second World War) will remain in the workplace for some years to come. Assuming that people normally retire at age sixty-five, the first baby boomers born in

1946 will reach retirement in 2011. However, as many people today retire as early as age 50 to 58, we have had "retired baby boomers" since 1996.

This large aging and retired population means that more people are competing for "supplemental" jobs to top up their income. In addition, many of these types of jobs also appeal to workers with disabilities who, for a variety of reasons, are not able to manage full-time or career-driven positions. The number of people between the ages of twenty-five and forty-four remains high and they occupy a large number of jobs. All these factors affect how you and your Asperger friend find work. Indeed, this will impact job opportunities for all people entering the workforce. Furthermore, shifts in demographics also mean that there is an ever-changing demand for new goods and services. In the case of an aging population, for example, there will be growing demand in the areas of prescription and over-the-counter drugs and supplements, hygiene supplies, travel and leisure, home maintenance, long-term health care insurance, retirement and assisted living communities, nursing homes, home health care, and funeral services. These consumer demands have a domino effect on the economy and, therefore, the labor market, creating new and different job opportunities.

The shift in attitude and employer demands has a significant impact on employment opportunities for people with Asperger Syndrome. First, the candidate needs to be prepared to have several jobs throughout his lifetime. He may even need to have more than one job at a time to get the hours, variety, and income desired. Second, today's jobs require higher education. All but two of the fifty highest paying jobs listed in the US 2003 *Occupational Handbook* require a college or university degree. The two that don't are air traffic controllers and nuclear power reactor operators. Because people with Asperger Syndrome may have difficulty applying general knowledge, acquiring a specific skill set today is more important than ever. The appropriate choice of post-secondary education or training for candidates with Asperger Syndrome will be crucial. For example, general arts diplomas or degrees usually do not adequately prepare a person with Asperger Syndrome for employment because these rely on the individual to apply lessons and knowledge to later create a skill set. Practical forms of education, such as cooperative programs, apprenticeships, and applied college programs, are excellent for people with Asperger Syndrome because they prepare them for a specific job. This is extremely important for people with Asperger Syndrome looking for a career. With the relevant practical skill set they can become anything from computer technicians, electricians, and bookkeepers, to lab technicians, auto mechanics, and embalmers. There are many growing industries that have suitable jobs for people with Asperger Syndrome who have the right training.

13.1.1 The common job market

There are two places to find jobs, the *common job market* and the *hidden job market*. Although your job search will focus primarily on finding jobs in the hidden job market, understanding the common job market is important because it holds its own value when finding work that works.

The common job market is openly and easily visible to the public. When beginning to look for a job, most of us look in our local newspaper to see what jobs are available. We might also surf the Internet, go to a job fair or walk into an employment office to look at the job postings. These are all reasonable places for the average person to begin a job search. This is called the common job market because it is where everyone looks for jobs.

The common job market offers valuable information when you are beginning your job search. If you pay attention, you will be able to use the common job market to lead you to hidden jobs.

The "hidden" value of the common job market is that it:

- tells you which companies are expanding and hiring
- tells you which companies have an equal opportunity hiring policy
- shows you local hiring trends.

As you might imagine, this information will be very useful to you in your job search. There are several established places where people begin a job search. Let's examine how they can assist you.

13.1.1.1 WANT ADS

Look in your local newspaper/s in the employment and career sections to see what types of jobs are being advertised. Specifically look for hiring trends. Perhaps you will notice that company "X" is hiring a lot of people, which means they might be expanding. Even if the company has not posted a position suitable for someone with Asperger Syndrome, there might be something on the horizon. It may be worth giving them a call. Use want ad postings to help you research and brainstorm companies.

13.1.1.2 JOB FAIRS

Going to job fairs is great experience because it gets you out there talking with employers. Job fairs are often put on by a particular industry, so this can be an opportunity for you to meet with a number of employers in your job target. Talk about a gold mine! Once you are talking, it is easy to determine how receptive the employer is to hiring someone with Asperger Syndrome. It also allows you to educate them a little to see how receptive they might be for future contact. It is a fantastic place to make contacts and to investigate potential opportunities that are *not posted*.

13.1.1.3 THE INTERNET

Employment on the Internet is big business and there are many web sites that cater to people looking for jobs. Most job-search sites allow you to perform a targeted search, which will bring up only the postings in which you are interested. This gives you insight into which companies might be potential targets for your search and then makes it easy for you to do further research by allowing you to click on the employer link. Once you are on the employer site, you can research the company. Pay special attention to the company's corporate or social responsibility program, if they have one. See if they do any work for the government. This can be a clue as to whether they might be motivated to hire people with disabilities. The Internet is an amazing tool to use in your search for finding work that works, not only because of the job openings it posts but because it makes your research much easier.

It is important to note that the main disadvantage of the common job market is that candidates with Asperger Syndrome will be competing with the general population for a position. This is a significant disadvantage because even though your Asperger friend might be considered competitive, it is very likely that he will still require some support to meet the expectations of the job. Employers who have posted an ad are typically looking for someone to fit in quickly. They are generally not prepared to make special workplace accommodations unless there is some advantage for them to do so. This usually sets the candidate with Asperger Syndrome apart from the general public and, I am sorry to say, this is usually a disadvantage when looking for work in the common job market for any person with a disability.

This is not to say that I have never placed clients through posted ads, because I have. Still, in my experience this does not happen frequently. The mistake many people with Asperger Syndrome make when applying for a job in the common job market is not to disclose their status for fear of not being offered the job. Perhaps this strategy puts them on the same level as their competitors initially, but once hired the problems inevitably arise and then the employee has to explain to an often disgruntled employer that he has Asperger Syndrome. This can quickly turn into a disaster. Disclosure is an extremely important aspect of the job-search process and was addressed in Chapter 12.

13.1.2 The hidden job market

As the name suggests, the hidden job market involves jobs that are not advertised. These are the jobs that employers may be thinking about but have not acted on, are not sure where to go to hire, are too busy to hire, or are on the verge of hiring but are not quite ready to make the decision. The employer may even be actively seeking the right candidate through networking channels. Each one of these scenarios presents an opportunity for the candidate with Asperger Syndrome but they can only be accessed through cold calling and networking. The remainder of this chapter will be focused on how to find jobs in the hidden job market because this is where you will most likely find work that works for people with Asperger Syndrome.

13.2 The information package

You will be speaking with business and industry professionals during the job search. To be most effective, you will need to approach them on a professional level, which means being prepared with a comprehensive information package. Presenting professionally from the beginning demonstrates that you are serious, efficient, and organized. This is a good first impression to leave with a potential employer!

Your information package will include:

- your candidate's resumé
- information about Asperger Syndrome
- information about available job support.

13.2.1 Candidate's resumé

You learned how to prepare an effective resumé in Chapter 12. This will be included in your package. A resumé is never folded, always printed in black ink on white paper and never has the candidate's picture on it. The same rules apply to an electronic resumé, one that is viewed on the computer.

13.2.2 Information about Asperger Syndrome

The employer will want to know more about Asperger Syndrome and this is a great opportunity for you to provide information that is a bit more detailed than what you said in your initial contact. The trick is to keep the information interesting, realistic, and easy to read. Try not to make the information too clinical or too long. You want this information to be enlightening not daunting. I like to include a "tips for employers" sheet in my information package so that the employer gets an idea of what to expect when working with a person with Asperger Syndrome. It's a way of dispelling fear in writing. You may want to customize the list with specific tips on working with your Asperger friend or relative.

13.2.3 Available job support

You need to put together information about any support services to which the candidate and the employer will have access on the job. I always include my company information and an outline of the support we provide to each of our clients. This includes details of our job coaching, employer education, staff support, telephone support, and long-term follow-up support.

Any government or private programs that offer an incentive to the employer for hiring an employee with Asperger Syndrome should also be outlined in the information package. If there are forms that need to be filled out by the employer, you may want to include a copy unless they look difficult or time consuming to fill out. You may want to fill out the paperwork yourself and then include it in the package. The employer only needs to sign the paperwork if a decision is made to hire the candidate. You want to leave the employer with the impression that hiring an employee with Asperger Syndrome is not going to create work for the company.

Finally, package the information in a large envelope and have it ready to send out. You may also want to have an electronic copy of the package ready in case the employer prefers email. Either way is acceptable.

13.3 Choosing your goal

Before starting the job search, you want to be really clear about your goal. You might think that the goal is simply a job, and this is truly the *ultimate* goal. However, there may be intermediate steps to reaching the ultimate goal. This will be determined by the needs of the candidate. Is the candidate's goal to obtain:

- an information interview to find out more about the company or a particular job

- an unpaid work experience to build up his employment portfolio

- a job trial to see if the employer would be willing to hire

- a job interview for paid employment?

Let's take a closer look at each of these goals.

An information interview is a helpful goal when the candidate is researching job or career ideas. In Chapter 11, you did the Career Direction Formula with your Asperger friend. There may have been some jobs on the viability chart that you marked with a "T" which meant that they required further training. An information interview is a great way to research what training is required to do the job, what the training might entail and what the job will be like once the candidate gets the training. An information interview is sort of like trying a job on without the commitment to buy.

Unpaid work experience can be useful and even necessary for anyone with or without Asperger Syndrome, to get work experience. This may be because he has no work history at all or no experience in the particular area of the targeted search. Employers like to hire people with at least some previous experience. When they are considering hiring a person with a disability and may be required to provide accommodation, the employer is reassured if the candidate has had some prior experience. This demonstrates that the candidate can do the job. Unpaid work experience also helps to build skills and an employment portfolio (resumé).

With regard to the job search, an unpaid work experience is an easier "sell." The employer is not making a commitment of paying the candidate so is often more open to the idea. Be prepared to offer job support in an unpaid work experience if your Asperger friend needs it. You want the experience to be a positive one for everyone. You also never know what the outcome of an unpaid work experience might be. Although this should never be an expectation, there have been many times that an employer has offered a paid position to a candidate placed in an unpaid work experience. You never know!

A *job trial* can be a great way to transition the qualified candidate into a job. Like an unpaid work experience, the job trial is also an unpaid placement. The difference, however, between unpaid work experience and a job trial is the outcome. In a job trial, the employer is *expected* to offer the candidate a paid position if things work out. These parameters are established up front. The job trial is usually set up when the candidate is qualified but has a longer learning curve and requires greater support. It allows both the employee with Asperger Syndrome and the employer the opportunity to see if the situation will work.

From a job-search perspective, this is an easier sell than going directly for paid employment; however, you are still asking the employer for a commitment. The fact that the employer gets to "try out" the employee can be appealing, but you need to be careful that the employer is taking this situation seriously and is willing to make a commitment of paid employment by the end of the trial period. A job trial should not exceed four weeks because you have already determined that the candidate is competitive and he should not work for free on a long-term basis. If you can offer the employer a wage subsidy, this is a great time to do it. Personally, I like to set up a short job trial and then have it lead directly into a wage subsidy. This is often the gentle persuasion the employer needs to make the commitment.

When your goal is a *job interview*, it implies that the candidate is ready to work competitively in a paid job. This is the "real deal" and, because you are reading this book, I suspect that this is your ultimate goal. You should still be prepared to offer job support and even a wage subsidy if it is available. Going directly for paid employment is the hardest sell of the goals listed because you are asking an employer for a commitment from the start. People get jobs this way every day and there is no reason that your Asperger friend, with your help, can't do it too when he is ready.

Write your immediate goal here:

13.4 The job search – Step 1

Your first objective in the job-search process is to obtain a meeting with the potential employer. To do this you will need to write a script. A script is important because you need to know beforehand what to say and how to say it. Some people are concerned that speaking from a script will sound phony. The really neat thing about a script, however, is that the more you use it, the better and more convincing it sounds. You end up sounding like you really know your stuff, something that will impress potential employers and instill confidence. It also ensures that you don't miss anything and curse yourself later.

Your own personal style will greatly determine how you present what you want. For many of us, selling does not come naturally and you may even find yourself very uncomfortable with the idea of having to sell something. This is exactly the reason you should write a script. Write that script, before you dial that phone!

What you project is how others will see you.

If you are genuine about finding work that works, it will come across in your presentation. If you project enthusiasm and positive energy, people will believe you are enthusiastic and energized about what you are doing. The energy you put forward is the selling tool that will serve you best. Just be yourself and be genuine.

Open your script with something friendly. This usually begins with a greeting like "Hi" or "Hello, my name is ___," "I'm calling from ___." But it's a bit more complicated than it appears. The way you open your script can trigger the recipient into "Oh no, a sales call" mode. So up front you want the person to know that you are not selling anything. And in fact, you really aren't selling anything. You are only exchanging information.

Here are a few opening lines that work for me:

> Hi my name is Gail Hawkins and I'm calling from Mission Possible. I'm wondering if you can help me?

> Hello, my name is Gail Hawkins and I specialize in employment services for people with Asperger Syndrome. Maybe you can help me out a bit.

> Hi, my name is Gail Hawkins and I am hoping you might be able to help me out.

Now go right into why you are calling. The reason for your call will of course involve the goal you determined earlier. You want to briefly say whom you are calling on behalf of (if you are calling for the candidate) and then why you are calling:

> I am calling on behalf of my friend/client/student/son Tyson, who has a disability called Asperger Syndrome, which is a mild social disorder. He is looking for an unpaid work experience/a job trial/a job in your industry.

Closing the script is where most people fall short. There is something about asking for what we want that makes humans quiver in fear. My philosophy is if you don't ask, then don't expect to get. Your goal at this point is to set up a meeting with the employer. So your "closing" is to ask for this meeting.

> What I'd like to do is set up a time to drop in and talk to you about Tyson. When would be a good time – middle of the week, end of the week? Morning or afternoon? What's best for you?

The trick is to deliver your entire script all at once, without breaks and without letting the recipient cut in or respond. Many times, you will get to speak to the person right then and there. Other times they will want to set up an appointment. You may also find at this time that you encounter some objections. This is what to do:

If they say: "I'm too busy right now."

Then you say: "I appreciate your time, the meeting will take twenty minutes and I can come at a time that suits your schedule."

If they say: "We're not hiring."

Then you say: "That's all right, I'm guessing that you know a lot of people in this field. I'm just wondering who you know who might be interested in talking to me? I would really appreciate any ideas, leads, or referrals you might have for me. This'll only take a moment."

If they say: "Send me a resumé and I'll think about it."

Then you say: "Let me tell you what's on it…" or "I'll fax/email it to you right now and call you right back."

Notice that I did not go into a lot of detail about Asperger Syndrome at this point. I don't want to overwhelm the employer or scare him off. At the same time, I want to provide enough information to appeal to the employer.

13.4.1 Some full script examples

Unpaid work experience:

Hi, my name is Gail Hawkins and I'm calling from Mission Possible. I'm wondering if you can help me? I am calling on behalf of my client Tyson, who has a disability called Asperger Syndrome, which is a mild social disorder. At this point I am helping Tyson to build his resumé through unpaid work experience. I'd like to talk to you about how Tyson could help out your company. When would be a good time to meet – middle of the week, end of the week? Morning or afternoon? What's best for you?

Job trial:

Hello, my name is Gail Hawkins and I specialize in employment services for people with Asperger Syndrome. Maybe you can help me out a bit. I am calling on behalf of my client Tyson. I read on your web site that you are an equal opportunity employer, so I thought you would be a great company to talk to about a job trial for Tyson. I know that you are very busy and I won't take up your time. When would be a good time to talk – middle of the week, end of the week? Morning or afternoon? What's best for you?

Paid employment:

Hi, my name is Gail Hawkins and I am hoping you might be able to help me out. I am calling on behalf of my friend Tyson who has a disability called Asperger Syndrome, which is a mild social disorder. I am helping Tyson look for work in your industry. He has two years' experience and is very motivated. I'd like to meet with you to talk about why it would be a good idea for you to consider hiring him and how it might save you money. When would be a good time to talk – middle of the week, end of the week? Morning or afternoon? What's best for you?

13.5 The job search – Step 2

Congratulations! You have managed to get a meeting with an employer. This is amazingly good news because you are getting closer to landing the job. You might be thinking that this is just an information meeting and not a real interview. Wrong! The employer will be evaluating you and the candidate and this is essentially the same as a real interview. There have been times when a meeting like this has ended in a job offer. Even if this meeting does not result in a job, it still could down the road.

Come prepared with your Asperger friend's resumé and a copy of your information package. Before the interview, meet with your Asperger friend and go over interview skills (review interview preparation in Chapter 12). It is important at the meeting that you do not out-stay your welcome. The meeting should not exceed thirty minutes. In fact, it is a good idea to let the employer know that you will be keeping track of the time. This is respectful and is a sign of professionalism.

Step 2 of the job search is how to prepare for and conduct a meeting with a potential employer. You will use a similar structure in preparing for the meeting as you did when writing the script.

There are several strategies that can be used in this initial meeting. The strategy you choose will depend upon how involved your candidate is in the job-search process and generally how well he will present to the employer. You need to discuss possible strategies with your Asperger friend and determine what his readiness level is before placing him in this situation. Your objective of this meeting is to get an official interview so you will need to use your judgment as to what strategy is best for each situation. There will be times when the employer expresses a preference. In this case, it is best that you accommodate the employer's wishes.

1. If the candidate is highly active in the job search, performs at a competitive level, and is ready to contribute, I suggest that he participate in the entire meeting.

2. If the candidate struggles to contribute but presents well, I suggest that you make arrangements for him to participate in the first half of the meeting and leave you alone to meet with the employer privately for the second half. This needs to be explained to the candidate and the employer before going to the meeting and both need to agree to this so it will not feel awkward. The reason you want to meet privately with the employer is that often the employer feels uncomfortable talking about concerns in front of the candidate. With the candidate out of the room, the employer will be able to ask his questions openly and therefore be in a better position to move forward.

3. The final strategy is to go to the meeting without the candidate. This has its advantages and disadvantages. Employers have a very

hard time imagining what someone with Asperger Syndrome will be like. The employer may feel nervous or concerned. Meeting the potential employee often reassures the employer and initiates a personal connection. The employer may feel more comfortable making a decision at this stage. On the other hand, if the candidate is not yet prepared and does not present well, this can intimidate or scare an employer and will be stressful and uncomfortable for the candidate. In this situation, the employer may need a little more information and background to be more convinced that hiring someone with Asperger Syndrome is a good idea. Being alone with the employer also allows you to check out the job, the employer, and the environment to determine its suitability and to speak freely with the employer about the candidate without making anyone feel uncomfortable.

Talk to your Asperger friend and decide together on the best strategy to approach this initial meeting.

If the strategy is to include the candidate in the presentation, either fully or partially, you want your Asperger friend to take as much of the lead as he is capable of and comfortable with taking. By this time, the candidate has prac- ticed the greeting process and will now put it to use. This first impression will stick, so try to make it the best one possible. The candidate should be dressed and groomed appropriately for an interview. The candidate should answer as many questions independently as possible, just like in a regular interview. With permission from the candidate you can fill in any blanks or prompt some of the answers when necessary but you definitely want to leave the employer with the impression that the candidate is a capable person, even if he requires a little help now and then. Don't talk *for* the candidate. Once the employer has had a chance to meet/interview your Asperger friend, you can move into the details of why you are there. Depending on the meeting strategy you have chosen, this might be the time to suggest that the candi- date wait for you in the lobby.

When you are ready to go into the details of why you are meeting with the employer, here are the points you want to cover:

- Why the candidate is suitable for a position in this company. This is the time to talk briefly about your Asperger friend's strengths. If he has a specific interest in the company this is also worth mentioning. "Tyson has always wanted to work at Bank of America." This is flattering and interesting to the employer.

- Share any knowledge you have about the company's social or corporate responsibility programs and explain why you think hiring this candidate fits in with the company culture or philosophy.

- Ask the employer to tell you about the company. You are interested in the types of jobs they have, the products or services they sell, and what is important to them when hiring staff.

- You may want to ask the employer if the company has had any previous experience hiring people with disabilities and how it turned out.

- What positions might the employer have that would be suitable for the candidate based on the information you have provided?

- The details of any short-term placement such as an unpaid work experience or job trial. This will include how many hours per week and how many weeks.

- The support services the candidate will require and how these will be supplied. This will include job coaching and employer accommodation.

- Details of any incentives you are able to offer, such as tax breaks or wage subsidies. Ask if these appeal to the employer.

- If your goal is paid employment, you should discuss shifts, hours, starting wage, dress and any other details that might be specific to the job such as safety or health requirements or licenses, permits, etc.

After you have presented the details of what you are looking for, you want to open the floor to questions. Feel comfortable asking if the employer has any concerns or questions. This is a great time to explore and address them. After reading this book, you will have a very solid understanding of how to work with someone with Asperger Syndrome and, more important, how to support your Asperger friend. You will find that you will easily be able to address the employer's questions or concerns. If there is anything you are unsure of, tell the employer that you will investigate and provide the answer quickly.

13.5.1 Closing the presentation

Now it's time to ask directly for what you came for. You have provided the employer with all the details and you have been professional, informative, and courteous. There is no reason to expect a negative response, so go ahead and ask your question in the way that is most comfortable for you.

- "Are you interested in setting up a work trial with Tyson?"

- "What are your thoughts on hiring Tyson at this point?"

- "Does a four-week unpaid work experience with Tyson appeal to you?"

- "When can I bring Tyson in to meet with you?"

- "What would be a good time for Tyson to start?"

- "How would you like to proceed?"

The more direct your question, the more direct you can expect the response to be. The employer may be ready to make the commitment right there and then or might need some time to think about or run the idea past some other people in the company. If the employer needs time to make his decision, try to nail down when you can expect an answer.

- "Would it be reasonable to call you in a few days to get your decision?"

- "How much time will you need to decide?"

- "Do you think you will make a decision over the next week?"

- "Is there anything more from me that you need to help you make a decision?"

- "When can I expect to hear from you?"

- "Would you like to contact me or would you prefer I call you to follow up on your decision?"

If the employer indicates that he is not interested, then you want to get a bit more information. You may as well; you've earned it by now and you are right there in the employer's office. Any feedback or additional leads are valuable to you.

- "Is there a specific reason you are not interested?"

- "Is there anything I can say or do that will change your mind?"

- "I understand that you do not have any openings right now. Is this something you might be interested in, in the future?"

- "You must know a lot of people in your industry. Who do you know that might be interested in speaking to me about Tyson? Any contacts or leads you can offer me would be greatly appreciated." If the employer offers you names, ask "May I use your name when I am calling these leads?"

13.5.2 A note on personal style

Some people find this script style too strong for them while others find it not strong enough. I was presenting a workshop on how to find work for people with Asperger Syndrome and a man in the audience got up and announced that if I called him using this script, he'd hang up on me. I was shocked, but realized that I had not yet demonstrated the script. Once I did the demonstration, the man who protested so strongly changed his opinion saying that it looked much stronger on paper than it sounded in person.

How you say your script has a lot to do with how it will be received. For example, when I say my script, the consistent feedback I get is that I sound friendly, professional, and motivated. It does not sound pushy. Much of this has to do with the up-beat personality and courteous manner I project. My enthusiasm and the passion for what I do comes across over the telephone. People tend to be drawn to a genuine and enthusiastic personal style. This is why it is so important that you write your own script with your own personal style and use vocabulary that feels natural to you. Make it your own!

13.6 Networking

Networking is probably the best way to find work that works and the easiest road into the hidden job market. Jobs are often in the minds of employers and the only way you can learn about those jobs is to talk to the people to whom employers are talking. You do this by networking.

Networking is simply an exchange of information, contacts, or experience. It is a means of making connections in a personal way and building relationships of support and respect to discover and create mutual benefits.

When finding work that works for people with Asperger Syndrome, networking is invaluable. For example, 95 per cent of the jobs I find for my clients are through networking and my guess is you will find the job you are looking for in the same fashion.

To make networking easy for you I have devised a simple five-step strategy. Follow these steps and you will be networking your way into the hidden job market before long.

- brain stretch contacts and avenues

- be prepared

- follow up

- be clear

- be organized.

13.6.1 Brain stretch contacts and avenues

I want you to make two lists. On the first list, write down the name of every possible person you know. Don't limit yourself to only the people who you think can help you get what you want. You never know who people know!

Family friends	Your physician	Former/current coworkers
Neighbors	Real-estate agent	Religious leader
Teachers	Your hairdresser	Massage therapist
Relatives	Alumni	Old school buddies

On the second list, write down places where you might meet contacts.

Church	Parties	Job clubs
Work	Continuing education class	Choir
Service clubs	Networking clubs	Reunions
The gym	Community centers	Fundraisers/events

13.6.2 Be prepared

It's important to remember that networking is a two-way street. A large part of networking is finding out about the person you are talking with and how you can help them move forward too. The golden rule, or "what goes around comes around" is good to live by particularly when networking. In a sense, you are trying to help others with leads, hoping that they will reciprocate. Ask lots of questions about the other person. It's interesting to get to know people, so ask what kinds of leads will help them in their business. For example, who is their best customer? This will give you insight into them, what they do and how you might be able to help them. It also gives you information and begins the relationship-building process. This is invaluable when finding work that works.

When you are meeting people through networking, this is a great time to use your script and presentation tools. Tell them what you are trying to accomplish and what they can do to help you. Educate them about Asperger Syndrome and let your enthusiasm and positive energy get them excited about helping your Asperger friend find work. People innately want to help others. It makes them feel good. Use networking as a means of educating people and getting them on your side.

The skills you have learned in this chapter have prepared you for any networking opportunities that arise, even when you are least expecting them. You never know who will be sitting beside you on the plane.

13.6.3 Follow up

After meeting with a contact, always follow up with a thank-you note. Everyone likes to be appreciated. Stay in contact with people and if they help you in your job search, let them know when you have been successful. People love to hear that they have contributed to someone's success.

13.6.4 Be clear

When you are talking to your contacts, help them understand by being clear about what you want. Be specific when at all possible. For example, "I'm looking for contacts in the banking industry, specifically data processing." If you can help your contacts walk away with a very clear idea of what you are looking for, they will recognize it when they come across it and will pass it along to you.

13.6.5 Be organized

Keep track of your contacts. Write down their names, telephone numbers, addresses, company information, and job title and make notes about when you spoke with them, what you spoke with them about and where you met them. I do this on my computer but many people use personal organizers to do this so they have their contact information with them at all times. If you do not have the technology to keep track of your contacts, then writing them in a book is just as good.

13.7 When your networking runs dry

You may find that you were successful finding work that works through your networking. People who become great "networkers" usually get what they want through connections, or through their connection's connections. Every once in a while, however, your network runs dry and you find yourself needing new contacts. Connections, you simply don't have. At times like these you need to do something called "cold calling."

A *cold call* means making contact with a person, either in person or by telephone, whom you don't know or with whom you have no connection. The first step is to create a contact list.

13.7.1 Creating a contact list

Before you begin calling, you need to know who to call. This is called prospecting. You did some of this when you were learning networking. The main difference is that in this case, you will not have a connection with the companies on this list. Begin by creating a list of companies that would have your target job. You can get these company names right out of the telephone book or *Yellow Pages*. You might find the companies in the newspaper or in trade magazines. Use your knowledge of the common job market to generate a list of companies that are appropriate for the job search.

Once you have this list, you need to find out with whom you should be speaking at the company. Perhaps the easiest way to find this out is to call the company and ask. This is a great way to start warming up to your cold calls. Here is a sample script to get this information.

> Hi, I need your help. My name is Jack Wallace. I'm helping a friend of mine who has a disability to find work. I've never spoken with anyone at your company before, and I'd like to change that situation. Who would you suggest I talk to so I can start the process?

It's as simple as that. Usually you are given a name. Before you get off the phone or transferred, make sure that you get the correct spelling of the name, the person's title or position in the company and phone number and/or extension so that you can call directly in the future. Be prepared to be transferred right away to the person to whom you wish to speak. When this happens, you will be switching from prospecting to selling. You must be ready for this because, if you are not, you might draw a blank and, believe me, this not an effective selling technique!

Now it's time for action!

13.7.2 The cold call

This is the call that everyone talks about hating and the situation I described in my story at the beginning of this chapter. Cold calls make people nervous because of a fear of rejection, of being yelled at, and of making a fool of oneself. Although these fears might be psychological, they are still real and if you let them, they can get in your way of finding work that works.

There is hope. Cold calls do not have to be as stressful as you might first imagine. The secret lies in your attitude. It's not so much what you are willing to do, but rather, what you are capable of doing. Knowing how to do something does not remove the fear you have about it, but it diminishes it and makes it more manageable. Once you become aware of your capability, your confidence will grow and so will your success. This is the cycle of confidence and it works!

With every cycle you need a starting point. This is where my system comes in. Remember your script? Now is a good time to use it. You have practiced your script in your networking calls. This is good because there is one very important tip to cold calling. You must memorize your script, and I mean *really* memorize it, word for word. If you don't, you will be concerned about what line you have forgotten or details you have missed because you will likely be a bit more nervous calling someone you don't know. If you are preoccupied with these things, it will be hard to concentrate on the information the potential employer is offering you. It should take only thirty seconds to deliver your script. You sit in the dentist's chair for thirty *minutes* and survive, so thirty *seconds* is nothing!

Now that you are fully equipped, the best way to make a cold call is to just do it!

13.7.3 The 3 Ps of cold calls – be patient, be persistent, and be polite

Be patient. It is not always easy to get through to your contact because people are busy, they don't know you, and will likely not make a huge effort to return your calls. You will get through to them eventually.

Be persistent. Study after study shows that things happen after the third call. Don't give up on call number two. If someone is not interested in what you are offering today, they may be interested next month or in six months.

Be polite. Above all, always be polite and courteous. Never get upset or show your frustration to the prospect or employer. This will get you in their bad books very quickly. People respond well to manners and a nice voice. You are what you project!

13.7.4 Voice mail

These days it is not easy to get hold of a person directly. You will encounter voice mail regularly in the job search. It's a good idea to leave a message for your contacts. This introduces them to you and helps to warm up the call a little. Don't expect them to call you back because they often don't. Don't let this discourage you – they are usually very busy people, and most of them are quite nice when you finally reach them.

A couple of pointers when leaving a message:

- Tell them you will call back if you have not heard from them by a certain time and date.

- Always be true to your word.

13.8 The job offer

When your Asperger friend receives a job offer there are a few points that are important to cover with the employer before accepting. Although negotiating wages may be awkward if you are also requesting job accommodation, it is still important that the employer is offering a reasonably competitive wage. If not, then the candidate must decide if the job is still worthwhile. Here is a list of points to clarify before accepting a job:

- the starting wage

- pay period and method of payment, for example automatic deposit, check, cash

- the start date, hours, schedule, shifts, etc.

- probationary period

- benefits and when they take effect

- dress code

- whether the employer wishes to have a job coach help with the transition into the job recommended.

Summary

- Become familiar with the common job market in your community and use it to research appropriate companies and build a contact list.

- Learn how to network and do it at every opportunity possible.

- Memorize your script so that you can concentrate your efforts on what is being said to you rather than what you are saying.

- You are what you project. Be enthusiastic and positive.

- Remember that any meeting with a potential employer is in fact an interview.

- Always come prepared to an interview.

- Include/consult the candidate in all major decisions regarding the job search.

- Let your Asperger friend take as much of the lead in the job-search process as possible.

- You know your stuff. Trust yourself!

14 Keeping the job

"The harder I work, the luckier I get." Samuel Goldwyn.

One of the first people I placed in a job was a young man named Harvey. He was one of the most likable fellows you could ever meet. Harvey was motivated and eager to learn, he presented himself well and he loved people. Like all of my clients, Harvey had Asperger Syndrome and all the idiosyncrasies and challenges that go with it, but he was determined that his disability would not get in the way of his being successful.

I placed Harvey in the mailroom at a large bank. It was a part-time job for two hours each day from 6 a.m. to 8 a.m. It took Harvey an hour and a half just to get to the job, so he traveled three hours each day to work for two hours. Many people would not have taken this job, let alone stuck it out because of these unusual hours. Most would have found the schedule ridiculous. But Harvey had an amazing work ethic. A job coach helped him transition into the job and establish the natural supports. Harvey traveled to that job every day and worked incredibly hard. He had a way of making everyone smile and within no time, everyone knew him.

After six months, the bank increased Harvey's hours to three hours a day, then to five. After a couple of years, he was working full-time with full benefits. Last year, Harvey was voted employee of the year in his department. He started that two-hour-per-day job eight years ago and made it into a successful career.

Harvey's story demonstrates how anyone with determination and a drive to succeed can do so. As with anything worthwhile, one must work hard for it. Success is not something that is handed to just anyone who decides they want it. It is something that is earned. Harvey *earned* his promotions and his career. He worked hard to better himself, he took responsibility for his challenges, and he built a foundation of skill that ultimately led to success.

Keeping a job is as important as getting one. Many candidates believe that if they can just get the job everything will be all right. Yet in many ways the work is just beginning. Much of what you have been reading in this book has been focused on finding work. Now let's look at how to keep it.

Finding work that works, goes hand in hand with keeping it.

You have learned many strategies and methods in this book to help people with Asperger Syndrome effectively in reaching their potential in the workplace. You have learned how to teach and to develop effective strategies. You can use these same methods to help your friend or relative with Asperger Syndrome, now a new employee, maintain her job.

14.1 Making a successful transition into the job

How the employee starts out in a job will set the stage for how well she will maintain it. Plunking someone into a job without setting it up for a smooth transition and longevity doesn't work. Once you find work that works, you want to do everything within your power to help the employee keep it. This is your new priority.

There are three steps to setting the stage for success once the candidate is on the job. These steps will create a smooth transition into the job in a clear manageable way for everyone involved:

- education
- establishing natural supports
- developing a support strategy.

14.1.1 Education and establishing natural supports

As was outlined in detail in Chapter 3, two of the primary roles of the job coach are to educate the employer and staff about Asperger Syndrome and to establish natural supports in the workplace to facilitate independence on the job. The employer and key staff need to be aware of how to communicate and direct an employee with Asperger Syndrome in order to help her reach full potential and be most productive to the company. The pay off is that the employer gets a very productive and dedicated long-term employee.

Establishing the development of natural supports is also crucial to long-term success. Natural supports in the workplace refer to the support network surrounding the employee on the job, predominately coworkers and management. Because the employee with Asperger Syndrome has difficulty building and fostering relationships in general, she will need the job coach to assist in creating these natural relationships on the job. To learn how the job coach goes about educating employers and establishing natural supports, you can refer to Chapter 3.

14.1.2 Developing a support strategy

When developing an on-going support strategy, you want to work closely with the employee's manager or supervisor because he knows exactly what is required from staff. The support strategy is what pulls everything together. It has four steps:

- define responsibilities
- establish routines
- review support needs
- off-site support.

14.1.2.1 DEFINE RESPONSIBILITIES

Sit down with the manager/supervisor and go over the employee's job description. Clarify each responsibility and get details. For example, if one responsibility is to pack boxes, then ask if there is a quota or expectation. If there is not, then ask how many boxes the other workers pack on average in an hour or a day. You want to know exactly what the manager expects beforehand. That way, you can develop a strategy that supports the employee in giving the employer what he *really* wants. The detailed questions you ask now will allow you to set appropriate targets and goals for the employee so that she can meet the expectations of the job.

If available, ask for a copy of the operations manual, employee orientation/procedures manual, or safety manual. These come in handy to answer questions regarding breaks, holiday time, payroll procedures, etc. Although you do not need to go over the entire handbook with the employee, it is helpful to have these resources on file to answer questions that may arise in the future. It may also fill in some of the gaps that you and the manager may have missed earlier.

14.1.2.2 ESTABLISH ROUTINES

Once you have a really clear picture of the job responsibilities and expectations, you need to develop routines that enable the employee to meet the demands of the job. Take each responsibility and break it down into steps, document those steps for each task, and put them in a binder for the employee. I call this the "Professional Binder." Essentially, it is a recipe book for each job responsibility to which the employee can refer if she has any questions or forgets how to do something. Coworkers can also use this tool to help the employee be more independent. Simply telling the employee to look up an answer in the binder may avoid having to go over something repeatedly. This prompt will help the employee to eventually become more independent.

In the Professional Binder, also include a sheet on taking initiative. This sheet lists other jobs that the employer would like to see done if the employee runs out of work. It also helps the employee to work more independently and take some initiative. The binder should include any company procedures and regulations that are relevant; for example, safety procedures, dress code, booking vacation, code of conduct, harassment and dismissal policies, etc.

By establishing routines up front, you lay the groundwork for the employee to succeed. She will know exactly what is required and expected and how to do it. The employee will also be clear about whom to approach when having difficulty. The Professional Binder is a great tool to promote independence and should be updated regularly with any new tasks or modifications.

14.1.2.3 REVIEW SUPPORT NEEDS

Over the first three months of a new job, you should be in contact with the employer and the coworkers to review support needs. You want to ensure that the key contacts on the job are feeling confident and supported while at the same time making sure that the employee is getting the appropriate support. The coworkers, or key contacts, will be your main connection to the employee at this point. Review with them the type and amount of support they are giving the employee. Make recommendations to help them be most effective with the employee. For example, it is common after a few months for everyone to relax a little as she becomes accustomed to the new situation. This is often when issues come up for the employee because she may be slipping into old habits. This may be the time for a reminder or "check-up" to help the employee out in a few areas, particularly in the area of social interactions. Whenever possible, the reminders should come from the key contacts. This cultivates the natural support system established earlier by the job coach. By reviewing the employee's support needs on an on-going basis, and keeping informed about how the key contacts are interacting with the employee, you will be able to advise how best to handle any topic.

14.1.2.4 OFF-SITE SUPPORT

It is time to move to off-site support when the employer is comfortable that the employee has adjusted to the job and is performing to expectations. Speak with the employer to make sure he is comfortable with phasing out the job coaching.

Once you have moved off-site, check in with the employer and the employee frequently to make sure everything is going well. Check with the employer to determine whether the employee is meeting her targets, exhibiting any unusual behaviors or presenting any other challenges. Don't wait for the employer to raise an issue! It may be much bigger by then and harder to handle.

14.2 The roles of the players

At the beginning of this book, you learned about the roles of the players involved in finding work that works. The following sections look at how each player can support *keeping* work that works.

14.2.1 Employee's role

The bottom line for employees with Asperger Syndrome when starting and keeping a job is for them to *take responsibility for themselves*. This means doing their best in the job and working hard to build the social relationships that are so hard for them to establish. They will require support in doing all of this, but we all need support from time to time.

There will be situations where, even though the employee does her best, the effort does not meet the requirements of the job. As disappointing as this might feel, it is not necessarily bad news. I advise my clients when this happens that it provides an opportunity to find a better fit. You can examine what did not work and either work to overcome those challenges or revise the job target to avoid those challenges. All experiences can be rewarding when you choose to learn from them. I recall a situation where a young employee with Asperger Syndrome was working in a data entry job entering bank check amounts. He had to meet a quota of entering so many checks per hour. Although he was very capable of performing the job, he found the pressure of having to meet a quota so stressful, that he started to get sick. His job coach supported his decision to leave this job because there is absolutely no point in continuing any job that makes you ill. What this young man learned was that, although he might have the skills to perform a job, a deadline or quota-oriented environment was not good for him. The job coach was able to take this information, restructure his job goals and find something more appropriate.

If necessary, before the employee starts out in a new job, help her understand what will be expected so that she can be prepared. For example, on the first day of a new job, the employee should:

- be on time

- be dressed appropriately

- act enthusiastic (within a natural comfort zone)

- be prepared to complete paperwork

- show interest in whatever she is being shown

- stay focused and pay close attention, even take notes

- be clear about what she is to do or where she is to go the next day.

During the first three months, the employee needs to demonstrate that she:

- can take responsibility

- can do the job

- is willing and able to learn

- can be flexible (within reason for someone with Asperger Syndrome)

- can meet productivity levels

- likes the job

- is motivated and committed to the job

- will be sure to notify the employer if going to be absent, and will be absent only for a good reason

- can be courteous to customers and fellow employees

- can observe all safety rules and follow company policies

- will be honest.

14.2.2 Coach's role

The job coach plays a major role in setting the job placement up for success. Everything discussed in Chapter 3 regarding making a successful transition into the job will be the responsibility of whomever is playing the role of job coach.

The job coach will:

- establish rapport with the manager/supervisor and key coworkers

- educate key staff members

- build natural supports

- define the expectations of each job responsibility

- clearly explain the expectations to the new employee, ensuring that they are understood

- break each job responsibility down into manageable steps

- effectively teach each job responsibility

- create the Professional Binder

- problem-solve issues as they arise

- conduct regular off-site check-ins

- be available to provide support as needed.

14.2.3 Family members' role

Family members play a vital support role in the success of long-term employment for the relative with Asperger Syndrome. The support and reinforcement they provide on the home front is essential. Families support the process of keeping a job by:

- supporting morning, evening and hygiene routines
- making sure the employee has appropriate clothes for the job
- paying attention to what is happening at the job so they might be alerted to any issues or problems. If anything comes up, they should contact the job coach immediately
- reinforcing the employee's independence by respecting and supporting her privacy as an adult
- being available to support (not control) the relative's decision-making and problem-solving when issues arise
- keeping the job coach informed of any behavioral changes they see in their relative, as well as of any medication changes or health issues that occur.

It is important for family members to reinforce a good work ethic and to explain situations that arise. Family members can use these things as tools to help their relative with Asperger Syndrome learn and prosper. They should also try to remain at arm's length to the employer. It is good for the employer to know that the family is supportive; however, direct contact with the employer should ideally be left up to the job coach whenever possible. There may be occasions when the employer wishes to speak with a family member, but the employer should initiate the contact and guide the process.

14.2.4 Employer's role

Hiring a person with Asperger Syndrome is an investment. The employer who is willing to nurture his new employee and put forth the time and effort into training will be rewarded with a very dedicated, reliable worker. The employer needs to be supported through the process of taking the candidate with Asperger Syndrome into his employ. The combination of the employer's commitment, the employee's motivation and drive to succeed, and the support you offer either on your own or through a job coach creates the formula for success.

The employer should be willing to accommodate his new employee by:

- providing key contacts, coworkers, who are willing to act as mentors

- giving the employee clear direction and perhaps alternative instruction such as written steps or checklists to help her reach full potential in the job

- being patient and supportive

- offering positive as well as constructive feedback

- supporting the job coach by giving direct, regular feedback so that issues can be addressed quickly

- treating the new employee equally and making an effort to include her in company social events.

14.2.5 Other professionals' roles

When the professional gets a call from a parent or from the employee with Asperger Syndrome it is often because communication has broken down somewhere along the line. The professional's main role, once the employee has found work that works, is to keep the lines of communication amongst the players open and connected. When anything is brought to his attention, it is always a good idea for the professional to check in with the other players to make sure everyone has the same information.

Professionals should always be an outside resource for the other players. They are a safe, neutral party to contact when the other players are unsure about something that is happening in the process. Professionals may provide support, counseling, advice, and referrals to the players. In many respects, the professionals are the support and information link amongst employees, family, job coaches, and employers.

> When our dreams become reality, it's amazing how real they become.
> Plant one foot firmly on the ground and reach for the sky.

Over the years I have placed many of my clients with Asperger Syndrome in jobs that to this day they still have. It is always the determination of the employee with Asperger Syndrome that ultimately makes her successful. I have seen part-time jobs turn into careers for my clients. I have seen jobs that were initially temporary turn into permanent fulfilling work because the employee with Asperger Syndrome had such a positive impact. The willingness of the candidate to be flexible and work her way into a job is often the avenue to victory.

"Keep your eyes on the prize," I remember hearing as a child. Ten years ago I never imagined that I would be writing a book. I didn't realize at the time that my vision of helping people with Asperger Syndrome find work that works would develop into a life-long passion. But I did know that it felt good to be doing my job. Intrinsically, I knew that if I stayed focused I would be successful and that my passion would motivate others to do the same. One of the many things that I have learned from my clients is to keep going regardless of what life puts in front of me. There is always a way to go through or around challenges, as long as you are motivated to do so. This is the recipe for success and I stand behind each and every person with Asperger Syndrome who wishes to pursue her dream. Anything is possible when approached with an open mind, an open heart, and the will to triumph.

Stay focused and determined and the dream will become a reality.

Summary

Support a successful transition into the job by:

- educating the employer and key staff members

- establishing natural supports

- defining job responsibilities

- breaking job responsibilities down into manageable steps

- creating a Professional Binder

- building a relationship with key staff members.

Help the employee with Asperger Syndrome keep the job by:

- clearly outlining the employer's expectations

- maintaining regular contact with the key contacts and manager/supervisor

- dealing with issues that arise quickly and efficiently

- giving regular feedback to the employee.

Recommended reading

Attwood, T. (1998) *Asperger's Syndrome: A Guide for Parents and Professionals.* London: Jessica Kingsley Publishers.

Bassett, L. (2001) *From Panic to Power: Proven Techniques to Calm Your Anxieties, Conquer Your Fears, and Put You in Control of Your Life.* New York, NY: Quill.

Beatty, R.H. (2002) *The Five Minute Interview: A Job Hunter's Guide to a Successful Interview,* 3rd edition. Hoboken, NJ: John Wiley and Sons, Inc.

Bissonnette, D. (1994) *Beyond Traditional Job Development: The Art of Creating Opportunity.* Chatsworth, CA: Milt Wright and Associates.

Boothman, N. (2000) *How to Make People Like You: In 90 Seconds or Less.* New York, NY: Workman Publishing.

Branden, N. (1994) *The Six Pillars of Self-Esteem.* New York, NY: Bantam.

Carnegie, D. (1982) *How to Win Friends and Influence People.* New York, NY: Pocket Books.

Cotton, P. (1992) *Getting There from Here: A Guide to Developing Natural Job Supports.* Durham, NH: Institute on Disability/UAP, University of New Hampshire.

Covey, S.R. (2003) *The Seven Habits of Highly Effective People: Powerful Lessons in Personal Change.* New York, NY: Free Press.

Devine, F.D. (2003) *Goof-Proof Interviews.* New York, NY: Learning Express, LLC.

Dunning, D. (2001) *What's Your Type of Career? Unlock the Secrets of your Personality to Find your Perfect Career Path.* Palo Alto, CA: Davies-Black Publishing.

Ehlers, S. and Gillberg, C. (1993) 'The epidemiology of Asperger syndrome. A total population study.' *Journal of Child Psychology and Psychiatry,* 34 (8), pp.1327–1350.

Farr, M. (2002) *Seven Steps to Getting a Job Fast.* Indianapolis, IN: JIST Publishing, Inc.

Gabor, D. (1983) *How to Start a Conversation and Make Friends.* London, UK: Sheldon Press.

Gershenfeld, A., Loparco, M. and Barajas, C. (2003) *Game Plan: The Insider's Guide to Breaking in and Succeeding in the Computer and Video Game Business.* New York, NY: St. Martin's Press.

Goleman, D. (1997) *Emotional Intelligence: Why it Can Matter More Than IQ.* New York, NY: Bantam Books.

Graber, S. (2000) *The Everything Resume Book: Great Resumes for Everybody from Student to Executive.* Avon, MA: Adams Media Corporation.

Grandin, T. (1992) 'An inside view of autism.' In E. Schopler and G.B. Mesibov (eds) *High Functioning Individuals with Autism.* New York: Plenum Press.

Grandin, T. (1995) *Thinking in Pictures.* New York, NY: Doubleday.

Kleinman, C. (2002) *Winning the Job Game: The New Rules for Finding and Keeping the Job You Want.* Hoboken, NJ: John Wiley and Sons, Inc.

Matthews, A. (1990) *Making Friends: A Guide to Getting Along with People.* Singapore: Media Masters.

Segar, M. *The Battles of an Autistic Thinker.* (unpublished)

Web sites

AS-IF is a wonderful, unique and comprehensive site out of the UK with fascinating information and insight. The site is written by a woman with Asperger Syndrome. *http://www.as-if.org.uk*

Disability Web Links is a Canadian site that helps viewers to search for a wide range of disability-related services, including employment services, in their region. *http://www.disabilityweblinks.ca*

Dr. Temple Grandin's web page *http://www.grandin.com/index.html*

Human Resources Development Canada's web site offers labor market information including labor market trends in Canada. It also has a section specifically for people with disabilities. *http://www.hrdc-drhc.gc.ca/common/home.shtml*

Job Hunters Bible is a well-established site by the author of *What Color is Your Parachute*, Dick Bolles. It is an excellent resource for conducting a job search on the Internet as well as general job-search information. *http://www.jobhuntersbible.com/index.html*

Mission Possible Employment Services is a web site offering information and employment services for people with Asperger Syndrome. *http://www.anythingispossible.ca*

Occupational Outlook Handbook is from the U.S. Department of Labor, Bureau of Labor Statistics. It offers a comprehensive look at the labor market and labor market trends in the United States. *http://www.bls.gov/oco*

Pediatric Neurology.com offers very easy-to-read and understand information on a number of neurological disorders including Asperger Syndrome. You can listen to samples of children with Asperger Syndrome speak to hear speech patterns. *http://www.pediatricneurology.com*

Resources

Australia

A.C.E. National Network: The Australian peak body association representing organizations that provide employment assistance and post-placement support to people with disabilities in competitive environments.
Phone: (03) 9411 4033
Fax: (03) 9411 4053
Address: PO Box 5198, Alphington, Victoria 3078
Email: *info@acenational.org.au*

Asperger Syndrome Support Network (ASSN): A group of parents who have a family member diagnosed with Asperger Syndrome have made this web site that offers information, support, and referrals. For contact numbers in the metropolitan and regional areas of Victoria call: (03) 9845 2766.
Address: Asperger's Syndrome Support Network, The Nerve Centre, 54 Railway Rd, Blackburn VIC 3130
Email: *assnvic@mssociety.com.au* (Australia only)
Web: *http://home.vicnet.net.au/~asperger/*

Australian Workplace (The) provides access to online services and information, guiding you to employment information, government assistance, jobs, careers, training, and working conditions. Very useful web site.
Web: *http://www.workplace.gov.au/Workplace/WPHome*

Centrelink is a government agency delivering a range of Commonwealth services to the Australian community. Their web site can make it easier to explore options and services and know what questions to ask. It lists programs and services available to people with disabilities, including employment programs and services such as wage subsidies.
Web: *http://www.centrelink.gov.au*

CRS Australia delivers vocational rehabilitation services to Australian citizens or residents who have an injury, disability, or health condition. They assist people who have a disability or injury to get a job or return to their job. CRS Australia has offices in 160 locations around Australia. The CRS Australia National Office is located in Canberra.

Street address: Level 2, Bonner House, 1–5 Neptune St, Woden, ACT 2606
Postal address: PO Box 111, Woden, ACT 2606
Phone: 1 800 624 824
Web: *www.crsrehab.gov.au*

Education Online the new Australian education web site.

Web: *http://www.education.gov.au/*
Web: *http://www.centrelink.gov.au*

WorkAble Electronic Network for vocational training and employment for people with a disability. This web site has a range of features for people with a disability and their families, and staff of service provider agencies.

Address: PO Box 29, Montacute, SA 5134 Australia
Email: *jdowsett@workable.org.au*
Phone: (08) 8390 2309
Fax: (08) 8390 2309

Canada

Asperger's Society of Ontario

Web: *http://www.aspergers.ca/*

Autism Society Canada

Web: *http://www.autismsocietycanada.ca/*

Canadian Council on Rehabilitation and Work (The): WORKink's mission is to facilitate communication and provide resources and information to enhance the equitable and meaningful employment of people with disabilities. WORKink provides its online visitors with labor market and career information, access to national, provincial, and territorial resources, and online experts' assistance.

Web: *http://www.workink.com/*

Disability Web Links is a Canadian site that offers viewers to search for a wide range of disability-related services, including employment services, in their region.
Web: *http://www.disabilityweblinks.ca*

Job Accommodation Network in Canada (JANCANA): Sponsored by the Canadian Council on Rehabilitation and Work, JAN is an international toll-free consulting service that provides information about job accommodations and employability of people with functional limitations. The service is available in both English and French.
Phone: 1–866–CCRWJAS (1–866–227–9527)

Job Accommodation Service (JAS): You can contact JAS to obtain information on questions related to job accommodations. JAS also provides you with links to Canadian sources on job accommodation, such as information about assistive devices, adaptive technology, and accommodation services.
Toll-free phone: 1–800–664–0925 ext. 225
Phone: (416) 260–3060 ext. 225
Email: *jasinfo@ccrw.org*

The National Educational Association of Disabled Students (NEADS): NEADS EdLink is a directory of disability service providers at Canadian colleges and universities. This listing provides contact information for service providers at Canadian post-secondary institutions.
Address: National Educational Association of Disabled Students
4th Level Unicentre, Carleton University, Ottawa, Ontario, K1S 5B6 Canada
Phone (voice/TTY): (613) 526–8008
Email: *info@neads.ca*
Web: *http://www.neads.ca*

Human Resources Development Canada (HRDC): This web site offers labor market information including labor market trends in Canada. It also has a section specifically for people with disabilities.
Web: *http://www.hrdc-drhc.gc.ca/common/home.shtml*

USA

Americans with Disabilities Act Disability and Business Technical Assistance Centers (DBTACs): For information on legislation, rights, and resources, visit *www.adata.org/index.html,* or call (800) 949–4232 (Voice/TTY). Callers are automatically routed to the DBTAC in their region. The DBTACs provide information, referral, technical assistance, and training on the Americans with Disabilities Act (ADA) to businesses, state and local governments, and persons with disabilities to facilitate employment for individuals with disabilities and accessibility in public accommodations and government services. The DBTACs also conduct training and promote public awareness on the ADA.

The Asperger Syndrome Coalition of the U.S. is a national non-profit organization committed to providing the most up-to-date and comprehensive information on Asperger Syndrome and related conditions.
Web: *http://www.asperger.org*

Autism Society of America (ASA)
Web: *http://www.autism-society.org*

Career One-Stop: This web site is a publicly-funded resource for job-seekers and businesses. Job-seekers can search for jobs – from entry level to technical to professional to CEO – locate public workforce services in their area, explore alternative career paths, compare salary data for different occupations, learn which careers are hot, get resumé writing tips and job interview strategies, and much more. Employers can identify job-ready workers with the right skills.
Web: *http://careeronestop.org/*

Davis Memorial Goodwill Industries, Inc.: Davis Memorial Goodwill Industries provides vocational evaluation, training, employment, and job placement services for persons with disabilities. An information packet describing Goodwill's services is available upon request.
Address: 2200 South Dakota Avenue, N.E. Washington, DC 20018
Phone: (202) 636–4225 (Voice)
Email: *jedavis@dcgoodwill.org*
Web: *www.dcgoodwill.org*

Department of Vocational Rehabilitation (VR): Vocational Rehabilitation is a nationwide federal-state program for assisting eligible people with disabilities to define a suitable employment goal and become employed. Each state capital has a central VR agency, and there are local offices in most states. VR provides medical, therapeutic, counseling, education, training, and other services needed to prepare people with disabilities for work. VR is an excellent place for a youth or adult with a disability to begin exploring available training and support service options. To identify the VR office in your vicinity, consult your local telephone directory or visit:
Web: *www.jan.wvu.edu/SBSES/VOCREHAB.htm*

JobAccess: The goal of JobAccess is to enable people with disabilities to enhance their professional lives by providing a dedicated system for finding employment. JobAccess provides a place where people with disabilites can seek employment and be evaluated solely on their skills and experience. The JobAccess Resumé Builder helps users to build and post a professional looking resumé that companies across the US will be able to browse.
Address: 1001 W. 17th St. Costa Mesa, CA 92627
Email: *generalinquiries@jobaccess.org*
Web: *www.jobaccess.org/*

National Center on Workforce and Disability/Adult (NCWD): The National Center on Workforce and Disability/Adult (NCWD) provides training, technical assistance, policy analysis, and information to improve access for all in the workforce development system. Areas of expertise include: accommodations and assistive technology, relationships with employers, helping clients with disabilities find jobs, and advising employers as to how to provide job-related supports. Spanish spoken; Spanish materials available.
Address: Institute for Community Inclusion, UMass Boston, 100 Morrissey Boulevard, Boston, MA 02125
Phone: (888) 886–9898 (V/TTY)
Email: *contact@onestops.info*
Web: *www.onestops.info*

Office of Disability Employment Policy: The Office of Disability Employment Policy (formerly the President's Committee on Employment of People with Disabilities, PCEPD) provides information, training, and technical assistance to America's business leaders, organized labor, rehabilitation and other service providers, advocacy organizations, families, and individuals with disabilities. ODEP's mission is to facilitate the communication, coordination, and promotion of public and private efforts to empower Americans with disabilities through employment. ODEP also serves as an advisor to the President of the United States on public policy issues affecting employment of people with disabilities. Spanish spoken.
Address: Department of Labor, 200 Constitution Avenue, NW Washington, D.C. 20210
Phone: (202) 376–6200 (Voice); (866) 487–2365 (Department of Labor, toll-free) (877) 889–5627 (Department of Labor, TTY)
Email: *infoODEP@dol.gov*
Web: *www.dol.gov/odep*

If you are employed and are experiencing difficulty on the job due to your disability, you might consider contacting the following organizations:

Access Board: The Access Board enforces the Architectural Barriers Act (ABA), ensuring accessibility in facilities built, altered, or leased using certain federal funds. It develops the Americans with Disabilities Act (ADA) Accessibility Guidelines (ADAAG), which are minimum accessibility guidelines for places of public accommodation, commercial facilities, state and local government facilities, and transportation vehicles and facilities. The Access Board is also charged with developing accessibility guidelines for telecommunications equipment and customer premises equipment. The Access Board offers training, technical assistance, and publications to individuals and organizations throughout the country on removing architectural, transportation, and communication barriers.
Address: 1331 F Street, N.W., Suite 1000 Washington, D.C. 20004–1111
Phone: (202) 272–0080; (800) 872–2253 (Voice) (202) 272–0082; (800) 993–2822 (TTY)
Email: *info@access-board.gov*
Web: *www.access-board.gov*

Equal Employment Opportunity Commission (EEOC): The EEOC is a government agency that handles discrimination complaints about employment based on age, sex, race, ethnicity, and disability. The 800 number will connect callers with their local EEOC office, which can discuss complaints. Spanish spoken; Spanish materials available.
Address: 1801 L Street, NW Washington, D.C. 20507
Phone: (202) 663–4900; (800) 669–4000 (Voice) (202) 663–4494; (800) 669–6820 (TTY)
Web: *www.eeoc.gov*

Job Accommodation Network (JAN): The Job Accommodation Network, a service of the Office of Disability Employment Policy (ODEP) at the U.S. Department of Labor, brings together information from many sources about practical steps employers can take to make accommodations for the functional limitations of employees and applicants with disabilities. JAN consultants provide technical details and assistance with accommodations and the implementation of products and procedures in the workplace. Callers should be prepared to explain the specific problem and job circumstances. Brochures, printed materials, and a newsletter are available free of charge. Spanish spoken; Spanish materials available.
Address: West Virginia University, P.O. Box 6080 Morgantown, WV
Phone: 26506–6080 (800) 526–7234 (Voice/TTY)
Email: *jan@jan.icdi.wvu.edu*
Web: *www.jan.wvu.edu*

UK

Department for Education and Skills (DfES): Government web site with information about employment and educational schemes and policies. Many links to other sites, including those of other government departments.
Web: *http://www.dfes.gov.uk*

EmployAbility: This site contains information, activities, links and contacts to help people with disbilities find employment-related services. It includes the program "Access to Work" (AtW), which provides support to disabled people and their employers to help overcome work-related obstacles resulting from disability.
Web: *http://www.nrec.org.uk/employability*

HEAG: The HEAG database lets you search for specialist services and accessibility support for students with disabilities in higher education in Austria, Belgium (Flemish), Belgium (French), Denmark, Finland, France, Germany, Greece, Iceland, Ireland, Italy, Netherlands, Norway, Portugal, Spain, Sweden, and UK.
Web: *www.heagnet.org*

Job Centre Plus: Offers specialist services for disabled people and contains information for both job-seekers and employers, with details of all the services that are available and a search facility to find your nearest Job Centre.
Web: *http://www.jobcentreplus.gov.uk*

Skill: National Bureau for Students With Disabilities (Skill) is a national charity promoting opportunities for young people and adults with any kind of disability in post-16 education, training and employment across the UK.
Web: *http://www.skill.org.uk/*

The National Autistic Society (NAS): The site includes information about autism and Asperger Syndrome, and about the support and services available in the UK for people with autism spectrum disorders including Asperger Syndrome.
Web: *http://www.nas.org.uk/*

General interest web sites

AS-IF is a wonderful, unique and comprehensive site out of the UK with fascinating information and insight. The site is written by a woman with Asperger Syndrome.
Web: *http://www.as-if.org.uk*

Career Development eManual is one of the most comprehensive career development web sites available. This site is developed and maintained by the University of Waterloo, Canada.
Web: *http://www.cdm.uwaterloo.ca/*

Job Hunters Bible is a well-established site by the author of *What Color is Your Parachute*, Dick Bolles. It is an excellent resource for conducting a job search on the Internet as well as general job-search information.
Web: *http://www.jobhuntersbible.com/index.html*

Mission Possible Employment Services is a web site offering information and employment services for people with Asperger Syndrome.
Web: *http://www.anythingispossible.ca*

Occupational Outlook Handbook is from the U.S. Department of Labor, Bureau of Labor Statistics. It offers a comprehensive look at the labor market and labor market trends in the United States.
Web: *http://www.bls.gov/oco*

Online Asperger Syndrome Information and Support (OASIS) is a comprehensive web site on Asperger Syndrome. It includes valuable information, reading material, updates and message boards.
Web: *http://www.udel.edu/bkirby/asperger/*

Pediatric Neurology.com offers very easy-to-read information on a number of neurological disorders including Asperger Syndrome. You can listen to samples of children with Asperger Syndrome speak to hear speech patterns.
Web: *http://www.pediatricneurology.com*

Index